Praise for *A Measureless Peril*

"Snow writes with verve and a keen eye. He is a kind of John McPhee of combat at sea, finding humanity in the small, telling details of duty."

The New York Times Book Review

"In this exhaustively researched and gracefully written book, Snow vividly re-creates the epic showdown between German submarines, sent to hunt merchant ships in the Atlantic, and the vessels sent to thwart them, one of which bore Snow's father. This is a hell of a story, at turns rousing, terrifying, fascinating, surprisingly funny, and deeply moving, and the postscript, telling of the peacetime fate of Snow's father, brought me to tears."

—Laura Hillenbrand, Salon.com

"*A Measureless Peril* . . . will keep you riveted. . . . [Snow's] description of key personalities is flawless."

—*Forbes*

"An accomplished historian with a welcome personal touch."

—*Kirkus Reviews*

"Snow ably uses his father's letters to reconstruct Atlantic duty in the final years of a vital battle for Allied victory."

—*Publishers Weekly*

"Richard Snow captures the sweep of battle—years long, thousands of square miles in extent—and its life-sized, daily events, from routine tasks to hellish violence, as seen through the eyes of the men who were there. The result is a stereoscopic view of a world-historical struggle and of the author's father, Lieutenant Richard B. Snow, USNR, a representative member of the greatest generation."

—Richard Brookhiser, author of *Founding Father: Rediscovering George Washington*

"By way of a great raft of sea stories, each impeccably told and perfectly turned, Richard Snow has transformed the faraway and half-forgotten world of the Atlantic convoys into a narrative as touching and exciting as it is melancholy and memorable. This is a valuable book: few better accounts have ever been crafted about this cruelest of wars, fought for year after year on the most imperturbably cruel of the world's great oceans."

—Simon Winchester

"Richard Snow's *A Measureless Peril* is epic, poignant, and until now the story he tells has been little known. At the same time, Snow's voice is warm, wildly entertaining, and achieves that rare magic effect in writing history: complete intimacy and authority. The book is chock-full of engrossing detail and the surprising stories spool out like private movies shot by our fathers, grandfathers, uncles, and brothers and sent back from the war—but arriving only now in this world of ours. Most of all, Snow's father, a courageous presence, is as literate and humane a voice as one could hope to meet in the darkest hours at sea. Snow smartly and thoroughly honors the men and women—and their families—who served in WWII."

—Doug Stanton, author of *Horse Soldiers* and *In Harm's Way*

"There is one very annoying and upsetting aspect to *A Measureless Peril*: it ends. However, I have to admit that when I am fascinated and excited by a book, and having the time of my life, I'm able to read really fast. What a fine writer is Richard Snow, and what a treasure this is."

—Alan Furst

"In this terrific tale, Richard Snow has written a splendid and exciting account of an unjustly overlooked story of World War II: the fight for the Atlantic. With a skillful narrative hand, he moves between scenes of combat and peril at sea (and under the sea) to moments of debate and decision at the highest levels of Washington and London. *A Measureless Peril*—the phrase is Churchill's—is a book to savor, and to remember."

—Jon Meacham

★★ A ★★
Measureless Peril

America in the Fight for the Atlantic, the

Longest Battle of World War II

Richard Snow

Scribner

New York London Toronto Sydney New Delhi

For Carol—

and, of course, Rebecca, who brightened the

last five years of Lt. R. B. Snow's life

Scribner
A Division of Simon & Schuster, Inc.
1230 Avenue of the Americas
New York, NY 10020

Copyright © 2010 by Richard Snow

First Scribner trade paperback edition May 2011

SCRIBNER and design are registered trademarks of The Gale Group, Inc., used
under license by Simon & Schuster, Inc., the publisher of this work.

For information about special discounts for bulk purchases, please contact
Simon & Schuster Special Sales at 1-866-506-1949 or
business@simonandschuster.com.

The Simon & Schuster Speakers Bureau can bring authors to your live event. For
more information or to book an event, contact the Simon & Schuster Speakers
Bureau at 1-866-248-3049 or visit our website at www.simonspeakers.com.

Designed by Nancy Singer

Manufactured in the United States of America

3 5 7 9 10 8 6 4 2

Library of Congress Control Number: 2009052995

ISBN 978-1-4165-9110-8
ISBN 978-1-4165-9111-5 (pbk)
ISBN 978-1-4165-9507-6 (ebook)

Except where noted, all insert photographs are credited to the National Archives.

Contents

★★ A ★★
Measureless
Peril

"What's the Matter with the *Davis*?"

Looking back on the Atlantic struggle

One hot, windy September afternoon in the early 1970s my mother and father came home to Bronxville from a two-week vacation in Maine. Bronxville is a town in Westchester County, half an hour north of Manhattan on what was then the Penn Central railroad. Like countless thousands of other couples, my mother, Emma, and my father, Richard, had quit the city in the hopeful months after World War II ended to raise their infant child in a house surrounded by suburban greenery and well-nourished public schools.

The beneficiary of this relocation came down to help them unload their luggage, and I was soon joined by Mr. Curcio, the superintendent of the apartment building in the village my parents had moved into after I'd gotten out of college.

Superintendent Curcio was a chatty, affable, powerfully built man (he once paused halfway up a flight of stairs to speculate with me at some length about the Mets' chances, all the time holding two air conditioners, one under each arm). He scooped a half dozen suitcases out of the Chrysler, and as we headed toward the apartment, something—the weather, perhaps—reminded him of having taken part in the landings on Sicily in July 1943, and he began to talk about it.

"Look, I'm a wop," he said cheerfully about his Italian heritage, "but let me tell you, once those wops on the beach were shooting at me, I was one hundred percent American. Guys begin dropping around me, and I start firing while I'm still in the water."

The story continued until the suitcases were in front of the door. We all said thanks, and then my mother put a protective hand on my father's forearm. "I'm so glad," she told Mr. Curcio, "that Dick was never in action."

AT A LITTLE AFTER eight thirty on the morning of April 24, 1945, a sailor said to my father, "What's the matter with the *Davis?*" He meant the *Frederick C. Davis,* destroyer escort 136, and she looked funny, canted forward and apparently stopped in the water. My father was watching her from the deck of another destroyer escort, the USS *Neunzer,* DE-150. The *Davis* lay a few hundred yards away, but not for long. "Jesus Christ!" said someone. "She took a fish." And sure enough, although nobody aboard the *Neunzer* had heard the explosion, a torpedo had struck the *Davis*'s forward engine room. Minutes later the *Davis* split apart and sank, taking 115 men to their deaths, while the *Neunzer* and seven other destroyer escorts—helped by planes from the escort carrier *Bogue*—set off on what would prove to be a ten-hour struggle against the submarine that had destroyed her.

While he unpacked in Bronxville, my father reviewed his role in this event for my mother, then added, with what seemed to me impressive mildness, "That's generally considered having been in action."

★   ★   ★

MY FATHER TOOK PART in the last great campaign of the Atlantic war. The *Neunzer* was one of a web of ships stretched across a hundred miles hunting an enemy that naval intelligence had reason to believe was going to launch rocket attacks against American cities. He was in at the end of the longest battle of World War II, indeed, of any war in history. If the Allies had lost that battle, they would have lost the war.

And yet, my mother's remark was not ludicrous.

Few people today remember the Atlantic war as a battle, and even at the time only some of those who were in it saw it as a coherent effort. The Pacific was the picturesque war, the one where naval victories took the form we think they should: battleships hammering it out gun to gun, aircraft carriers deciding in a morning the fate of nations. Louis Auchincloss, already a lawyer, soon to be a novelist, but at the time the navigator on an LST (landing ship, tank) remembered, "Changing oceans was like changing navies. In the European theater the army and air force were everything; the navy, only a police escort. . . . Never shall I forget my first glimpse of the Pacific navy in the atoll Ulithi where the lines of battleships, cruisers, carriers, and auxiliary vessels seemed to stretch out to the crack of doom."

Conquer an island; then conquer another island; then sink some battleships. That was a proper sea war. The Atlantic effort by contrast was strange and diffuse, week upon week of boredom endured in constant discomfort, fires on the sea at night and yet nothing there in the morning, eventually the unheroic sight of Halifax through the fog if you were lucky. It was a sea fight whose results were recorded on land. But it began on the first day of the war and ended on the final one, five years and eight months later. In the Pacific, the Battle of Midway broke a Japanese fleet in five minutes.

But the Allied aim in the Atlantic was not to destroy an enemy on the high seas. It was to keep a delivery system going:

to get grain and aviation gas, chocolate and rifles and tires, oil and boots and airplane engines, from America to Europe. The trucks in this operation were merchant ships, some of them ancient, none of them carrying the martial glamour of a PT boat, let alone a cruiser.

One who did see the high consequence of this dogged chore was Winston Churchill. He said that the U-boat campaign was "the only thing that ever really frightened me during the war." While the Atlantic battle was going on, he wrote, "How willingly would I have exchanged a full-scale invasion for this shapeless, measureless peril, expressed in charts, curves, and statistics." The charts and statistics showed how many ships the German submarines were sinking, as against how many the Allies could build. It was "a war of groping and drowning, of ambuscade and stratagem," said Churchill, "of science and seamanship." If the stratagems failed, if the seamanship faltered, Britain would starve and the European fighting fronts would fall to the German army.

In *Commander in Chief*, his fine book about the American high command in the war, the historian Eric Larrabee wrote the arresting sentence "The Battle of the Atlantic was the war's inner core, an only partly visible axle on which other contingencies turned." That image has stayed with me since I first read it twenty years ago, although I can also see the battle as a vast drill bit or screw, with grooves a week or a month apart, turning and turning through the mortal years, always from America toward Europe, driving convoys eastward. Some of the vessels it carries will get through fifty trips without a scratch; some will burn and sink in front of vacationers on Miami Beach. Sometimes destroyers will protect them; sometimes there won't be enough destroyers to spare for the job; and sometimes the destroyers won't do any good at all, darting this way and that as the U-boats lance into the heart of the convoy and with a torpedo or two turn the months of manufacturing the ammunition and trucks and locomotives and radios and the days of loading them and all the time spent building the vessel that carries this cargo and the lifetimes of raising the crewmen who are attending it into a horrible inanity.

The battle killed nearly eighty thousand people: drowned them, crushed them, burned them, froze them, starved them in lifeboats. Far beyond the brutal vacancy of ocean that extinguished all those lives, an empire of strenuous ingenuity fizzed and crackled, whole cities running night and day given over to trying to outsmart the slim, dark shapes that Allied seamen so rarely saw.

It took three nations to end the U-boat campaign—the United States, Canada, and Great Britain—and Britain's role in the immense task seems better remembered than America's. In some ways this is just; in some, it isn't.

The particular fight my father was in that April went just the way it should have. This despite the loss of the *Frederick C. Davis*. By then what Lincoln called the "terrible arithmetic of war" had established that an American destroyer was a small price to pay for a German submarine. Over the previous four years the U.S. navy had learned a great deal about how to cope with U-boats. Not one ship that took part in this final wide sweep had existed before the war began. I don't just mean the vessels themselves, but the *kind* of vessels they were. The escort carriers—"baby flattops" that carried a fraction of the number of airplanes that rode in the immense fleet carriers that were going about their famous work in the Pacific—had been improvised to meet the crisis, and so had the class of ship my father served on, the destroyer escort, the DE.

This book tells the story of the American effort in the Battle of the Atlantic. The destroyer escort figures prominently in it because the ship represents a combination of practicality and ingenuity that America brought to the war; and, of course, my father was on one. He isn't in this story through mere sentimentality on my part. I believe that he embodied the kind of war America fought and the kind of people that allowed us to win it.

Richard B. Snow (I escaped the inconveniences of being called Junior by grace of having a different middle name) was an architect. Before the war, his only connection with the sea was having ridden across it in ocean liners to study the violin in Paris. Born in 1905, he was old for active duty, and moreover he was married. Yet when the war came he pulled such strings as he could find, and although he had reached the wintry heights of his late thirties, he managed to wangle sea duty. In time he became a "plank owner" (part of the original crew) on a brand-new destroyer escort. His wife wasn't happy about this, but he promised to write her every day they were apart, and he came surprisingly close to fulfilling this pledge. Recently I began to read those letters for the first time.

Before he went into architecture school, my father had studied at Columbia College with the critic, poet, and novelist Mark Van Doren, who encouraged him to become a writer. The letters suggest what it was that caught Van Doren's eye. They're fluent, sardonic, fond, observant, full of irony about many things but never about his work at sea, and not quite like any other war letters I've ever read.

But like the unique but widely produced ship he served aboard, my father's letters encapsulate a vast common experience. This architect became a capable officer, and thus his career echoes those of the eighty thousand other Americans who became naval officers during those years—and of the twelve million Americans who were in uniform by war's end. Five years earlier these warriors had no more thought of joining the military than of joining the circus. They at once brought about and were formed by the biggest, swiftest change that has ever overtaken our society.

If my father can speak for them, though, he can't do it yet, because the story starts long before he traded his T square for a sextant. He will make only a few brief appearances before he ventures out into the Atlantic, that beautiful, malevolent thirty-million-square-mile battlefield where he and those like him were to win a great and underappreciated victory.

Flower Show

The dangerous state of the U.S. navy
on the eve of war, 1939

The planes that spotted the U-boat that sank the *Frederick C. Davis* and the ships that pursued it were still minerals in the ground in the spring of 1939. The people who ran them were raising poul-try, teaching school, selling cars or stocks or hot dogs. In Flushing Meadows, in Queens, New York, some of them were putting the finishing touches on pavilions designed to advertise the virtues of nations that in a few months wouldn't exist. For the New York World's Fair was about to send up its brief sparkle between the paired darknesses of global depression and global war.

This tremendous undertaking—three hundred buildings, sixty miles of new roadway, the vision of a benign future made concrete on top of a sometime municipal garbage dump to the tune of $155 million—changed a great many lives, among them my father's.

He had graduated from the Columbia School of Architecture in 1931, about the worst possible year for a young man embarking on the profession. The sort of people who commissioned new buildings were hard-pressed merely to maintain the ones they owned. Unlike many newly minted architects, he had a salaried position, but the prospects throughout the field looked bleak. Indeed, they seemed so barren to the parents of Emma Louise Folger, the girl who was about to become Mrs. Richard Boring Snow, that they forced her to break the engagement.

He got rid of the apartment he had rented for them, dated other women, scratched up jobs—a shoe-store redesign was a particular windfall—and soldiered along. In 1936 he read that the World's Fair Corporation, bolstered with a lot of New Deal money, was going to help architects by mounting a contest: design an "Applied Arts Building" for the fair and, if you place high enough, get a commission to build an actual pavilion. He contacted some friends and acquaintances in the profession and formed a team; they worked up plans and submitted them. One (very) fine morning, riding on top of one of the double-decker Fifth Avenue buses that cost a nickel more than their humdrum counterparts serving lesser streets, he opened the *New York Times* to discover he'd won.

Well, not "won" exactly, but he had received an honorable mention, which was enough to get him a commission for the Focal Foods Building. This pavilion was not what the name might suggest to the modern reader—a gathering of tapas and sushi bars—but an exhibition meant to teach Americans who had been through a hungry decade something about basic nutrition. The lesson had the virtue of being entertaining, for the building contained an elaborate animated display by the designer Russel Wright. Strongly influenced by the surrealists of the day, Wright had put together a landscape where giant fur-covered eggs greeted the visitor and bright red lobsters circled in the sky over distant mountaintops. Outside stood the exhibit's emblem, which was less antic: a quartet of gilded steel wheatstalks, designed by my father, severe art deco abstractions that stood one hundred feet high.

The fleet was in on opening day, April 30, 1939, and although for the sailors this was, in a way, demanding duty (the ships had to be made immaculate before they tied up at the Hudson River piers), hundreds of men got liberty and went out to the fair. It seems likely that they would have been more attracted by, say, the Crystal Lassies peep show than by flying lobsters, but surely many of them gave at least a glance to those metal wheatstalks glinting in the spring sunshine.

This was the first time my father's career intersected with that of the Atlantic Squadron. Of course he had no idea that before so very long the groups of sailors he saw wandering through this pageant billed as "The World of Tomorrow" would be part of his today, once it became clear where all the fair's pastel boulevards actually led.

THE SQUADRON HAD COME to New York for the best imaginable "flower show." That's what the sailors called it when their ship got dispatched to take part in a civic occasion. The phrase had been born in a Florida senator's request that a "battleship or other suitable vessel" be sent to his verdant state to add heft to an actual flower show. For years the navy had been generating goodwill by responding to such requests: battleships for the big cities, destroyers for smaller ones.

The ships that steamed up through the Narrows and into the Hudson that April gave a good indication of the state of the U.S. navy at the time. For one thing, far fewer were on hand than there should have been. At the last moment many of the scheduled attendees were recalled to the Pacific—the more glamorous ocean, as far as navy men were concerned, and a place increasingly troubled by Japan's imperial ambitions. The fleets of both oceans had just taken part in a six-day simulated battle that had suggested the rising influence of the aircraft carrier and the waning one of the battleship. Throughout the entire exercise, not one battleship had found the opportunity to fire the big guns that justified its existence. The destroyers, not surprisingly, did best what destroyermen best liked to do: a gallant dash at the enemy line, loosing torpedoes, then dodging away between the (in this case, imaginary) columns of water thrown up by heavy shells. On less flashy duty, things hadn't gone so well. During a bored and lax patrol of San Juan harbor, the *Reuben James* was "sunk" by a submarine. None of the vessels assigned to hunt submarines had done well.

The ships looked fine at the Hudson piers, buffed and bright with signal flags. But they weren't young, and they'd been worked hard, going on cruises that sometimes ran ten thousand miles, training men who were then often grabbed away for Pacific duty.

Here is the battleship *Arkansas,* commissioned in 1912. Earlier in the year, when she'd been directed to train midshipmen on the .50-caliber antiaircraft guns, her captain made the reasonable suggestion—couched in the inevitable passive voice of any military communication—that if .50-caliber antiaircraft practice is required, "it is felt that .50 caliber anti-aircraft guns should be supplied."

Tied up near the *Arkansas* is a sister ship, the *Wyoming,* commissioned the same year. Half her twelve-inch guns have been removed to comply with the naval treaties of the past two decades. These international accords, designed to discourage aggression, are the children of acrimonious wrangling, parents to immediate cheating, and are satisfactory to nobody who is participating in them.

And here are the destroyers. They seem small next to the battleships, but they're worth particular attention. They will forever be known as four-stackers or four-pipers, even though not every one was born with four funnels (the single characteristic that they all share is their flush deck, a clean line sloping from high bow to low stern). Products of the ferocious spasm of industrial energy that accompanied America's entry into World War

I, almost all of them were finished too late to take part in it, and many of their fellows are sleeping flank to flank in rusting rows up the Hudson or out in San Diego, thoroughly embalmed for years, but not quite dead.

They are handsome. Even from our vantage point of nearly a century they don't look quaint, although many warships built just a couple of decades earlier can bring to mind antique wind-up toys.

They are not easy ships to work. Their sailors all know a brief poem, by no means affectionate:

> *Pitch, pitch, goddamn your soul.*
> *The more you pitch, the less you roll.*
>
> *Roll, roll, you mean old bitch.*
> *The more you roll, the less you pitch.*

Before too long, they will bend the course of human events far beyond the capacities suggested by their middle-aged fighting powers.

THE SEAMEN WHO SERVE them, the lucky ones prowling around the city now, their less-favored counterparts showing visitors about the battleships and destroyers, are most of them old hands, members of a guild that goes back to the age of fighting sail. Scraps of their uniforms and many of their assumptions have come down from the War of 1812.

During the next few years they will accept with resigned competence a torrent of newcomers—people who talk about "stairs" instead of "ladders," of "back that way" instead of "aft"—and in time make sailors of them, too.

The life they live seems fantastic to us now, these men of what would soon be called the Old Navy, the prewar service that is half folklore and half dirty joke. What popular memory remains has them moving through a perpetual riotous shore leave of whores and bars and brawls (a tradition illuminated at its least attractive by the painter Paul Cadmus), and in some navy towns citizens are still hammering into their lawns signs that read SAILORS AND DOGS KEEP OFF THE GRASS. This seems an almost insane provocation, one whose outcome is as inevitable as it is predictable, yet a seventeen-year-old enlistee named Emory Jernigan saw them in Norfolk, Virginia. "Many signs were vandalized and urinated on," he reported, adding that he was "high on the list of sailors" who had done so.

Too Dumb to Stay
on the Farm

The making of a sailor, 1940

Jernigan joined the navy in 1940. Things were already heating up by then, but he nonetheless went through the same process that had been turning out American sailors for generations. Unlike the overwhelming majority of them, Jernigan wrote a memoir about his navy experiences and thus speaks for the multitudes who preceded and followed him into the ranks of the OS—the "ordinary seaman," who is the foundation upon which all naval enterprise ultimately rests.

E. J. Jernigan, a Chattahoochee, Florida, farm boy, was six years old when the stock market disintegrated. "Our garden assured us plenty to eat," he wrote, "even though we had no money, no electricity, and no car."

Attracted early to the military, Jernigan tried to join the navy at sixteen. The recruiting officer he spoke to was sympathetic, but Jernigan was too young. "We'll be starting the new kiddy cruises in December," the sailor told him. "I can come back for you then."

A kiddy cruise, it turned out, took you in at seventeen and let you out four years later, at twenty-one. Jernigan went home, persuaded his parents to sign his enlistment papers, and turned up in early December with other boys who wanted to go to sea. "Of the 21 of us trying to get in the Navy that day, 3 made it." This would have been about right for the time; in Depression America the service, with its regular pay and regular meals, had plenty of candidates to choose from. During the twelve-month period that had ended the previous June, the navy looked over 159,409 volunteers and accepted 14,512—less than 10 percent.

Jernigan was sworn in by a lieutenant and sent by train to the Naval Operations Base in Norfolk. He ate in the dining car, watching cows and farms and water tanks wheel past, buoyant in the knowledge that he was now earning $21 a month.

Norfolk was dirty, and it stank. "A young man like myself out of the backwoods wasn't used to the smell of warehouses, stored fruit, and exhaust fumes." The base itself was smart and well maintained, although the barracks, built for World War I, seethed with cockroaches. There, he was taken in hand by a man so thoroughly Old Navy that he had come back from retirement to find that his rating, chief turret captain, although permanently conferred, had not actually existed for years. Chief Turret Captain Mettick welcomed his new charges by explaining, "We were too damn dumb to stay on the farm, let alone to become sailors."

Then, after a brief nestle among the roaches, they were up at 4:00 a.m. This was boot camp, with all its routine discomforts and humiliations: shots, venereal disease inspection ("'Pull it back, milk it down.' If you didn't do it right, the pharmacist's mate would grab you and jerk it half off. He did this to get your attention. It was extremely effective"), on the double to collect uniforms—whites, blues, peacoats—issued with perfect contempt for any consonance in size between the clothes and their future inhabitants, and then, perhaps worst, the barbershop: "The barber was the most sadistic man I ever met," said Jernigan, rather surprisingly adding that his remorseless shearing was "the best way I could think of to break a man into the hard job he had to do." The bald products of the barber's work "even looked alike"— uniform new parts for a machine whose building never ceased.

Jernigan and the other men in his newborn platoon each got a seabag, "shaped like a long bucket made of canvas and tied with a drawstring at the top." These would follow their owners down the years, for everything they had went inside them; there were no closets, no footlockers, just the bags. Amid much cursing and scorn, the men learned how to pack them. Chief Martin would seize one man's jumper, fling it to the floor, and stamp on it screaming, "Roll the damn thing right or give your heart to God and your ass to me!" Rolling it right meant along the seam and then, for seabag stowage, tying it with twine, like a butcher's roast. Two other vital items went in with the cylinders of clothing: a sewing kit and a small ditty bag with shoe-polishing equipment. All sailors knew how to sew (to the end of his days, my father would darn and redarn his socks far beyond the boundaries of respectability); and their black shoes had always to glow with a liquid sheen, an effect achieved by hours of brushing and polishing and alchemical acts such as the application of Aqua Velva. Finally, there was *The Bluejackets' Manual*, which, Jernigan said, "was our Bible."

Bound in flexible covers so it could squirm in among the stacked coils of uniform, the 1940 edition of the *Manual* contained 784 pages of maritime wisdom. At "ninety cents, postpaid," as it said on the title page, it was an impressive bargain, with color plates of signal flags and the markings on shells, drawings and photos showing the firing chamber of a rifle, platoon formations, and, of course, an infinitude of knots. The book opened with instructions on how to behave under such headings as "Knowledge" (it "comes only through study and hard work"),

"Self-control" ("Do not fly off the handle"), "Justice" ("Play the game hard but play it squarely"), "Faith" ("Count on yourself to be one of the best man-o'-war's men in the whole Navy"), and "Cheerfulness" ("If you cannot smile, at least try to. You can surely keep the corners of your mouth *up*").

This last dictum was not always easy to follow. From the moment the master-at-arms came clattering through the barracks clubbing the steel bunks to wake the men, the day was one long, loud, wearing scramble: push-ups, jumping jacks, squat-and-walk (and at all other times, run); learning rifle drill on bolt-action weapons from the Great War; learning to row under the scalding tutelage of a man Jernigan described as "the ugliest, meanest seaman in the Navy"; learning how to talk ("a bed was a bunk; upstairs was topside . . . you drank water from a scuttle-butt. The window was a porthole. To work was called turning to; the kitchen was a galley; a light was a lantern; a light on a ship was a running light"); learning to take a swat on the ass from the flat of the chief's saber without making a move to retaliate.

Christmas came: "We slept until noon and turkey time. Everyone was sad, happy, and lonely at the same time and thankful when the Navy routine started anew. That December 25, 1940, was to be our last peaceful Christmas until 1945."

Back to drill, to marching in formation, and to—in the wake of some particularly egregious breach of military order—scrubbing the sidewalk with toothbrushes. The weeks passed. Jernigan began to realize that he liked some things about navy life: the food was fine; the jumper—so tight that pulling it "over your head was like skinning a squirrel"—looked good; he found the archaic complexity of the bell-bottoms satisfying ("with a flap that had thirteen buttons and was big as the opening in a coal chute. When you had to get to your talley-whacker, you unbuttoned a vertical row of buttons right and left and a horizontal row at the top"); his peacoat ("I was never cold in one"). The hat was another story; he could never manage to get the little white disk firmly secured on his head.

Then, after a week of close-order drill, came graduation. The men checked each other's blues, flicked motes from their shoes, gave a final rub to the stocks of their rifles, laced and relaced their leggings. Finally they marched past the reviewing stand. The captain of the base was there, along with "many flag rank officers, their wives, and kids." It was over too quickly, and they wanted to march past again. Instead they threw their caps in the air, hugged each other, and felt the first stirrings of affection for Chief Turret Captain Mettick.

Jernigan drew $15 and went back to Chattahoochee on leave. Nobody met him at the station. "It was a homecoming without anything happening. I'll never forget how disappointed I was. My little brothers and sisters said, 'Oh, you look thinner than you did when you left. Your hair's too short.' The girls didn't take to the uniform like I thought they would. I had a bad 15 days and went back to Norfolk."

Which was home now. He and his buddies would get liberty (*liberty* was permission to go ashore for less than forty-eight hours; any longer stretch of time was *leave*) and head to the Shamrock Beer Garden, which was "big enough to plant corn in and lined from one end to the other with sailors sipping suds." Beer gardens in Norfolk "were easier to find than a traffic light."

So were women. The chief had told them, "The girls in Norfolk can give you more grief in ten minutes than the Navy can in four years." He held up a condom, ordered them to use one every time, "and then check in at a pro[phylactic] station. They are open all night. The pharmacist's mate will show you what to do. If you catch VD, the navy will put you on restriction and stop your pay until you are cured. You will make up the time at the end of your cruise."

Thus encouraged, they visited places where half-naked women chatted with them until they made a choice, paid their $2, and found themselves back on the street within half an hour. As for any more permanent arrangement, "if the Navy wanted you to have a wife, they would have issued you one."

Jernigan went to a tailor and had the man run him up a set of good dress blues, despite the stern passage about this in *The Bluejackets' Manual*: "Many men want 'tailor-made' clothes and spend large sums ashore to get them. In most cases the cloth in these clothes is not as good as in the clothes purchased from the supply officer. The pattern is usually not strictly regulation, and these men frequently get in trouble over this." This admonition was universally ignored.

Jernigan wore his new blues when, in March, he reported to Philadelphia for duty aboard BB56, the USS *Washington*. She was a brand-new battleship, still under construction, and the crew at first slept in barracks ashore. "Every ship is like a city, large or small. Even a tugboat is a little town all its own," wrote Jernigan, who had found his way to a big town, one with fifteen hundred inhabitants. It would take him months to become familiar with this town, but a lot of his neighbors were already at home there.

These knowledgeable old-timers reflected a stasis throughout the navy that turned out to be a gift in the Pandora's box of the Depression. For years there had been scant chance of getting ahead. "You had to be perfect," Jernigan said, "or you were called on the mat. I knew many shipmates with 12 to 15 years in service who were seamen or third class petty officers, not because they weren't good but because the Navy didn't advance you that fast." These long-seasoned professionals would be the tough hide of an ever-expanding balloon filling with neophytes who needed to be taught jobs on which the survival of a nation depended. It was a good thing they were there, for that time was coming soon.

Building Hitler's Navy

Superbattleships vs. submarines, 1933–39

Adolf Hitler didn't much like ships. "I am a hero on land," he said once, "but a coward at sea." He had a wonderfully retentive mind for nautical detail, but his grasp of strategy was that of a general, not an admiral. He saw his country as historically threatened by France and Russia, and his response was to set about building a peerless army. Even his air force, powerful enough to frighten half the world in 1939, was essentially designed to support the operations of his troops in battles on the ground. Nor did his searing formative experiences in World War I make him feel more warmly toward naval matters.

By 1914 Germany had built a battle fleet that, if not as large as Great Britain's, had better ships, better armor on them, and better shells for them to fire. And what had this superb High Seas Fleet done? Come out once in full strength, in 1916, and, at the Battle of Jutland, badly roughed up the British fleet, but then fled for home and stayed in port while the months ground by and morale corroded and, in the war's last days, mutinied and refused to go back to sea.

Only one branch of the service had kept faith until the very end: the submarines. Indeed, they came close to putting Britain out of the war long after the surface fleet had tried and failed.

Nevertheless, despite his often-expressed scorn for battleships, Hitler was vexed by the theories of a naval officer who was not only long dead but an American. As a teacher at the Naval War College in the 1880s, Alfred Thayer Mahan had come to believe that "control of the sea was an historic factor which had never been systematically appreciated and expounded." He wrote a book to correct this. *The Influence of Sea Power upon History* came out in 1890.

Mahan's thesis was simple and strong. Maritime commerce is the life of a nation; choke it off and the nation will wither. The key to dominating the seas, though, is not commerce raiding—that is, attacking the ships that carry the commerce—but rather keeping a powerful battle fleet that can destroy the battle fleet of an opposing nation. This force should not be frittered away chasing after merchant ships, but should instead concentrate itself, stay together, and strike a decisive blow. Once the main force of the enemy is shattered, the rest will follow.

Of all the American books ever published, perhaps only *Common Sense* and *Uncle Tom's Cabin* have had a comparable impact on events. Mahan's argument was taken up everywhere. America settled upon the all-big-gun battleship as its main strategic weapon at sea and started building them. Britain not surprisingly embraced his thesis; so did Kaiser Wilhelm II, who had a copy of *Influence* placed aboard every German warship. Mahan played a role in the American defeat of the Spanish navy in 1898 and the Japanese annihilation of their Russian opponents at Tsushima in 1905, and in bringing the German and British fleets together at Jutland in 1916.*

---

*The battleships he summoned up are museums now, or long since melted down for razor blades, but Alfred Thayer Mahan is still very much with us: in a 1902 article called "The Persian Gulf and International Relations," he invented the term *Middle East*.

Even though Hitler knew that commerce-raiding submarines had come far closer than the High Seas Fleet ever had to tipping the balance in Germany's favor during the Great War, Mahan's potent theory continued to influence him. So did Mahan's disciple Erich Raeder.

In 1939 Raeder had been commander in chief of the German navy for eleven years. He was sixty-three years old, a thoroughgoing professional who had joined the service in 1894 and seen it grow into a force that could threaten Britain's three-century command of the seas. He had fought at Jutland aboard a cruiser and had taken over the hulk of his navy when it barely existed. He despised Nazism, thought it mere thuggery, but he saw in Hitler a man who could bring back the old High Seas Fleet, and then perhaps the Jutland-to-come would go the other way.

Hitler listened to Raeder, listened and was drawn as when speaking with his architect Albert Speer about the wide boulevards and colossal buildings that would transform German cities once the world was set aright. Hitler and Raeder talked of battle cruisers, of seventy-two-thousand-ton superbattleships, of aircraft carriers.

The predecessor to this dream navy had committed suicide. After Germany surrendered in the winter of 1918, the High Seas Fleet had been interned up in the Orkney Islands at the great British naval base of Scapa Flow. The next spring, when the skeleton crews of those ships learned of the terms of the Versailles Treaty, they scuttled them in protest. The peace treaty had all but abolished the German navy. The service was cut to fifteen thousand men and a handful of aging ships. These could be replaced when they got to be fifteen years old, but only with smaller counterparts. There could be no German submarines at all.

The victorious nations, looking back at the monstrous cost of the past four years, began to talk about devising disarmament agreements that would extinguish the possibility of another war.

That these treaties failed in the end is not nearly so surprising as what they actually accomplished.

President Harding is generally remembered as being affable and lazily incompetent, but he certainly got what he wanted here, which was an armament reduction of radical severity. Henceforth, navies would be confined to a maximum tonnage—eventually, in capital ships (those of ten thousand tons or more with guns larger than eight inches), 500,000 tons for Great Britain and the United States, 300,000 for their recent ally Japan, 175,000 for Italy and France. These ratios would be echoed in the permissible tonnage of smaller warships. This meant not only naval self-restraint on the part of the signatories, but naval self-destruction. The United States alone would have to scrap fifteen battleships and another fifteen capital ships that were still being built. Britain would be obligated to destroy nineteen of her battleships, but the Mistress of the Seas was all for the plan because it would allow her to maintain her naval superiority without the exorbitant competitive shipbuilding that had roiled the century's first years. In 1921, at the Washington Naval Conference, England signed, America signed, and so did France and Japan and Italy. And for a while, they all played by the rules.

To be sure, a lot of haggling and bad faith continued about lesser vessels, especially cruisers and submarines. The matter didn't get settled until 1930, when, after having veered toward the total abolition of submarines, the delegates at the London Naval Conference settled on a 52,700-ton limit per nation, and all of them signed Article 22, which in retrospect seems a most extraordinary exercise in wishful thinking: "a submarine may not sink or render incapable of navigation a merchant vessel without having first placed passengers, crew and ship's papers in a place of safety."

Of course, this clause would not have affected Germany because she was permitted no submarines. Her little navy, reborn in 1921 and christened the Reichsmarine—the State Navy—tried to figure out a role for itself. It would most likely fight against France and Poland, the planners decided, and when it came time to replace their ships, they looked to build successors that could fill the role of the outlawed U-boats in a war of commerce: fast surface raiders. But as the decade wore on Germany more and more blatantly experimented with submarine development, too. Under a fairly transparent front company, research went forward in Holland. Boats were built in Finland and Spain and tested by German sailors dressed as tourists. A submarine school opened in Turkey.

Meanwhile, Raeder moved away from the limits imposed by Versailles. In late 1932 he got permission from his government to build six capital ships and six squadrons of destroyers, and to establish a secret submarine school on German soil. A couple of months later, Hitler came to power. He encouraged Raeder, while urging him to keep on good terms with Britain. There would never again be a war between the two countries, Hitler said; German naval planners weren't even permitted to envision one in their exercises. In March 1935 Hitler repudiated the terms of Versailles, announcing that he would build Germany the army, air force, and navy she deserved. Three months later British and German delegates met in London, and Hitler's new foreign minister, Joachim von Ribbentrop, offered to establish a comforting three-to-one ratio between British and German tonnage. The result was the Anglo-German Naval Treaty, which also allowed parity in submarines, Germany having agreed to the Article 22 stipulation about not attacking merchant ships. In keeping with the tenor of that anxious decade, Britain was both pleased and relieved. No less a figure than David Beatty, who had been first sea lord for eight years, declared to the House of Lords, "We owe thanks to the Germans. . . . That we do not have an armament race with one nation in the world at least is something for which we must be thankful." That same year the Reichsmarine adopted a sharp-fanged new name: the Kriegsmarine. The State Navy had become the War Navy.

The Germans kept their word for about as long as they usually did in that era. At the end of 1938, Raeder presented his Z plan to Hitler. It called for a massive expansion of the fleet. Plenty of U-boats, but also ten battleships, four aircraft carriers, nearly seventy destroyers—a million tons all told by the time the job was done, in 1948. Hitler approved, but with one change: the fleet must ready by 1946. There would be no war until then, he promised—and never one with England.

"The Simple Principle of Fighting Several Steamers with Several U-boats"

Captain Doenitz works out his strategy,
1918–39

★ ★ ★

The Z plan came as a highly unpleasant surprise not only to the British, but also to Captain Karl Doenitz. He knew very well that Germany would be at war before 1946 and that Great Britain would almost certainly be the enemy. He knew how he wanted to fight that war, too, and it had nothing to do with aircraft carriers.

Karl Doentiz, who was to be the single most important man in the Nazi navy, was born in Berlin in 1891, the son of an engineer. He joined the kaiser's navy in 1910 and became a lieutenant three years later. Assigned to the cruiser *Breslau,* he quickly impressed his captain, as he would every officer he served under. After a year's service in the Black Sea (where he met his wife-to-be, the daughter of a general), the *Breslau*'s skipper wrote, "Doenitz is a charming, dashing and plucky officer with first-rate character qualities." In the fall of 1916, with Jutland fought and Germany looking more and more toward her submarine fleet, the young officer was ordered to U-boat school in Flensburg, up on the Baltic. After a three-month course, he was sent to *U-39* to serve under Captain Walter Forstmann.

It was an opportune posting at an opportune time. Forstmann was one of the most celebrated and capable of all U-boat commanders, and Germany, after years of trying to keep from angering a neutral America, was soon to declare unrestricted submarine warfare.

Two days after setting sail, the *U-39* sank an Italian freighter. There followed ten busy months, at the end of which Forstmann gave Doenitz as warm an assessment as any U-boat man could hope for: "Sailed and navigated the boat calmly and confidently, is reliable as watch-keeping officer and understands the management of his subordinates . . . Lively, energetic officer, who enters into each duty with diligence and enthusiasm . . . Popular comrade, tactful messmate." These were all the main qualities necessary for success as a submariner, and not least of them was the tact: it was not just a matter of good manners, but nearly as necessary as oxygen in the claustrophobic little society of a U-boat.

After a year with Forstmann, Doenitz got his own command, of a mine-laying submarine, and did so well that after just two cruises he became captain of a better boat, the *UB-68*. During his time at sea, he had thought a great deal about submarines and how they should best be used. "Up till now the U-boats had always waged war alone," he wrote years later. "They set forth and ranged the seas alone, they battled alone against the antisubmarine defenses, and they sought out and fought the enemy alone."

The evening of October 3, 1918, found the *UB-68* lying motionless under a fingernail of moon fifty miles off the southeast corner of Sicily. Doenitz was waiting for two things: a British convoy bound westward from the Suez Canal and, what was probably a more exciting prospect to him just then, the arrival of another U-boat. This operation, he wrote, would be "the first

ever undertaken by two U-boats together." The other U-boat
never showed; engine trouble had kept it in port. The convoy did,
though. At about 1:00 a.m. Doenitz's lookout spotted a British
destroyer. "Soon more shadows loomed up in the darkness, first
more destroyers and escort vessels, and finally the great solid silhouettes of the merchantmen themselves—a convoy of heavily
laden ships from the East, from India and China and bound for
Malta and the West."

He took the *UB-68* in unseen past the guarding destroyers
and got between two lines of merchantmen. He went after one
in the farther line and had the satisfaction of seeing "a gigantic,
brightly illuminated column of water" rise beside it, "followed
by a mighty explosion." As a destroyer came pelting toward him,
Doenitz took his boat down and slipped away from the convoy.

When he cautiously surfaced, he saw the lines of ships moving away to the west, and followed them. He always preferred to
attack on the surface, "but dawn came too soon; as I came up on
the convoy, it became so light that I was compelled to submerge.
I then decided to try and attack, submerged at periscope depth.
Things worked out very differently, however."

The dive to periscope depth came close to being his last.
Perhaps he made a mistake, perhaps his engineer did, or perhaps the crew was not sufficiently trained. The result was that
"we suddenly found ourselves submerged and standing on our
heads. The batteries spilled over and the lights went out." He ordered all tanks blown—the water in them replaced with buoying
air—and could then only sweat it out, watching his first lieutenant play a flashlight on the depth gauge while a thousand fathoms of water drew his boat down. The hull could stand up to a
dive of 180 feet, perhaps 200. Under the lieutenant's light the
unforgiving needle dropped steadily past 170, past 200; it went
by 220 and 230 without pausing; 250; 260. Somewhere beyond
270 it began to quiver, stopped, and then rose from 300 feet even

more swiftly than it had gotten there. The submarine rocketed to the surface and burst up into full daylight in the middle of the convoy, having over the past few hours provided a succinct working demonstration of the strengths and weaknesses of this capricious weapon.

"All the ships, destroyers and merchantmen alike, were flying signal flags, sirens were howling all round us. The merchant ships turned away and opened fire with the guns they had mounted on their sterns, and the destroyers, firing furiously, came tearing down upon me. A fine situation!"

Doenitz had no choice. "I gave the order, 'All hands, abandon ship.'"

The *UB-68* sank. Doenitz lost seven of his crew. "That was the end of my seagoing career in a U-boat in the First World War. That last night, however, had taught me a lesson as regards basic principles."

He had time to mull over those principles while a prisoner of war for the next ten months. Then he returned to the naval base at Kiel, a ghost town now with the fleet that had once occupied it rusting on the bottom of another harbor and a few remaining submarines going under the wrecker's torch. Still, this was headquarters of the new navy. It was permitted just fifteen hundred officers, but Doenitz's reputation made him an obvious choice. The director of personnel asked "whether I would like to remain in the service."

Doenitz replied with a question: "Do you think we shall soon have U-boats again?"

"I'm sure we shall. Things won't always be like this."

The time Doenitz had spent in submarines had made him a passionate advocate of them, and that passion was still warm when he came to write his memoirs nearly forty years afterward. It is something of a surprise to see it flash out amid his austere prose: "This was all that I needed to persuade me to serve on in the navy. . . . I had been fascinated by that unique characteristic of the submarine service, which requires a submariner to stand on his own feet and sets him a task in the great spaces of the oceans, the fulfillment of which demands a stout heart and ready skill; I was fascinated by that unique spirit of comradeship engendered by destiny and hardship shared in the community of a U-boat's crew, where every man's well-being was in the hands of all and where every single man was an indispensable part of the whole. Every submariner, I am sure, has experienced in his heart the glow of the open sea and the task entrusted to him, has felt himself to be as rich as a king and would change places with no man."

It would take him quite a while to return to that favored company. The Versailles Treaty allowed no submarines, and he was posted to their surface counterparts, torpedo boats. As before, he flourished, drawing the same sort of praise from his superiors that he had when the kaiser was still in business: "exemplary service outlook and fullest devotion to duty"; "full of hearty merriment at appropriate times"; "respected and popular." It was the same story when he took a staff course under Erich Raeder in 1924: "Clever, industrious, ambitious officer," Raeder wrote of his new student. "Of excellent general professional knowledge and clear judgment in questions of naval war leadership." Raeder became commander in chief in 1928, and Doenitz got the Fourth Half-Flotilla—torpedo boats again, four of them, with twenty officers and six hundred men under him. In exercises he was directed to mount a night attack against a "convoy"; he found it and "destroyed" it.

Next he was posted to shore duty in a job much vaguer than commanding torpedo boats: "My tasks included measures of protection against inner unrest [that is, within the service]." Whatever he was doing, it was "truly a time filled with hard work," and it gained him a commendation that stands in curious contrast with the tenor of his earlier praise. It came from the sinuous, canny, unknowable William Canaris, the admiral who would take over German military intelligence in the war they were all busy hatching and be put to death for his role in the 1944 plot to assassinate Hitler. "Very ambitious," Canaris wrote of Doenitz, "and consequently asserts himself to obtain prestige, finding it difficult to subordinate himself and confine himself to his own work-sphere. . . . His strong temperament and inner verve frequently affected him with restlessness and, for his age, imbalance. Must therefore be brought to take things more calmly and not to set exaggerated demands, above all on himself. . . . Character is not yet fully formed."

Perhaps Doenitz offers a glimpse of the person Canaris saw in his account of the hours that preceded his capture, when he says the aborted meeting with the other U-boat would have been the first time submarines had ever operated in concert. It wasn't true. Joint attacks on convoys had been going on for months; the captain of the U-boat he'd been scheduled to meet had taken part in two of them. Doenitz made the claim in a memoir written after he had been the head of his navy—and, indeed, of his nation. That he still had to assert the credit for inventing group U-boat tactics suggests the gnawing of a restless, hungry ego.

If Canaris alone spotted this, he was an observer with experience that lay beyond the boundaries of most officers in the German naval fraternity. For Doenitz, it was back to the usual fare of high compliment: "magnificent intellectual and character gifts," said his annual report for 1934, the year he took command of the light cruiser *Emden*. She was about to be sent around Africa and the Indian Ocean as a traveling emblem of Germany's resurgence. But first, her captain was summoned to meet the new chancellor.

Doenitz was not only of a different generation from his commander in chief, Raeder, he held very different political views (Raeder would mockingly refer to Doenitz as "Hitler Boy"—but only after the war was over). Doenitz felt no disdain for Hitler or his party, and he would warmly agree with Hitler's policies throughout the war—save where they differed with his own about how the navy should be employed.

Doenitz returned home in the summer of 1935 to be given a big assignment. "You, Doenitz," Raeder told him, "are to take over the job of raising our new U-boat arm."

Despite Doenitz's paean to the virtues of the service, he wrote, "I cannot say I was altogether pleased." His hesitations did not come from any doubt about the efficacy of submarines. "I believed in the fighting powers of the U-boat. I regarded it, as I had always regarded it, as a first-class weapon of offence in naval warfare, and as the best possible torpedo-carrier." Rather, he was keenly aware of the chimera of the heavy surface fleet. This view extended even to the submarine itself in the German admiralty, which wanted to build immense U-boats—U-cruisers—that could fight gun battles with big surface ships. Doenitz found this ludicrous.

It was not a hasty judgment. He'd been thinking hard, both pragmatically and imaginatively, about U-boats, applying those "basic principles" that had been driven home to him nearly twenty years earlier while he was upside down in darkness under a drizzle of battery acid with British destroyers awaiting him on the surface if he could ever get back there.

He believed the U-boat existed solely to deliver torpedoes. The same low freeboard that made the vessel so hard to spot in attacks—which should take place on the surface, at night, close in—made it a poor gun platform and worse reconnaissance vessel. Nor was a U-boat fast enough to work effectively with a surface fleet, although it should always cooperate with its fellows in joint attacks such as the one he'd been looking forward to the night before he'd been captured. And now that radio had come of age, these could surely be coordinated from some central command post,

What, then, was the most desirable kind of U-boat to build? Doenitz was sure he knew, and he explained why with clarity and bite: "The submarine is the sole class of warship which is called upon only on the rarest and exceptional occasions to fight one of its own kind. The question of the strength of the corresponding type of ship possessed by a potential adversary, which plays so important a role in the design and construction of all other types of warships, is therefore of no importance whatever when it comes to deciding the size and fighting power of a submarine." Despite the universal naval temptation to build ever-bigger ships, "many of those characteristics from which the submarine derives its own particular value as a fighting unit tend to decrease in value once a certain size is overstepped." The bigger the submarine, the longer it takes to dive, and the harder it is to maneuver.

Amid such considerations, what he had on hand when he took over that July were twenty-four boats either in commission or soon to be: twelve Type IIs, of 250 tons and three torpedo tubes in their bows, "a very simple and successful vessel, but very small"; two Type Is—four bow and two stern torpedo tubes, but, at 712 tons, too big to handle easily; and ten Type VIIs, "approximately 500 tons; four bow and one stern tube; surface speed 16 knots; radius of action 6,200 miles." "An excellent type," Doenitz concluded of this last with fond economy. Whenever he could, he would fight the Atlantic war with Type VIIs.

But of course he needed men who knew how to handle them, and with the little two-hundred-tonners he began training them. In the wholly dedicated assiduity he brought to this task, we can see the justice of all that approbation from satisfied superiors, and perhaps catch a whiff of the zealotry that Canaris noticed.

In September Doentiz inaugurated the Weddigen Flotilla—named for a U-boat hero of the last war—in Kiel at the Anti-Submarine School ("later," Doenitz wrote, apparently unconscious of a kind of grim humor in the name change, "to become the Submarine School"). No group of recruits ever worked harder. "Every part of the training program was systemically, steadily and thoroughly carried out. . . . Every U-boat, for example, had to carry out 66 surface attacks and a like number submerged before . . . its first torpedo-firing practice."

The boats were at sea all the time, and Doenitz was always there aboard one or another of them, teaching the tangible ("the invisible attacks at periscope depth and with minimum use of periscope") and the intangible ("the commander being required to try to develop a kind of sixth sense with regard to whether he had or had not been observed when on the surface"). None of Doenitz's pupils had any prior experience with submarines, but as one of them wrote decades later, "The knowledge acquired during this single year of training, in which the crews were tested to the limits of human endeavor, was the foundation in so far as choice of types, armament and training are concerned, upon which the future structure of the U-boat arm was built."

By 1939 Raeder had ships and men enough to take part in an elaborate exercise that pitted fifteen U-boats against an Atlantic convoy. By the war game's end thirteen of the boats, directed by radio, had surrounded their target. Doenitz's report on this success spelled out briefly what he intended to do in the coming war: "The simple principle of fighting several steamers with several U-boats . . . is correct. The summoning of U-boats under the conditions of the exercise was successful. The convoy would have been destroyed."

To win a naval war against Britain he would need a great many U-boats: three hundred was the precise number he settled on and held to. "In arriving at this figure I assumed that at any given moment one hundred U-boats would be in port for overhaul and to give the crews a period of rest, a further hundred would be on their way to or from the theater of operations, and the remaining hundred would be actively engaged in operations against the enemy. Given this total, however, I believed that I could achieve a decisive success."

But now things were moving too quickly for his plans. In late April 1939 Hitler repudiated two of his treaties: the 1934 Non-Aggression Pact with Poland, and the 1935 Naval Agreement. On August 23 he signed a nonaggression pact with the Soviet Union. On September 1 he invaded Poland.

Doenitz had already ordered his boats to sea. Still, he was clearly shocked when, on September 3, at his headquarters in Wilhelmshaven, fifteen minutes after the British ultimatum to Germany had run out, an aide gave him a telegram from German naval intelligence. The British Admiralty had broadcast the signal "Total Germany." Doenitz wadded up the piece of paper and began to pace back and forth, muttering, "My God! So it's war with England again!" He left the room.

Raeder, receiving the same news in Berlin, was even more distressed. Now he was no more likely to get his superbattleships and aircraft carriers than he was to be handed Excalibur. "The surface forces," he wrote, "are so inferior in number and strength to those of the British Fleet that, even at full strength, they can do no more than show that they know how to die gallantly."

Doenitz recovered himself after half an hour and came back into his office. "We know our enemy," he calmly told his staff. "We have today the weapon and the leadership that we can face up to this enemy. The war will last a long time; but if each does his duty, we will win."

Still, his three hundred U-boats had vanished into impossibility along with Raeder's carriers, and he would be bitter about those unbuilt ships to the end of his days. "The navy was like a torso without limbs," he wrote years later. "The U-boat arm possessed in all forty-six boats ready for action [and] only twenty-two were suitable for service in the Atlantic." Could he do more "than subject the enemy to a few odd pinpricks"?

Very much more, the months and years to come would show.

On the Devil's Shovel

U-boat life, 1939–45

Doenitz had a single goal, and a single tool with which to achieve it. He believed that his country's sole chance of victory lay in what he came to call a "tonnage war"—destroying freight, and sinking the ships that carried it faster than they could be replaced.

To that end he had worked out his fleet's tactics and helped develop the extraordinary vessel that would carry them out. If the U-boat was soon to become an object of dread to its enemies, the submarine had always been a fearfully harsh ally to the men aboard it.

A torpedo is as complex as a fine watch, full of machinery as a sausage is of meat: the explosive charge in the head is served by intricacies of piping and gears, gyroscopes, elegant little power plants driven by steam or compressed air or electricity.

A U-boat is a big torpedo. We may remember from pictures the high, sharp bow rising from the water, the conning tower with its cage of railing, the deck and its gun mount, but this is all a carapace and has no more to do with the heart of the boat than the hood of a car and its headlights have to do with its engine and power train. The cladding covered the pressure hull, a cigar-shaped, two-hundred-foot hermetic tube widest at its middle, and there only fifteen feet across. Inside it were two long, head-high diesel engines, standing side by side with a narrow walkway between them, an arsenal of torpedoes, fifty-ton batteries beneath deck plates, and a baffling infinity of pipes and valves and vents and gauges and generators. Foot for foot a U-boat was more complicated and expensive to build than any other warship. All this tortuously compressed hardware had to be in and functional before any thought could be given to inserting the people who had to tend it.

On his small surface ship my father, as a lieutenant, would get his own stateroom, which he shared with another officer. A U-boat had no stateroom. The captain alone enjoyed the luxury of a padded bench about the width of a soda-fountain counter to sleep on, and a curtain to pull across it.

At sea, nobody could move aboard a U-boat without having to squeeze around jutting equipment or another crewman. There were two toilets, but only one was available at the beginning of a war cruise because the other would be filled with food—as would be the rest of the boat. Cans of condensed milk clinked against the torpedo tubes, and crates of cabbages colonized the tiny wardroom, where the officers used the table alternately for plotting courses and eating meals.

Those toilets were problematic even when free of provisions because they were extremely tricky to flush and couldn't be worked at all if the boat was submerged beyond eighty feet. Flushing required a dozen separate actions with pumps and levers, and if the proper sequence wasn't followed, the consequences could be disproportionately severe. In at least one instance, mishandling of the flushing (in *U-1206,* by no less a figure than the captain) led to the destruction of the boat. In good weather the crew preferred to use the "outside" toilet, a wooden ring mounted on the deck.

This was often accessible because U-boats were not submarines as we know them today, vessels that can stay submerged for weeks at a time. U-boats ran underwater with electric engines powered by those enormous batteries, but not for long: perhaps sixty miles at six miles per hour. The big diesels could push them far faster, but only if they were on the surface. Running submerged on diesel power would asphyxiate the crew in minutes.

Nevertheless, submarines had to spend a great deal of time below the surface. In the coming war against America, they would loiter on the bottom the whole day off the Carolinas or Massachusetts, rising as the sun set to track their quarry. Those were long days for the crews. Everything dripped, everything stank. Clothing was always damp and soon dirty. The men wore what they called "whore's undies," boxer shorts dyed black to make less evident their increasing filthiness. The captain—who lived on top of his men in an intimacy unknown to any other service—would encourage any number of stationary diversions: cards (although that wonderful wellspring of ill feeling, gambling for money, was largely forbidden), chess, painting, reading of course, although the dim lights required to preserve the batteries often made this more pain than pleasure. At regular intervals meals would emerge from the two-burner stove in the galley—which was no more a "galley" than the wardroom was a "room"—to be enjoyed in a close pungency of aging vegetables, piss, fuel oil, much-breathed air, and the real but less definable smells of boredom and tension. Bomber crews endured the same thing, but they were back home after a few hours. Submariners lived on what some called "the devil's shovel" for three months straight.

The preparations for a war cruise reflected the boat's uniquely inhospitable soul.

The stay in a home port was never brief. Routine maintenance was done during a U-boat mission, but not as the term was understood in the surface navies. There, sailors got a sense of the least enticing aspects of eternity by chipping paint down to what was hopefully called "clean bright metal," laying on primer, then new paint, then chipping again close by, and chipping, and chipping some more. Nobody chipped paint in a U-boat, where the most mundane operations required constant attention to the craft's endlessly complex innards. Each return to port meant an overhaul of the entire boat.

This was good for the crew, who got long leaves, and every possible support to help enjoy them. The realities of the service had combined with years of recruitment propaganda to make submariners even more highly regarded in Germany than Luftwaffe pilots. At the end of a cruise, special trains would be standing by to take them to their hometowns—or, if they preferred, to requisitioned châteaus turned into lavish resorts.

As the time for the next mission approached, the seamen would return to their bases and put up in shoreside barracks for the next few days, or on ocean liners converted into floating dormitories. No man spent a night more than he had to aboard a U-boat.

The overhaul completed, the boat would begin taking on supplies. Torpedoes first—fourteen for the Type VII boats, twenty-two for the IXs. The latter were roomier vessels, but the additional matériel crammed inside them made the experience of serving aboard identical. The U-boat existed solely to carry torpedoes, and these were stowed everywhere: winched up to a forty-five-degree angle and slid into the pressure hull to lie beneath the flooring of the bow room, and in the stern, and of course in the tubes. Others went between the pressure hull and the outer cladding.

These machines, as efficient-looking as bullets, and with the same aura of lethal inertness, were actually as restive as a cargo of live cougars, and the crew had to start tending to their incessant demands just hours after the boat sailed.

Next came the shells for the deck gun, often the famously effective 88mm (virtually everyone who ever came under fire from an 88 remembered the weapon with deep respect and equally deep loathing). Each of the rounds—about 250 in all—came aboard packed in its own watertight container. Well packed, too: recently divers retrieved several from the ocean floor, still potent and full of menace, fresh as the day they were stowed, ready to claw apart a freighter scrapped fifty years ago.

Food followed, the nonperishables first—canned corned beef, powdered eggs, 150 pounds of canned cheese—some twelve tons in all. The third watch officer had to find places for the hundreds of cans and crates. On these most scrupulously designed boats, surprisingly little attention had been paid to food storage; aside from some cramped cupboards and a tiny refrigerated meat locker, the stowage had to be improvised. Once the third watch officer had achieved this, he had to keep his hundred places of sequesterment in mind for the rest of the voyage, shifting their contents about as the food was consumed so uneven weight would not throw off the boat's trim—that is, the delicately maintained equilibrium that would keep it making its way underwater without bursting to the surface (as it often wanted to do) or plunging to the bottom (as it always wanted to do).

On the third and last day of provisioning, after the diesel fuel had been pumped aboard, the fresh food came on. This went everywhere: through the first weeks of the voyage hams swung from the overhead pipes in the forward torpedo room, and sacks of onions and lemons and potatoes crowded lumpily against the bulkheads. Clusters of sausages dangled the length of the boat, which would set out carrying the curious combined atmosphere of a luxury grocery store doing business inside a gargantuan automobile engine.

"Luxury" because the U-boats got the best provisions Germany had to offer. It made little difference, though, especially with the fresh food. In the perpetual metallic damp, nothing kept for long. The sailors called their bread "rabbits" because each loaf soon grew a coat of white fur, and the men excavated in past this pelt to dig out edible scraps. In days, everything had been basted with the effluvium of the boat. "The food?" said a crewman on *U-106*. "The food was good—as long as you liked the taste of diesel."

Before the diesel oil could do its seasoning, it had to drive the engines. The crew called them the Jumbos, and they deserved the old American superlative: eighteen-foot-long, four-stroke, supercharged diesels, six cylinders on the Type VIIs and nine on the IXs, producing fourteen hundred horsepower each on the former, twenty-two hundred on the latter. Kicked into life by a jolt of compressed air, they set up a clamor that could destroy the hearing of those who tended them (the antique name *stokers* still attached itself to these men), and they threw off enough heat to give the men rashes and boils. They were fickle, too. Although they did little to warm the boat in winter, they could run engine-room temperatures up past 140 degrees in warm weather.

The engines were the province of the *Leitender Ingenieur,* the chief engineer, who, because of the boat's importunate complexity, was second only to the captain in the hierarchy of officers. A great deal was demanded of the LI and his "technical branch," which accounted for a good half of the crew. One is said to have improvised replacement ball bearings by melting pellets out of metal foil stripped from cigarette packs. More common was the quandary that faced Paul Mengelberg, a diesel mechanic on *U-26.* "We had one time when we were forced to replace a piston pin . . . on the bottom of the Mediterranean, which took us about eighteen hours. It was a problem changing this diesel piston pin because the pin would not budge. . . . So eventually we had an idea. The whole piston was removed and immersed in hot oil, then boiled on the cook's stove. Then we took it out of the oil, filled the hollow part of the pin with ice from the cook's icebox to shrink it just enough, and bingo, with a sledgehammer and a bit of luck the pin came out!"

Just aft of the engine room, and usually spared such heroic expedients to keep it functioning, was the electric-motor room. Unlike the hammering diesels, the electric motors that drove the ship when it was underwater were relatively quiet, and duty here was less exhausting, although no less exacting: a failure to shift quickly from diesel to electric power during an emergency dive could mean an instant end to the boat and all aboard it. The motors drew their current from the banks of batteries that ran along the hull beneath them. The formidably successful U-boat skipper Peter "Ali" Cremer, who made it through the whole war (occasionally bringing home his boat under circumstances so difficult that his crewmen had a saying: "Ali's better than life insurance"), wrote, "If one speaks of a certain superiority of the submarine or *Unterseeboot* in being able to hide under the water, one must in the same breath mention its weakness." A main one was electricity. "The electric motors derive their energy from the batteries, which are heavy and bulky, limited in size . . . by the narrowness of the boat. Under heavy loads their energy is soon exhausted and they are obliged to surface to recharge them." On a type VII this took eight hours running on the surface, with one of the diesels banging away clutched to the electric motor, which, when it wasn't driving the boat, worked as a generator.

Forward of the engine and motor rooms was what the crew called the *Zentrale*. The boat's demanding neurological system was run from this control room. The periscope was here; actually, one of two periscopes: the larger—the crew called it the *Spargel*, asparagus, for its bulbous head—was used for navigation. It let in a good deal of light and thus afforded greater visibility, but it left a strong, telltale wake. The leaner, more businesslike-looking attack periscope, with its range markings, was almost always the skipper's choice during a torpedo run.

The LI spent hours in the control room, keeping an eye on the planesmen. The two of them maneuvered the hydroplanes at bow and stern that raised and lowered the boat. Each sat before a burly wheel, but this got touched only in emergencies: if things were going as they should, the planesmen did their job with a pair of electronic push buttons.

Nearby, the helmsman controlled the rudder, also with buttons. During a surface attack, he took another station, directly above in the conning tower. There he followed orders from the captain, who would have climbed the ladder that led through the conning-tower hatch up onto the open bridge.

Forward of the control room were the captain's quarters. The plural might be misleading: this was a tiny closet entirely filled by its furnishings of a bunk, cupboard, and dollhouse writing desk. Nonetheless, it was shielded by the green felt curtain, which, once drawn, gave its occupant the sole scrap of privacy a U-boat had to offer.

It was of course no accident that the captain lived a few feet away from both the control room and the radio room, the latter as important to a U-boat's operations as the former. All through the war Doenitz used radio as the reins with which he kept close control over all his boats. This would cost him dearly later, but in the early days was an effective, indeed indispensable, part of what looked to be a winning campaign.

Every U-boat sailor came aboard with a good deal of stiff training behind him, but the amount doled out to the *Funker*—the radioman—suggests his importance to the enterprise. After taking a series of intelligence and psychological—and, of course, hearing—tests and three months of what was essentially boot camp, he would go to Flensburg for a full half year of naval radio school there. After that it was on to Gotenhafen for the training administered all prospective U-boat crewmen, then back to Flensburg for more specialty work on telegraphy.

Before he could go to sea, he had more courses to take, ones useful in the other "room" near the captain, where the listening devices lived. These could pick up the mutter of a convoy passing sixty miles away, a single ship at twelve miles, and could distinguish between the dutiful turning of a freighter's propellers and the higher-pitched whir of a warship's. Also to the *Funker* fell the duty of working a keyboard in a wooden box that might have reflected the efforts of a moderately adept weekend carpenter. This was the Enigma machine. It coded and decoded radio messages. At its most operatic, war is a whole city in flames, or two battleships tearing majestically toward each other carrying four thousand souls into combat. But this ratty-looking little shoeshine kit would often be the hinge on which the fortunes of the Atlantic campaign swung.

Its operators occasionally made insectile clickings as they coded or decoded messages, and nobody forward in the torpedo room gave it much of a thought. Here was U-boat life in its swarming essentials. Twenty-five men lived in this chamber, but there were only twelve bunks. These were shared, one watch coming off duty and climbing onto cotton wafers still warm from the previous occupant. Most of the torpedoes—ten out of fourteen in a VII—were here, too, carrying a plywood floor on their backs during the beginning of the cruise. This artificial floor so raised the deck height that the men often had to move about on hands and knees.

Four torpedo tubes ran thirteen feet into the room. The cruise began with each one charged, and its inhabitants wanted plenty of attention. This meant that every couple of days every torpedo had to be drawn from its tube and gone over. And here was an odd contradiction of U-boat life: on the most mechanically sophisticated vessels yet built, the men often had to work at the level of Incas prying a boulder out of a swamp.

The torpedoes were moved by hand, and they weren't small.

Out the missile would come from its tube (or, with even greater effort, up from beneath the decking), each one weighing some two tons and costing, Captain Cremer said, "in present-day terms [as much as] a medium-sized house."

Like a medium-size house it had a multitude of systems that had to be kept in order. Some "eels"—their universal nickname among the men who served them—ran on compressed air; others, the G7es, were electrical, like their mother boat carrying a hull full of batteries. These latter were preferable, for they left no wake at all, nothing to tell their targets they were coming. Every torpedo came to the boat having run sea trials conducted by—a word remarkable even in German military vocabulary—the *Torpedoespruslungkommando*, and accompanied with its own logbook, conscientiously maintained. It had to be. A torpedo was delicate, always "treated like a raw egg," Cremer wrote, and with its hydroplanes, rudders, and such, a simulacrum of the submarine that bore it. But unlike its parent, it could run at thirty knots. And unlike its parent, its bow was full of torpex, a compound of TNT and cyclonite salted with aluminum flakes and packing enough of a wallop to sink anything afloat.

But what a job to get it to its target! Once a torpedo had laboriously been exposed, the "mixer"—as a torpedoman was known—would fuss over its mechanisms, setting aright anything that had worked its way loose or out of alignment during the missile's brief solitude. Then it had to be slathered with grease, hoisted up, and swung back into its tube while men not on duty squirmed out of the way. The torpedoes were so precious, so sedulously maintained, that it is not surprising the men managing them would sometimes instinctively reach out an arm to try to protect one from the boat's lurching and get the arm broken. When this happened, the *Funker* was summoned. U-boat crews were so sparse for the jobs they had to do that the radioman doubled as doctor. This meant he'd read a book or two and had charge of some bottles of medicine. The thinking seems to have been that someone with a delicate hand on a telegraph key would be equally deft with a severed artery. One *Funker* had to amputate a crushed foot while a fellow radioman relayed instructions from a surgeon two thousand miles away.

This was exceptionally demanding duty, but so were all the other duties on a boat. Only the *Smutje,* the cook, whose job kept him busy pretty much around the clock, was excused from standing watch.

Whenever the ship was surfaced, four lookouts posted themselves in the tight horseshoe formed by the bridge railing (with sardonic wistfulness, this platform had been christened the *Wintergarten*). Standing back to back, shoulder to shoulder, each man was responsible for scanning a quarter of the horizon. Sometimes the sea would be calm and the weather mild and the work thus only deeply boring. But it was the Atlantic after all, and the lookouts' perch was only a few yards above it, fastened to what was essentially a big cylinder. In heavy weather the rolling, corkscrewing boat would put the watch neck-deep in water so that the men had to hold their binoculars aloft until they got a chance to put them back to their eyes for a few seconds. If the streaming glasses showed an airplane, everyone scrambled off the bridge, dispensing seawater among all down below, and wheeled shut the hatch as the air came blasting out of the ballast tanks.

Cremer described diving with a pro's precision: "When the boat is surfaced, the bottom of the ballast tank is open and air, kept in from above, prevents the water entering. The boat is floating on an air bubble. To dive, the air is allowed to escape at the top through vents. Water takes its place—the boat sinks and disappears." And best do it quickly. Not that any activity aboard a submarine was cavalierly conducted, but no drill was taken with quite such ferocious seriousness as the one that got the boat out of sight. No captain was ever satisfied with the results, either, although thirty seconds seems to have become the standard on a VII, thirty-five on a IX.

Then back to the surface, and the watch back out on the bridge, and remember, always, no matter what the weather, to strap yourself into the lines and harness that will keep you tied to the boat. The Atlantic could get the better of such measures, though. On *U-653*, butting its way west through bad February seas, the first watch turned out in its heavy rain gear. The men they were relieving saw to it that they were properly buckled up, then gratefully went below. Hours into the watch Heinz Theen, the navigation officer, became aware of a diminution in the noise of the sea. The helmsman told him that the watch had closed the conning-tower hatch a few minutes earlier. "I was puzzled," said Theen, "and climbed up to open the hatch and was startled to find nobody on the bridge. I could see no one from the first watch. The bridge was empty! *U-653* had spent seven minutes sailing blind. Despite well-fastened harnesses, four seamen had been snatched to their deaths by the cruel sea in an instant."

For the first years of the war, the men who endured this life—and death—were volunteers. In time, crewmen would be drafted into U-boat service. What never changed was the men's willingness to go back out. At the end, when the chances of living through a war patrol were perhaps one in four, the boats still sailed, the crews determined as ever to serve their nation, and their torpedoes, of course, every bit as dangerous as they had been in the summer of 1939, when the long campaign had begun.

The End of the *Athenia*

The sea war begins, 1939

★ ★ ★

Fritz-Julius Lemp, commander of the *U-30*, opened the U-boat campaign. He had been at sea for nearly two weeks when he spotted his target. On August 22, propelled by the pressure of the coming war and ordered to maintain strictest secrecy, he had taken the *U-30*—one of Doenitz's "excellent" VIIs—from Wilhelmshaven and headed north in a wide circle that brought him close to arctic waters, up around the Shetland and Faroe Islands before swinging down into the Western Approaches, the vast stretch of Atlantic through which almost all traffic coming to Britain had to pass. There he waited, day after mild, quiet day, restless and eager. On September 1 the boat's radio operator brought Lemp a signal and the captain entered its message in his log: "Negotiations failed. Hostilities against Poland." Three days later word came that Britain had declared war, and an hour later Lemp received his orders: "Do not wait until attacked. Make war on merchant shipping in accordance with operational orders."

The envelope containing the orders was in his quarters. He got it, broke the seals, and there, over Doenitz's signature, were his instructions: he was to fight, but to do it following the rules of engagement that had come out of the 1930 London treaties, which included the old Article 22 that so limited the blow from nowhere that was the U-boat's greatest strength. Germany went to war agreeing that no merchant or passenger ship could be sunk out of hand. This mandate allowed many exceptions, however. Any merchantman sailing in the protective presence of an escorting warship was fair game, as was any troop transport. If a submarine captain suspected a merchant ship of carrying war materials, he could order her to stop and be searched. If the ship fled or uncovered deck guns, it could be sunk. So, too, could it if the search turned up contraband, but only after everyone aboard was safely off and assured of rescue.

The *U-30* was lying on the surface. Lemp went up to the bridge and stood with the watch while a lovely late-summer afternoon waned. He was twenty-six years old, sturdy, quick-tempered but humorous, and popular with his crew. Like everyone else aboard, he had trained for years to be able to achieve just one thing.

By 1900 hours—seven o'clock—the wind had begun to rise, and a haze came down with the dusk. An hour or so of daylight was still left and was more than sufficient to show Lemp the ship—the big ship—that was coming his way. It was steaming west at about fifteen knots. Lemp called his gunnery officer to the bridge, and the two of them tried to figure out what they were looking at. Or perhaps they were trying to convince themselves that what they were looking at was what they *wanted* to be looking at.

The size: it had to be a troopship. But doing what? Rushing reinforcements to Nova Scotia in the opening minutes of the war? But wait—it could be, probably was, an "armed merchant cruiser." Doenitz, who throughout the war would meet with his captains every chance he got, had done so with Lemp just before he sailed and had warned against these innocuous-looking vessels that nonetheless mounted guns powerful enough to do in a submarine if they caught it on the surface. Moreover, the deepening dusk made it clear that this ship was running without lights. Why do that if she had nothing to hide: an ocean liner went about its proper business lit up like an amusement pier.

The men left the bridge and dropped down into the conning tower. Lemp took the *U-30* to periscope depth and made for the ship with only one near-invisible pencil of mechanism above the surface. It showed him that his target—for surely it was a target now—still had no lights burning. Captain Lemp closed to one thousand yards, gave his orders, and fired the first four shots of the Atlantic war. Three shots, actually, for one torpedo jammed in its tube. Two of the others ran wide, but a third found its mark.

The 13,500-ton, 526-foot-long Donaldson Atlantic Line steamer *Athenia* had been built in Scotland in 1923, but her public spaces had a prewar feel to them, as if an Edwardian country house had floated out to sea. In the cabin-class lounge a grand piano stood beneath a domed glass ceiling supported by ornamental wrought ironwork; the baroque dining room had what the Donaldson brochure described as scagliola marble columns. None of this splendor was overly imposing. The *Athenia* was a friendly ship, and during her years in Atlantic service had come to be known for her informality. The famous tended to choose other vessels—Charlie Chaplin and Greta Garbo would not be found on the *Athenia*—but families felt welcome and comfortable in her salons and smoking rooms.

But those aboard the *Athenia* had no sense of ease as tugboats nudged her out into the Clyde from Glasgow on September 1. The government had made such firm guarantees to Poland that it could scarcely back down, and Hitler had never backed down yet. The British ultimatum would run out in hours, and a lot of people wanted to put an ocean between themselves and what was coming.

Yet they had fewer and fewer ways to do so. Ships had been

taken out of service by the British Admiralty. The *Queen Mary,* for instance, was already drafted into a war that had not yet begun. The master of the *Athenia,* who bore the almost comically appropriate British captain's name James Cook, was taking in two hundred extra passengers for this crossing. The ship's gym had been turned into a dormitory, and hastily knocked-together bunks were being put in odd corners.

Captain Cook got his crowded ship away about noon; it would become more crowded still as it took on passengers at Belfast and Liverpool before heading out into the North Atlantic, bound for Montreal.

Everyone was feeling the weight of the hour. As the *Athenia* slid away down the Clyde, dockworkers stared at the passengers along the rail. "Cowards!" they shouted from their dun wilderness of gantries. "Cowards! Cowards!"

The *Athenia* left Liverpool with 1,102 passengers, among them 300 Americans and 150 European refugees, some of these last so poor, one passenger noticed, that they walked the decks with bare feet.

The morning of the third brought a lifeboat drill, the third since the *Athenia* had left Glasgow. At a little after eleven Captain Cook got word from his radioman and, like Captain Lemp, learned that Britain and Germany were at war. He called his officers together. A notice was posted outside the purser's office, and the crew set about readying the lifeboats, checking that they were equipped with food and water and flares, and making fast the plugs that stoppered the holes drilled in the hulls to let rainwater and spray drain out.

All this unsettled the passengers, of course, but the day was mild—warm, even, in the lee of the superstructures; they were headed for a neutral port (Canada would not join the war for another five days); the sea looked benign. Families had been broken up in the press of events, mothers and children sharing cabins with other mothers and children, the husbands bunking elsewhere, but now they were, most of them, together on deck. Games started up. Some of the Americans had been able to book passage not only for themselves but for their cars, too, and they felt good about that. People had a drink, or a pot of tea, and watched the children scrambling about and felt better.

Captain Cook did not. He calculated that he still had some hours before he was beyond the likely reach of any German submarine, and they were long hours.

The light changed; the bridge was still bright but the lower decks hung in shadow. People began to think about dinner.

The torpedo struck at 7:39, entering No. 5 hold and detonating against the engine-room bulkhead. A dirty gray-white pillar of water, a half-solid chowder of pieces of pipe, decking, luggage, and people, came boiling up through No. 5 hatch and rose fifty feet above it. Passengers who had been sitting on the hatch cover enjoying the evening went up with it, and many dropped back into the hold to float, naked and flayed, in the water that was already deep in the hull.

Margaret Hayworth, a ten-year-old Canadian girl, was with her mother and three-year-old sister on the tourist deck. The explosion did not kill them, but part of the debris it blasted upward laid open Margaret's forehead.

Many others than those on the hatch cover died immediately. Mrs. E. J. Wilkes, the wife of a New York physician, was sick and lying on her bed down in third class with her nine-year-old son, Daniel, keeping her company while Dr. Wilkes was off having his dinner. The explosion blew down the cabin wall. Daniel saw his mother crushed but managed to squirm clear of a tangle of broken things and grab hold of a chair, which, lifted by the rising water, floated him out into the passageway.

A Mrs. Fisher had sent her young son topside so recently that, at the concussion, she ran from her cabin in time to see the boy at the end of the corridor. Then the lights went out. She never saw him again.

The lights had failed all over the *Athenia;* the explosion had cut the oil lines that fed their generators. The ship was already settling by the stern and listing heavily to port. Watertight doors clanged down, trapping crewmen everywhere.

People panicked, pushing up black stairways from the black dining rooms. Chief Steward Rankin stood, back to the wall, holding aloft lit matches as the weeping, shouting crowd stumbled past him toward the promenade deck. Rankin saw one woman stop, back out of the throng, stand across the stairs from him and start lighting matches of her own. Guided by these two frail torches, the passengers made their way out into the dying daylight. When the last of them had passed, Nancy Bishop of Toronto waved out her match and said to Rankin, "Well, cheerio, I'm away to collect my lifejacket." She would not survive the night.

The panic began to ebb once passengers started gathering at the lifeboat stations, although they saw distressing things. Amid all the hurry, one man sat in a deck chair, apparently studying his newspaper, but dead. A man in his underwear tried to claw his way into a boat until a bosun knocked him out and he lay on the deck while women and children stepped over him.

As the lifeboats filled, a sailor helped the wounded Margaret Hayworth into one, then handed in her mother. Her other daughter, the three-year-old, Jacqueline, was still on the deck. Mrs. Hayworth called to the sailor, and he passed over a child—but the wrong one. As the boat began to lower, Mrs. Hayworth had seconds to make a decision: jump off and go to the three-year-old, or stay with her injured child. She stayed.

As another boat pulled away from the tilting *Athenia,* its occupants saw a twelve-year-old girl weeping at the rail as she watched her mother and three brothers disappearing into the dusk.

Captain Cook had his radioman send out a distress signal and drew a response from the *Knute Nelson,* a Norwegian cargo ship less than fifty miles away: "The old man doesn't believe you've been torpedoed—but he's coming to your assistance anyway." Then the captain asked about the emergency generator, and minutes later the auxiliary lights shone down on the decks, hard, dead white, and comforting.

A passenger named Barbara Bailey—thirty-four years old and, after considerable friction with her father, a London lawyer, on her way to Calgary to care for her brother's children—was about to step into the last seat in her assigned boat when she heard a woman behind her starting to sob. She turned and said, "You go ahead." The weeping woman held back. Bailey urged her on, saying it was all right: "Nobody loves me." Taking her place in the boat, the woman said, "It's not true nobody loves you—Jesus loves you."

By nine o'clock all but four of the ship's twenty-six lifeboats were away, some overloaded, some with only fifty people in a craft designed to hold eighty-six. A few, hastily launched, were nearly swamped. Before long, the women in them would be bailing with their shoes.

Captain Cook helped load the last boat, worried that there might be a final frenzy among the remaining passengers. There was nothing of the sort. A couple of them refused to get in at all until they were assured that everyone else had gone.

Then Cook and his officers were alone on the bright, sloping deck. The *Knute Nelson* would be up about midnight. How long did the *Athenia* have to live? She lurched and settled farther as some of the officers took a final tour. In one of the dining rooms they saw plates of food still sitting on the tables—deeply appealing to them after the exertions of the evening, despite being surrounded by a bog of spilled soup and crushed glassware. They went back up and found the rest of the crew gathered at No. 3

hatch. The moon was out now, and they could see the lifeboats a half mile off, pale on the dark water. Someone had an inspiration: "Has Davy forgotten to lock his bar?" He had, and soon whiskey was being passed around.

They sat for a while and listened to the big American cars, torn loose from their lashings, banging back and forth in the hold below.

The radioman told the captain, "I've sent out this message to the *Nelson:* 'We are now abandoning ship. Will screw down key contact and help you locate us.' They've replied good luck." A few rafts were still left. Cook glanced around the ship that had been his favorite command. "All right then," he said, "I think that will do."

Barbara Bailey had finally found a place in a lifeboat. She was close enough to the *Athenia* to see Captain Cook climbing down the side, his sextant case under one arm. "There he goes with the swag," called out someone cheerily, and Bailey laughed. Not many in the boat joined her; it was shipping seawater, and a refugee woman in the bow began a keening chant that added to the eeriness of the night: the greasy shine of the water inches below the gunwale, sluggish with oil bled by the *Athenia,* the liner's decks empty under the emergency lights, and, far off now, the lift and fall of red flares from the scattered boats.

Toward midnight they saw a brightening on the horizon, and a ship rose over the rim of the sea. The sailor in charge of the boat urged the passengers to row. Many refused and even tried to keep others from lifting their oars. The sailor, surprised and angry, shouted, "If you can't row to save your own bloody necks, do it to save somebody else's!" Barbara Bailey glumly realized this mutiny was her fault. When she'd spotted the lights of their rescuer, she had blurted out, "It's the *Bremen!*" The German liner was in New York harbor when the Polish crisis broke, and the English newspapers had been full of speculation that she would make a dash for home. The refugees, almost all of them Jewish, had made the unarticulated, instantaneous decision that they would rather die out there than go back to Germany.

But the ship wasn't the *Bremen;* it was the *Knute Nelson.* As she made her way toward the nearest boats, the *Athenia*'s emergency generators drank off the last of their gasoline, and the liner went dark.

Barbara Bailey's boat came alongside the Norwegian freighter at about two thirty. The sea was mild by Atlantic standards, but it was still a demanding business to hoist people up a ship's flank in the middle of the night. When Bailey's turn came, she found her way blocked by the corpse of a woman. "That's all right," someone said, "you'll have to step on it to get off." "I won't," she insisted, but she did.

Now a coruscating, anomalous newcomer appeared on the scene, the yacht *Southern Cross.* She belonged to a man sometimes called "the Rockefeller of Sweden," Alex Wenner-Gren, who had done sufficiently well with his Electrolux vacuum cleaner company to buy the yacht from Howard Hughes. He had been making for Bermuda, spurred by his American wife, who'd awakened from a nightmare in which she met a man holding a bleeding child and demanded they leave Europe immediately. The yacht joined the freighter in the rescue operations.

At four o'clock lifeboat 5A rowed up alongside the now-empty boats bumping at the *Knute Nelson*'s hull. The ship, carrying no cargo, rode high in the water, the blades of its propellers slowly turning just beneath the surface. Crewmen had thrown a line and the boat taken it in when word went around the freighter's bridge that a lifeboat was sinking somewhere in the darkness beyond the bow. The captain ordered full ahead, and as the *Nelson* surged forward, 5A went under her stern. The propellers kicked the boat into the air, split it in two, and threw ninety people into the sea before threshing several of them back into the blades.

Dawn was coming up now, and by its light Daphne Sebag-Monteifiore, one of the rescued passengers on the *Southern Cross*, saw a young woman still sitting by herself in a lifeboat. As Sebag-Monteifiore watched, the woman stood up, cried out, "My baby!" and threw herself into the sea to drown.

Full dawn, a fine one, inspired a survivor to write "flushing vast battlements of cloud." Beneath these battlements two newly arrived British destroyers picked up the last of the castaways, while a third patrolled for submarines. The captain of the *Knute Nelson*, with 430 people aboard his ship, dropped his plans to sail to Panama and headed for Galway. Barbara Bailey would be back with her difficult father in a couple of days. She found herself perfectly happy with the prospect.

Wenner-Gren had 380 survivors drinking hot soup on the no-longer-immaculate decks of his yacht. He had no way to support such a crowd. The destroyers transferred some of them and started for Glasgow. That still left over 200. An American freighter had just showed up. Maybe it could take them.

And so the drab old *City of Flint* became not only the vessel that saved America's first victims of the war, but went on to show a nation that wanted nothing to do with this European quarrel just how complicated keeping out of it was going to be.

Captain Gainard's
Killer Dillers

An American freighter comes to the rescue, 1939

Joe Gainard would not have been sitting on a hatch cover in a war zone. Born in Massachusetts—he would call his memoir *Yankee Skipper*—he had been at sea for most of his fifty years, and he remembered the lessons he'd learned in the Great War. One was "you must not cross a hatch" because an explosion in a ship's hold will probably throw it, and you, into the air. When the troopship *President Lincoln* had been torpedoed in 1918, Gainard was "particularly interested in the discipline aboard the sinking vessel. With lifeboat crews hurrying to their stations, not a single man that I saw was tempted to take a shortcut across a hatch."*

Gainard had been in the navy then. Now he was with the merchant marine, master of the *City of Flint*. She was a Hog Islander, one of the freighters assembled in the Pennsylvania yards designed

---

*The sinking also made him doubt "the story they tell—that the suction of a sinking ship pulls lifeboats and floating rafts under. I floated off the stern and there was no suction I could notice."

to help build "a bridge of ships" to Europe when America had entered the Great War. The squared-off, slab-sided Hog Islanders were famous the world over for their ugliness, but twenty years of peacetime work had shown them to be tough and dependable. The level of luxury they offered is suggested by the fact that the *City of Flint* had accommodations for exactly six passengers.

Gainard took command of her in March 1939. "There's no way to start on a ship as good as trying the coffee," he wrote, and he found the coffee on the *City of Flint* very much to his liking.

His first voyage took him to Hamburg. Before he even dropped anchor, he got a taste of the climate there. When the *City of Flint* stopped to pick up the pilot, the captain greeted him "in the traditional manner of the sea" as the man came on the bridge: "Good morning, Pilot. My name is Gainard. Glad to have you aboard. The ship is stopped. The wheel is amidships. We're bound for Hamburg."

The pilot said only, "Full speed ahead."

Gainard turned to his third mate. "Mr. McAllister, this is the pilot, who apparently has no name. He is ready to go full speed ahead."

In the wheelhouse the pilot became more communicative. "You Americans are fools," he told Gainard. "You are in the hands of international Jews and you don't know it. But we Germans know it."

Gainard asked, "Did you come aboard as a pilot or a political speaker?"

They steamed along in silence for an hour before the pilot found something more to say. "You Americans think we are starving in Germany, but we have more and better food than you."

A little later Gainard took McAllister aside. "When the coffee comes up, I want only two cups—one for you and one for me."

When the steward arrived in the wheelhouse, the pilot said, "I'll have a cup of coffee, Captain."

"I don't think so," said Gainard, and politely explained that he couldn't face the humiliating possibility of serving his guest coffee inferior to what he was accustomed to. The pilot had to steer them into Hamburg warmed only by his zeal.

"I made two voyages to Germany," Gainard wrote, "and that was the only official who acted that way. Everybody else was friendly." But he didn't forget the conversation.

August found the *City of Flint* in Glasgow getting ready to sail for home with a cargo of wool and whiskey when the captain was told to call the Maritime Commission offices in London. It was a Sunday, nobody was there, so he phoned the American embassy, then wished he hadn't. Eddie Moore, Ambassador Joseph Kennedy's secretary, was "too agreeable, too glad to hear from me, and too cordial." Soon Gainard learned the reason for his effusiveness: "Well, the Maritime Commission has given us permission to send thirty passengers home on your boat."

Gainard protested vehemently. For days anxious people had been begging him to take them aboard, and he'd turned them down: the *City of Flint* had no room for passengers. But Moore put the screws to him. "Joe has promised!" (And Joe was, after all, a Massachusetts man.) "Are you going to let Joe down?"

Gainard returned to the ship and told his indignant first mate, B. L. Jubb, and his alarmed steward, Joe Freer, that not only would they have to find accommodations for thirty passengers, but that some of those passengers would be college girls who had been squeezed out of the *Athenia,* which was then taking on stores just across the pier. Fortunately, Freer was a provident man and laid in so ample a supply of food that Gainard had to fight with his line's agent to get the requisition filled.

The girls—four of them, it turned out—came aboard to have a look around. Gainard had hoped to discourage them, but they were not easily discouraged. He gave them coffee in the saloon, and "all the other officers found excuses to come in for coffee, too, while we were there." Captain Gainard began to relax. "There was more laughter in the saloon that evening than the *City of Flint* had ever had before. These girls were absolutely irrepressible, nuts, but nice ones."

In the days that followed, the crew laid planking over the steel plates of the shelter deck, put bunks on top of the new flooring, and strung lights above the bunks. The girls would sleep in the captain's cabin.

The *City of Flint* sailed thirty-six hours after the *Athenia*. As the freighter made its way down the Clyde, Gainard said, "I got my first warning of what I was going to be in for." One of the college girls began dashing from rail to rail to see the river traffic. Gainard called to her and warned that the deck of a freighter was no place to racket about heedlessly. She spotted the brand-new *Queen Elizabeth* falling majestically astern. As she ran to get a better look at it, she called over her shoulder, "Oh, Captain! Don't be such an old fuzz bug!"

On the third night out the old fuzz bug was savoring his victory over his officers and several passengers in two straight rounds of a word game called Guggenheim when the radio operator handed him a message. He went to the bridge immediately, to be joined by Jubb, who already had men preparing the lifeboats. The radioman said his counterpart on the *Athenia* had tied down the key; Gainard swung the *City of Flint* toward the signal. Going at top speed—eleven and a half knots—he calculated he would arrive at about nine the next morning.

"I guess," said the first mate, "we'll have to take some of these passengers quite a long distance."

Gainard nodded.

"We can build a lot of bunks on the shelter deck," Jubb said, and left to get started. Gainard went down from time to time to check progress. "We didn't build any single beds down there like you see in a steamship cabin or a railway sleeping car. The bunks were made in long sections, six or eight or ten people to sleep side by side. We built a board platform for the bunks, stretching canvas over the boards, stretching it taut so that only three or four boards were needed to support six or eight persons. Some places we had solid beds, other places the canvas stretched from one side to the other almost like a hammock."

As word spread that they were on their way to help a torpedoed British ocean liner, passengers and crew alike turned out. "Everybody on the ship worked that night," said Gainard.

A shorebound type named R. L. Jenkins, who had been below ~~complete since they'd left the Clyde, approached Gainard.~~ "Captain, I'm a physician as well as a psychiatrist. What can I do to help?" Delighted to have a medical man aboard, Gainard asked him if he could set up a ship's hospital. Dr. Jenkins said he could, and by morning he had. When the captain visited the galley, he found stacks of sandwiches under napkins, and soup and coffee on the boil. The college girls were up and about and would seem to stay so for days. Gainard posted them as messengers for the watch, relieving the seamen assigned this duty for other tasks, such as building the bunks. To finish that job, Gainard wrote, "We put up small lath boards between the bed sections, marking them off about twenty-four inches apart. Because these divisions were not too high we were able to spread one blanket so it would cover two people, sometimes three. We didn't have enough blankets to assign one to each bunk."

By dawn, they had built 255 bunks.

They saw the smoke of the *Southern Cross* at 8:40 and got up to the crowded yacht half an hour later, just as Gainard had estimated. Every crewman aboard the *City of Flint* volunteered to help ferry over the survivors—the lifeboats had been swung out for hours—and the captain chose the largest, on the theory that "there is something encouraging about a six-footer at an oar."

First to come aboard was a girl whose eyes were glued shut with oil. The master of the *City of Flint* stepped forward to greet her with what he hoped was a brisk, reassuring formality: "Good morning. I'm Captain Gainard, and I'm glad to have you with us."

He had told the four college girls and the five other women aboard to be ready to bring female survivors aft, take off their clothes, get blankets around them and soup inside them, and show them to their bunks. As Kay Calloway (of Lexington, Kentucky, "one of our most efficient passengers") started to do this, Gainard said to the dripping newcomer, "You look American. Where are you from?"

"I'm ashamed to tell you" was the surprising answer. Gainard said she didn't have to be, that wherever she came from was not her fault.

"I am German," she said.

"Well, that doesn't make any difference," Gainard assured her; there would be only Americans and their guests on his ship. "You can get dried and cleaned up and fall in with everybody else just the same as if you were born in the United States. There need not be talk of nationalities here. We're very glad to have you." Then, in happy inspiration, he added, "Won't you help the other girls?"

The women washed her eyes clear of oil and gave her fresh clothes, and she was helping cheerfully and effectively long before the boats had finished plying between the *Southern Cross* and the *City of Flint*. It took seven hours to bring everyone aboard. At first Gainard's paying passengers did most of the work helping get the survivors settled, but before long the rescued were pitching in, too.

One man asked Gainard if he could be excused for a few hours because his wife was "very nervous," and he thought he should stay with her. Gainard said of course. The next *Athenia* passenger to come over the side told the captain what had made the wife nervous. The couple "had been in a lifeboat near the *Southern Cross*. Not far away another lifeboat overturned, with thirty children aboard, including their two children—both under ten years of age. The man jumped overboard and saved ten or twelve of the little ones, but did not find his own two."

Gainard at once sent word to the man not to worry, that plenty of help was at hand, but by the end of the next day he and his wife were at work: "They were two of the best aides on the voyage, keeping busy every day, all day long."

Most everyone was. Eating the first day was sandwiches and chaos, but by the second, mess rooms had been set up under the direction of Professors H. H. Plough and George Child of Amherst College. The passengers ate in strictly timed relays, seven and a half minutes a seating before bringing their plates to the college girls, who would wash them and set them out for the next brief shift. Mealtimes proved a good opportunity to get the new arrivals sorted out. When everyone was finally accounted for, it turned out the *City of Flint* had taken aboard 286 passengers. Gainard set course for Halifax.

Survivors of different nationalities tended to keep together, and soon their sections, rather than being numbered, bore signs that said POLISH CORRIDOR, SUDETENLAND, and the like. The sole Greek on board got to sleep under a placard that read ACROPOLIS. An Episcopalian minister, his wife, and a friend were in HEAVENLY REST. Gainard wrote, "We had a section for Austrians and another for the Canadians, marked 'Montreal,' 'Quebec,' or wherever they came from. The American Jews put up a sign reading '7th Avenue.' Clerks and stenographers had their quarters marked 'Madison Avenue,' 'Times Square,' and 'Fifth Avenue.' . . . Then we had 'Boyle's 30 Acres'* and 'The Bowery,' the last a terrible place: all my male passengers and the officers who had been dispossessed of their rooms landed there sleeping on cargo—whiskey cases and bags of cement."

The wounded went in the hospital, but Margaret Hayworth, the

---

*The hastily built wooden arena in Jersey City where Jack Dempsey fought Georges Carpentier in 1921.

ten-year-old with the cut forehead, did not look seriously injured to the captain, and he berthed her on the wheelhouse grating with her mother. An hour later, Gainard stopped by the wheelhouse and noticed that Margaret had kept one hand absolutely immobile since he'd last seen her. He called Dr. Jenkins, who found the child had a fever. One of the college girls kicked two women off the wheelhouse settee and put Margaret and her mother there. (Word would eventually come through that Margaret's three-year-old sister, left at the rail on the *Athenia,* was safe aboard one of the British destroyers.)

Making his rounds, Captain Gainard gradually realized that three of his sailors were sharing a single pair of shoes, passing them along to whichever man had the watch. They had given the two other pairs to passengers.

A captain of the New Hampshire National Guard organized a nightly patrol of the sleeping quarters; women formed two-hour watches and kept the toilets and showers clean around the clock. Every morning the passengers on the shelter deck would come topside and shake out their blankets while, under the direction of Helen Kemper, a California schoolteacher, their quarters were swept. "No ship was ever more clean or more orderly," said Gainard. "We ran things Navy fashion. I would hold 'Captain Inspection' every day at 'air-your-bedding time,' walking through the 'streets' of the shelter-deck bunks, and later going with the Doctor on deck to see the people there."

Dr. Jenkins didn't like the look of Margaret Hayworth and moved her to a room near the hospital. When his patient's temperature reached 105 and stayed there, the doctor said he had to perform a "spinal puncture."

In the ship's machine shop, Jubb and Freer made an instrument under Dr. Jenkins's direction. He performed the operation, and Margaret's temperature went down.

All the children on the ship were short of clothes. Jubb did what he could about this by sewing shoe tops out of pipe-covering canvas, with red and blue bunting shredded into laces. The college girls proved quick learners and joined in the cobbling. But "after running around on a Hog Island ship where you require boots if there's a heavy dew," Gainard said, "the youngsters' feet got wet. The next day we took their shoes off them and cut up a hospital rubber sheet to make inner soles."

Professor Child started a ship's newspaper. George Cree, a baker from Albany, New York, took over the night shift at the ovens so the ship's baker and second cook could get some sleep. The passengers staged a talent show one night, a limerick contest the next. Fellow passengers and crew provided the subjects, as in the tribute to Kay Calloway:

> *There is a young maiden named Kay*
> *With a form that is light as a fey,*
> *They sunk her in water*
> *(They hadn't of oughter)*
> *But her presence makes us all gay.*

Because people are people, one woman complained to the captain that she'd paid for first class on the *Athenia* and wasn't getting anything like it. Gainard gravely explained that the shelter deck *was* the first-class section of the *City of Flint* and got one of his better sign painters to identify every entrance to it as FIRST CLASS. Amazingly, this expedient completely mollified the protester.

Margaret Hayworth had been better since her spinal tap. But five days into the voyage her condition worsened. She slept and cried and asked once, "Mummy, did it really happen?" In the early hours of September 9 she died.

Her mother begged the captain not to bury her child at sea. He consulted with the doctor and the first mate, and "we made an embalming solution so that the body could be prepared for burial on land. The body was wrapped in three-inch bandages of sheets and covered with powdered cinnamon, then again well sprinkled with clove and the shroud again wrapped in bandages which were then wet, and then dry bandage was wrapped around the shroud again. It was then placed in salt, secured in a box placed in the forecastle head, inaccessible to anyone but the Master and the Mate. On arrival at Halifax the body was taken to the undertaking home provided by the Donaldson Line, where no other attention was needed." Gainard thought it best the passengers not be told.

The next day the U.S. Coast Guard cutters *Bibb* and *Campbell* took up company with the *City of Flint*. Gainard had not asked for the escort—the *Southern Cross* had alerted the Coast Guard—but he was glad to have it. "I was mighty proud of being an American when I looked at those sturdy vessels steaming along with us."

The college girls were certainly excited to see them. They were now known throughout the ship as the Killer Dillers. ("Killer Diller was a slang phrase that had something to do with swing music," Captain Gainard helplessly explained.) The cutters signaled asking if the *City of Flint* needed anything. Toothbrushes, was the heartfelt reply, and over they came, along with medical supplies and fresh vegetables. "The Killer Dillers were right on the job as welcoming committee, but the Coast Guard men carried on with their work. I won't say that someone didn't get to talk a little, or that perhaps some of the bright young officers of the Coast Guard didn't get telephone numbers or addresses. I don't see how they could have avoided it."

Captain Gainard had never been master of a liner, but he knew how things were done on one. "Now on West Indies cruise ships, Fifth Avenue shops send famous models with dozens of costumes to parade in the salon, for afternoon style shows. We had the models, but the trunks of course were missing."

The headlong week had tapped deep veins of resources in the Killer Dillers. Jubb had apparently always been resourceful—ship-handler, shoe- and scalpel-maker, carpenter, embalmer—and now he sat with the girls, sewing dresses out of signal flags and mess jackets and the sheets of burlap used to separate cargoes. They held their fashion show around No. 4 hatch while the officers on the *Bibb* and the *Campbell* watched through their binoculars with all the attention they would be giving to periscopes in the years ahead, and the *City of Flint* stolidly pounded westward, the sole merchantman in the first American convoy of the war.

They made Halifax on the thirteenth. Captain Gainard had a very different experience coming into port there than he had approaching Hamburg half a year earlier. "Good morning, Pilot," he said. "Our speed is 11 knots and we are a turbine ship. This ship holds her headway quite a while."

"Thank you, Captain. Full speed ahead, if you please. They are prepared for you at the dock. You have no papers for Halifax, of course, but that will be attended to easily. It's a nice day we are having, and you don't look so bad yourself."

There was no delay disembarking the passengers, and a great deal of food awaited them on the pier. Thanks to Steward Freer, the meal was an amenity rather than a necessity.

The *City of Flint* cast off at six that evening and headed for New York with six *Athenia* survivors and twenty of the original paying passengers, all of them disoriented by the sudden mute enormousness of the ship. Gainard reached New York on a Saturday and sailed on Monday for Baltimore, then to Norfolk, where he found waiting a letter that "said 'thanks' in a language sailors of every nation understood."

UNITED STATES MARITIME COMMISSION
Washington

Dear Captain Gainard,

We wish to inform you that the Maritime Commission has directed me to instruct you to provide a special din-

ner for the crew of the S.S. CITY OF FLINT. . . . This dinner is to be given in recognition of the excellent service
and co-operation of the crew in providing for the comfort of the survivors of the S.S. ATHENIA.

As the crew will be paid off at Norfolk, the dinner
should be arranged at that port, and it is suggested
that you make the necessary arrangements for the dinner through Southgate Nelson Corporation, Managing
Agent. We are notifying that company to cooperate with
you in this regard.

It was a fine dinner. There was plenty of liquor, but nobody
got drunk, and this gave Gainard one final reason to be proud
of his men before they dispersed. "The dinner over, the crew was
paid off—and a new crew signed on. Some of the men left the
ship, others came to take their places. Cargo carrying must go
on. That's the job of a vessel like *The City of Flint*."

The memory of this particular crew would stay with him,
though. Of the passengers, too: "Oh, I never think of that crowd
of girls that I don't remember something they did or said that
makes me laugh."

And so a little world dissolved, its energies and improvisa-
tions, its goodwill and incessant toilet-scrubbing, its forced in-
timacies and all the soup and coffee and sandwiches and First
Officer Jubb's rubber shoes and Dr. Jenkins's homemade medical instruments. Along with his passengers, Captain Gainard had
been given a peek into the future—a glimpse of how his nation
would handle the war that was coming its way.

But history wasn't through with him yet.

Prison Ship

*The difficulties of keeping out of the war,
1939–40*

Whatever exhilaration Captain Lemp might have felt about hitting his quarry didn't last long. Minutes after the torpedo struck, the *U-30*'s radioman picked up the target's distress signals, wrote down what they were saying, and handed the piece of paper to Lemp: "*Athenia* torpedoed 56.42 north, 14.05 west." He had attacked a British passenger ship. "What a mess!" he said.

Well, there was nothing for it now, except to get out of the area, which the *U-30* did. Lemp weighed the idea of radioing a report and decided against it.

The news was all over the Western world by the next morning, when the German high command issued its first statement about the *Athenia*: "There were no German submarines in the area at that time. It is likely a British submarine fired the torpedo as a propaganda measure to influence U.S. neutrality." And so the myth was maintained, with a dispiriting number of people believing it right up until the Nuremberg trials finally put the canard to rest.

Germany had accused England of the crime even before the final tally of its victims. One hundred and twelve people died that night: nineteen of the crew; ninety-three passengers, sixty-nine of them women, sixteen children. Twenty-eight Americans had perished.

Captain Lemp continued his cruise, and he was punctilious when, a couple of hours before dawn on September 11, he saw the British freighter *Blairlogie*. Scrupulously following the rules, he signaled the ship to stop, put warning shots across the bow, and gave the crew all the time they needed to take to the lifeboats before firing a torpedo. As the ship went down, he took the *U-30* slowly among the boats, distributing schnapps and cigarettes to their occupants, and even fired flares until a neutral ship, the *American Shipper*, came up to help.

Three days later it was the *Fanad Head*'s turn. Once again, Lemp made sure everyone aboard was safe in the lifeboats, then towed the boats beyond any possible danger while his men placed explosive charges in the freighter. Before he was done, he had even captured two British airmen. While bombing his ship, both planes had, incredibly, blown themselves out of the sky.

Still, Lemp was full of misgivings as he dropped anchor in Wilhelmshaven on September 26. A band was playing brightly on the pier, but Admiral Doenitz was waiting there, too.

Doenitz greeted his captain. "He asked me to speak in private," wrote the admiral. "I noticed immediately that he was very unhappy, and he told me immediately that he was responsible for sinking the *Athenia*. . . . I dispatched Lemp at once by air to report to the SKL [naval high command] at Berlin. At the same time I ordered complete secrecy as a security measure."

It can have been only the smallest comfort to Captain Lemp that he was going to justify his actions to his commander in chief, Raeder, rather than to Hitler. But justify them he did—armed merchantman, no running lights—and this turned out to be enough. Lemp was surely helped by his government's having so unequivocally denied being responsible for the sinking. Raeder spoke with Hitler after questioning the *U-30*'s commander, and the two men reached the same conclusion as Doenitz: secrecy. This went as far as swearing the crew of the *U-30* to silence, and replacing the relevant passages in the boat's logbook with faked ones that omitted any mention of the *Athenia*.*

Having disobeyed no orders, Lemp was of course subject to no court-martial. Soon he was back at sea.

Hitler himself disavowed the sinking. Still amazed that Britain had actually kept its word to Poland and gone to war, he had little desire to inflame neutral nations, and none at all to bring so powerful a one as America into the fight. The same day the *Athenia* went down the German navy was told, "By order of the Fuehrer, passenger ships until further notice will not be attacked even in convoy."

The order didn't hold for long. Like Captain Gainard, Captain Lemp had briefly pushed open the heavy lid the present keeps on the future. What he had done to the *Athenia* was how the Atlantic war would be fought.

As soon as he could, Doenitz began to chip away at his confining orders. Before September was over, he told his boats, "Armed force should be used against all merchant ships using their wireless when ordered to stop. They are subject to seizure or sinking without exception." By year's end he had got far sterner: no schnapps and cigarettes for lifeboats, no flares to summon help. "Rescue no one and take no one aboard. Do not concern yourselves with the ship's boats. Weather conditions and the proxim-

---

*This was one of apparently only two times the Kriegsmarine took such a measure during the whole of the war, and it wasn't skillfully done. The Nuremberg prosecutors pointed out that not only had Lemp's signature transformed itself on the substitute entries, but they were the only ones in the log where the dates were recorded in Arabic rather than Roman numerals.

ity of the land are of no account. Care only for your own boat and strive to achieve the next success as soon as possible! We must be hard in this war."

Doenitz had every reason to expect his requests would get a respectful hearing. His submarines had achieved far more than the "pinpricks" he had fretted about. During the war's first month fifty-three Allied ships went down.

Warsaw surrendered on September 27. The victory came swiftly enough to surprise even Hitler. The next day he traveled to Wilhelmshaven at the urging of Admiral Raeder, who wanted his branch of the service to get some attention after a campaign in which the navy had played little part. From Doenitz's point of view, the visit couldn't have gone better. The weather-stained ships came in, their crews bearded (U-boats had neither enough room nor fresh water to allow regular shaving), high-hearted, sanguine. Doenitz got the chance to tell Hitler face-to-face of his long-fomented plans to gather his boats in group attacks against convoys. Hitler's naval aide, Karl-Jesko von Puttkamer, who accompanied him to Wilhelmshaven, said that the Führer "carried back to Berlin an excellent impression of the leadership of the U-boat arm as well as the liveliness and spirit of the crews."

That impression never left him. This most savagely capricious of men supported his U-boat admiral to the very end. Doenitz spoke that day in Wilhelmshaven of his ideal goal of three hundred submarines. Hitler would eventually give him nearly twelve hundred.

ONE OF THEM WOULD kill the weary old *City of Flint,* but not for a long time yet. She was a neutral vessel, with big American flags painted on her sides now, and lights rigged to play on them at night.

Rather missing his Killer Dillers, Captain Gainard took on his new cargo and signed on his new crew. The protean Jubb left, but Steward Freer stayed aboard.

Gainard sailed for Britain on October 3. The *City of Flint* had cleared the Newfoundland Banks and was well along the great-circle route that would eventually raise the southern tip of Ireland when, on the afternoon of the ninth, one of Gainard's officers pointed out a cloud that seemed to be moving faster than its fellows. It turned out to be smoke from a ship, and the men on the bridge speculated whether it was French or British.

In a couple of years German surface vessels would be encountered out in the middle of the North Atlantic about as often as flying saucers were. But these were early days, and the *City of Flint* had run into the *Deutschland*.

The naval agreements had put a ten-thousand-ton cap on warship construction, but within this stricture Raeder had worked with the greatest ingenuity. One result of his planning was the pocket battleship, which carried far heavier weaponry than any vessel of its weight ever had before. The *Deutschland* mounted six eleven-inch guns, and as she came steaming along at twenty-five knots, all of them were pointed at Captain Gainard.

When the German captain saw the emphatic American blazon on the freighter's side, he swung his guns inboard. "You must not use your radio," he signaled. Then: "I am going to send a boat."

Gainard came to a stop, then went to his cabin and changed from dungarees into his dress uniform. He thought his visitors would be dressed that way, and so they were. Although he had been stopped at gunpoint—the most intimidating gunpoint the world had to offer—the men who came over the side were far more civil than the Hamburg pilot had been.

"Glad to have you aboard," Gainard said, and the senior of the three officers matched this politeness: "Captain, I am sorry to cause you inconvenience, but this is war. I must ask to see your papers." Gainard showed him the manifest: wax, apples, asphalt, tobacco, lard, flour, grease, oil, tractors, lumber . . .

The German lieutenant looked grim. "This is bad. You have twenty-thousand drums of oil on board. What kind of oil is it?"

"Lubricating oil."

"This is bad. And this flour, what is it?"

"White-bread flour."

"Under the laws of my country, you are guilty of carrying contraband."

Gainard protested that it was an American ship, and that the cargo was perfectly legal under American law.

This didn't impress the officer, who signaled the battleship and received in return a message asking if the *City of Flint* could make room for "thirty-eight male passengers." The lieutenant explained they were from the *Stonegate,* a British merchantman the *Deutschland* had sunk a few days earlier.

Gainard said he could.

The officer was concerned. "This is a big passenger list, and you are a freight ship."

"I've carried more," Gainard told him.

The *Deutschland* signaled again: "The ship will go to Germany."

The captured English sailors came across, along with a prize crew about twenty strong under Lieutenant Hans Pushbach, who spoke good English and used it to explain that no one must interfere with his men: "If you do, I will kill you."

The *Deutschland* departed. Lieutenant Pushbach sketched a line on a chart of the North Atlantic. "We go to Germany, and we go like this."

Gainard may have been a prisoner of sorts, but he was still captain. He shook his head. "Not with this ship under these conditions." He drew a course far to the north of the lieutenant's, through less traveled sea-lanes. "If we get into trouble and the ship is sunk, no government will know who was responsible, for most of my people would be dead and so would yours. There's no telling what might happen. We want peace between our countries, so we're not going to meet any belligerent ship if it can be helped and you will have to use force to make me do it."

Lieutenant Pushbach agreed and the strange voyage began. It proceeded in silence because, as Gainard half-explained a few months later, "something had happened to the *Flint*'s radio between the time the *Deutschland* was sighted and the time the prize crew came aboard. The German radio operators evidently didn't know enough about radios to fix it; consequently, they were unable at any time to receive messages from Germany."

They went north into the ice fields off Greenland, through the mists of the season, and the equally shifting and puzzling mists of neutrality. The Germans assured the Americans that they'd have their ship back as soon as the cargo was confiscated, but the Americans were restive, and the captain had to defuse several plots to take the ship over from its well-armed guards. Along with pistols and machine guns, Pushbach said he and his men were carrying grenades so powerful that just one would kill everybody aboard (although you'd think that this might make the Germans reluctant to use them).

Nevertheless, a kind of homey routine settled in. Dark, drizzling mornings would find the American captain, the German lieutenant, and Captain Randall, the British master of the vanished *Stonegate,* shivering together on the bridge drinking coffee and agreeing they had been fools to take up their calling. "Why did I ever leave my father's farm?" Randall wondered once. "The politicals," said Pushbach. "Ah! They have the jobs. Comes my next incarnation, I will be a political. Let the other fellow go to sea." Gainard agreed: "Just think. Steam-heated trains, soft seats, warm subways, no wind or snow, no cold rain . . ."

Then, on a fine high blue morning, with the icebergs glowing green about them, the three sailors would speak pityingly of "the poor earthbound landsmen."

Despite such camaraderie, Gainard wanted his ship back. He persuaded his captors the *City of Flint* was running low on water, and after eleven days they dropped anchor at Tromsoe, Norway. There was plenty of water, but Gainard knew that if they put into a neutral port for it with no real need, neutrality statutes mandated that the prize crew should be seized and taken off the ship. But the Norwegians did no such thing, merely topping off the tanks and telling the *City of Flint* a few hours later to get moving. They did, however, take off the British sailors for repatriation before escorting the freighter back out of their territorial waters.

Pushbach knew Norway would broadcast the news of what had happened to the *City of Flint*. Nervous about British patrols, he ordered Gainard on through a mean southeast gale, finally coming to rest in a place American seamen would soon know all too well: Murmansk, Russia. Gainard was delighted when the Russians took the Germans ashore to be interned, as the Norwegians should have done. For five days the *City of Flint* stayed there, being assured by the local authorities that it was a "free ship," but forbidden to leave. Then the German crew reappeared: Russia and Germany had recently consummated the nervous embrace of the Hitler-Stalin pact. The Russians put the Germans and their colossal grenades back aboard and told the Americans to get out.

Back to Norwegian coastal waters—Pushbach was quite right in his belief that the British and Americans alike were now following the war-blown ramblings of the *City of Flint,* and he didn't want to meet the Royal Navy. At last, he ordered the ship to anchor at Haugesund. The Norwegians warned them off, but Pushbach thought he had no choice. At midnight on November 3, a boarding party from a Norwegian minelayer stormed the *City of Flint*. "It was slick, the way they did it," wrote Gainard. "Simply woke the Germans up, took away their artillery—and told them they had lost their rights by anchoring without legal cause and contrary to Norwegian neutrality laws." Gainard, his crew, and his ship were free to go about their business.

The world had moved along while the *City of Flint* was picking its way through the ice floes, and neutrality laws with it. The captain could no longer take his cargo to Britain in a ship under American registry. He sailed north along the coast of Norway instead, to try to sell it in Bergen. That didn't happen quickly, and the *City of Flint*'s men celebrated Thanksgiving and Christmas in the port—Steward Freer put up two magnificent meals—before they could at last head for home. On January 27, 116 days after setting sail, Gainard entered the port of Baltimore. He arrived angry. During his ordeal he had possibly been most deeply annoyed when his German captors insisted that a big tractor in the hold of his freighter was meant to be converted into a tank, but this was worse. The night before she dropped anchor, he had heard over the radio the ubiquitous newscaster Lowell Thomas saying, "The *City of Flint* is coming through the Virginia Capes again back from her Odyssey, just a rusty piece of junk, bound for the boneyard."

"A freight ship is no *thing*, Mr. Thomas," Gainard replied. "She's my home. And if the *City of Flint* was good enough to carry . . . stranded Americans out of the war zone, if it's good enough to be the home of a crew of officers and sailors, and good enough to carry the cargo of American manufactures to all the world—she's no pile of junk!"

Nor was she bound for the boneyard. She and a thousand very much like her were entering a sea battle of unprecedented length and ferocity. So, too, was Gainard. It may have taken some of the sting out of Thomas's words when, for his service aboard his Hog Islander, Captain Joseph A. Gainard was awarded the Navy Cross, the first to be given in the war.

The Neutrality Patrol

Guarding the western hemisphere,
1939–40

Franklin Roosevelt had heard about the *City of Flint*. When the *Bibb* and the *Campbell* had come out to see it home, one of Captain Gainard's guests, Alta Magoon, needed to have an ankle x-rayed. One of the cutters had the equipment, but to use it she had to get permission to be the first woman ever allowed aboard a coast guard vessel. Apparently this could be granted only by the president.

Roosevelt would have been tickled by this duty. He liked everything connected with the American seafaring tradition. Springwood, his home in Hyde Park, New York, contained some two thousand prints and paintings of warships from sailing days. He had been assistant secretary of the navy under Woodrow Wilson and greatly enjoyed the post. During the early years of his presidency he had not shown himself much interested in military matters—he had more than enough to contend with—but he always found time to go over the navy promotion lists. A couple of years down the road General George Marshall, nettled by FDR's clear preference among the services, would ask him, "At least, Mr. President, stop speaking of the army as 'they' and the navy as 'us.'"

The war found his navy early.

The tremors shaking the world had been going on as long as Roosevelt had been in office. His inauguration in 1933 took place a day before Hitler came to power, and Japan had invaded Manchuria two years earlier. In December 1937, with their armies besieging Nanking, Japanese bombers sank the USS *Panay* while the Yangtze River gunboat was trying to get American citizens out of the tormented city.

There have been times in our history when the deliberate sinking of an American warship—and it had been deliberate—meant war, period.

This wasn't one of them. A frustrated FDR asked his cabinet, "If Italy and Japan have evolved a technique of fighting without declaring war, why can't we develop a similar one?" But it was largely a rhetorical question. Roosevelt could gauge the mood of the nation he led as shrewdly as any politician who ever lived, and although it might be unsettled and even violent, it was not warlike.

A general feeling held that back in 1917 America had been duped into going to war by the House of Morgan, the munitions industry, and cynical political hacks in their thrall.

This conviction was not confined to the extremes: the Communist left that saw in any powerful capitalist nation a threat to the Soviet Union and the far right as incarnated in Father Charles Coughlin, the immensely popular "radio priest" (he drew a bigger audience than *Amos 'n' Andy*) with his winning trace of a brogue and a heart full of malice encapsulated in his references to Franklin Roosevelt's "Jew Deal."

The sense of betrayal bubbled up quite early. In 1924 Laurence Stallings and Maxwell Anderson enjoyed one of the greatest theatrical successes of the decade with their play *What Price Glory,* which, as Stallings's *New York Times* obituary put it, "painted World War I as an inelegant brawl between two hard-bitten veterans—Captain Flagg and Sergeant Quirt—over a slut who might have been called Europe."

Then there was the tremendous success of both the novel and the movie *All Quiet on the Western Front* (Germans didn't want to do this any more than we did), and a bestseller by Thomas Boyd called *Through the Wheat* that showed the grim absurdity of the war from the other side, and *Company K* by William March, which portrays the American effort with a brutal nihilism that still has the power to shock. Even Stephen Vincent Benét, a patriotic writer in perhaps the least patriotic decade since the republic began, published a poem in which the speaker dreams he sees corpses stringing "their wire on disputed ground—I knew them then." Why have they come to trouble him, he asks. "We know your names. We know that you are dead. / Must you march forever from France and the last, blind war? / 'Fool! From the next!' they said."

All these works carried the same message: the war had been an obscene waste of time; we must never do it again. Keep away from Europe's squabbles.

The belief took more concrete forms than literary ones. Starting in 1935, Congress began passing acts aimed at making it impossible for the United States to get involved in any foreign war. The first of these Neutrality Laws forbade American ships to sell or carry armaments to any country embroiled in conflict, but allowed the president to decide when the act should be applied. The next one took that power away from him. Roosevelt didn't like this, but support was running so strongly in favor (the Third Neutrality Law passed 376 to 16 in the House, and 63 to 6 in the Senate) that he let the issue drop and signed the bills.

On September 5, 1939, two days after Britain declared war on Germany, the president proclaimed the Neutrality Act in effect. Then he set about doing his best to dismantle it. Summoned to a special session, Congress unhappily reconvened in a Washington still clammy with summer heat, and FDR asked that the act be repealed in favor of a cash-and-carry arrangement that would allow a belligerent power to buy munitions so long as it paid up front and took them away in its own ships. This would, of course, greatly favor the British, who controlled the sea-lanes of the Atlantic. It would also, as Congress well understood, permit the release of previously ordered arms and thus irrigate with millions of dollars a workforce still in the shadow of the Great Depression. In a month, Roosevelt had his way.

That same September 5 FDR announced the Neutrality Patrol. This was a project he had warmed to long before. Back in April, with Warsaw still intact, Europe still in what passed as a state of peace, and the Atlantic Squadron preparing itself for the World's Fair, the president had told his cabinet he was planning to order "a patrol from Newfoundland down to South America and if some submarines are laying there and try to interrupt an American flag and our navy sinks them, it's just too bad . . ." He was a man of circumspection, misdirection, and improvisation, but in the confusing months to come he would never abandon this basic idea.

He said nothing about sinking U-boats being just too bad on September 5. His directives, as filtered through the Navy Department, established a zone two hundred miles out from shore (by any standard, a generous interpretation of territorial waters), but suggested only that the U.S. vessels keep track of the comings and goings of ships that entered it.

This nonetheless seemed more than enough of a job to Rear Admiral Alfred W. Johnson, in command of the Atlantic Squadron. He didn't have enough ships, and he didn't have the means to effectively support the ones he did (his fliers based at Key West fueled their planes from trucks that trundled back and forth to Fort Lauderdale, where civilian contractors sold them the gas). Nor were there enough men. Hastily reconditioned four-stack destroyers were putting to sea with crews of 56 rather than their full complement of 103. And among those 56 were only the sparsest salting of old hands that knew their way around a warship.

It came as a considerable shock to Roosevelt's chief of naval operations, Admiral Harold R. "Betty" (a surprising number of high-ranking American navy men had infantile nicknames) Stark, when, later in September, FDR indicated a swath of Atlantic that at one point ran a thousand miles off the Carolinas and airily asked, "How would the navy like to patrol such a security zone?" Stark, a highly capable man, was also a restrained, careful one. He merely told the president that this would take a great many ships.

In fact, the assignment would require—as the navy concluded when word of it got out—three hundred ships and perhaps four thousand planes. In other words, the whole fleet, plus three times as many airplanes as the service possessed. Some wishfully thought that the mission was presidential hyperbole, but on October 9 FDR issued a memo that began, "I have been disturbed by..." and contained the words "slowness," "lag," "weakness," and the like, all in regard to getting the patrol up and running.

So the ships, more and more of them, shouldered their way through steepening seas while summer blew away and autumn came in and a bad year moved toward a worse one. The Atlantic Squadron was stretched to the limit, its undermanned ships couldn't find enough time for proper gunnery and tactical training, and there was little torpedo practice because there were hardly any torpedoes to practice with. Yet, more and more men were learning the ropes in a task and on an ocean that would demand all their efforts for the next five years and more.

MOST OF THE ACTION in this peculiar new war seemed to be taking place at sea. England and France had mobilized to protect Poland, but there was scant chance of that, and in any event they didn't try. Americans watched skeptically as the "Phony War"—it was an American phrase—settled in. During the coldest winter anyone could remember, English soldiers and equipment crossed the Channel to France, and French troops reinforced the miles and miles of passageways and bunkers that made up the Maginot Line. There were none of the great wheeling maneuvers and ferocious clashes that had marked 1914; there was not much of anything at all.

Spring came. Over here, the New York World's Fair reopened for its second and final season. Its theme had changed from "The World of Tomorrow" to the somehow rather plaintive "For Peace and Freedom." The Czechoslovakian and Polish pavilions still stood, cenotaphs for their vanished nations. The Soviet Pavilion of the first season was gone, replaced by something called American Common, a two-and-a-half-acre square dedicated, according to the official guidebook, "to the perpetuation of a democratic idea. . . . From a liberty pole in the center of the site flies the highest flag on the Fair grounds." Russel Wright's flying lobsters apparently hadn't had legs; his exhibit was gone, too, and my father's wheatstalks now served as the puzzling herald for a Coca-Cola bottling operation. No nicely shined-up fleet was in the Hudson on opening day.

Overseas, the war had dropped any aspect of phoniness. On April 8, Hitler attacked Denmark and Norway. Denmark fell in hours, Norway in a few weeks. Raeder lost a good many of his surface ships in the fighting along the Norwegian coast, but it made no difference to the outcome.

The Germans had launched their campaign in the last freezing days of the bitter winter. Now the season gave way to a glorious spring, bright and mild and radiant all across Europe. This was *Hitlerwetter,* Germans told one another, the kind of fine dry days and clear nights that had smoothed his battalions' path into Poland.

On May 10 the Nazi armies struck west into three neutral countries—Luxembourg, which fell without a struggle, Holland, overwhelmed in five days, and Belgium, taken in eighteen—and France, where they broke the front in forty-eight hours. In the last war, the Germans had striven exorbitantly toward the Channel for more than four years, and never got there. This time, it took them ten days.

On May 15, Winston Churchill sent Franklin Roosevelt a telegram asking for "the loan of forty or fifty of your older destroyers."

"A New Chapter of World History"

The destroyer deal goes forward, 1940

Churchill had been prime minister for just five days, and a power in the British government for less than a year. He had been one before, of course, most significantly as first lord of the Admiralty in the last war, until the costly misfortunes of the Gallipoli campaign put him out of office. In recent years, while the word *appeasement* still carried the kindly connotations of a well-intentioned attempt to right old wrongs, he had widely been regarded as a bloody-minded troublemaker. "We must arm," he'd called. "Britain must arm. America must arm." After the Munich settlement of 1938 had appeased Hitler by giving him Czechoslovakia, Churchill said, "Britain had a choice between shame and war. She chose shame. She'll get the war, too."

As soon as she did, a few hours before the *Athenia* was torpedoed on September 3, Prime Minister Neville Chamberlain, the failure of his policies stark before him, reluctantly invited Churchill to return to the Admiralty. A week later, the new first lord received an unusual letter, from the president of the United States, that began, "My Dear Churchill, It is because you and I occupied similar positions in the World War that I want you to know how glad I am that you are back again in the Admiralty. Your problems are, I realize, complicated by new factors but the essential is not very different. What I want you and the Prime Minister to know is that I shall at all times welcome it if you will keep me in touch personally with anything you want me to know about. You can always send sealed letters through your pouch or my pouch."

Churchill answered quickly and with warmth (perhaps not wanting to deploy the resonances of his title in an informal correspondence, he signed his response, a little coyly, "Naval Person"), but at first relatively few communications passed between the two men.

The Norwegian campaign ran its sorry course, the British attempts to take back the country slipshod to the point of fecklessness. Much of the blame for this lay with Churchill, but the failure meant the end of Chamberlain's government.

Churchill became prime minister on May 10. Early on the morning of the fifteenth he was awakened to take a telephone call from Paul Reynaud. The French premier told his English counterpart, "We have been defeated. We are beaten. We have lost the battle."

Churchill did not yet believe the French would surrender. But they *might*. He saw clearly what would follow: his country, on its own, shoring up its defenses behind the narrow ribbon of water that separated it from a hostile continent, facing—and this was the brightest possible prospect—a siege that would last for years.

After lunch that day, he wrote his telegram to Roosevelt. This extraordinary message for one head of state to send another pretty much said, Your nation has to save mine. "Although I have changed my office, I am sure you would not wish me to discontinue our intimate private correspondence. As you are no doubt aware, the scene has darkened swiftly. . . . The small countries are simply smashed up, one by one, like matchwood. We must expect, though it is not yet certain, that Mussolini will hurry in to share the loot of civilisation. We expect to be attacked here ourselves, both from the air and by parachute and air-borne troops in the near future, and are getting ready for them. If necessary, we shall continue the war alone, and we are not afraid of that.

"But I trust you realise, Mr President, that the voice and force of the United States may count for nothing if they are withheld too long. You may have a completely subjugated, Nazified Europe established with astonishing swiftness, and the weight may be more than we can bear. All I ask is that you should proclaim non-belligerency, which would mean that you would help us with everything short of actually engaging armed forces. Immediate needs are, first of all, the loan of forty or fifty of your older destroyers to bridge the gap between what we have now and the large new construction we put in hand at the beginning of the war."

Churchill knew America had the destroyers; 170 of them were laid up at the time the war started, and 68 sent back to sea once the Neutrality Patrol began.

Where were Britain's destroyers? The nation had ended the last war with 433 but a straitened peace had cut the number to fewer than 200 by 1939, and even when rearmament began, destroyers were low on the list of new vessels, partly because the Admiralty preferred to put what funds it had into larger ships, and partly because of the complacent fallacy that the U-boats had been taken care of the last time and wouldn't pose much of a threat in any future war.

The destroyers Britain did have had been battered by the awful winter, and in the Scandinavian campaign four were put out of action by damage, and seven sunk outright.

Ever since the Neutrality Act had been ramified to allow sales on the cash-and-carry basis, England had maintained a purchasing mission with its offices at 15 Broad Street in Manhattan. At its head was that rare creature, a man disliked by nobody. Arthur Purvis had been born in London, but his Scottish wellsprings disarmed Americans of a generation more leery than ours of what they saw as English hauteur and high-handedness. The mission's first days had been hectic, as Garment District salesmen came downtown to pitch bras, and one elderly man stopped by repeatedly to offer an exemplary mule that was "a very great bargain." Purvis had done reasonably well in recent months, but destroyers were a different matter from machine tools and wire. It required an act of Congress to sell them.

Roosevelt hardly stood in terror of Congress, but he was a human seismograph where public opinion was concerned. He might want to get Churchill the ships, but he couldn't afford to be branded as a warmonger in the presidential election that was coming up in November.

Yet he had reason to be hopeful. At the time of Munich the Roper poll—which FDR trusted more than the Gallup—had shown that two-thirds of all Americans opposed selling any arms to any belligerents. In late September 1939, after the war had begun, Roper reported that this had changed: two-thirds now wanted the United States to help the Allies, but less than 3 percent thought we should do it by going to war. Most Americans then held the tacit belief that however malign the German government might be, they were insulated from any mischief it could work by the French army, so indefatigable in the Great War, and the Royal Navy, which was, after all, the Royal Navy.

Now, with the Western democracies being blown out like a stand of birthday candles, Germany suddenly seemed both closer and scarier.

Still, the president replied cautiously: "I have just received your message and I am sure it is unnecessary for me to say that I am most happy to continue our private correspondence as we have in the past.

"I am, of course, giving every possible consideration to the suggestions made in your message. . . .

"With regard to the possible loan of forty or fifty of our older destroyers. As you know, a step of that kind could not be taken except with the specific authorization of the Congress, and I am not certain it would be wise for that suggestion to be made to the Congress at this moment."

Beyond the considerable legal difficulties in turning over the ships was another, unspoken one: the possibility that we might be giving them to the Germans. The Allied chances seemed slim, and a great many Americans thought them poorer than that. When in late May German forces trapped hundreds of thousands of French and British troops in the Channel around Dunkirk, Ambassador Joseph Kennedy sent FDR a cable saying, "Only a miracle can save the BEF [British Expeditionary Force] from being wiped out or, as I said yesterday, surrender." But something like a miracle was taking shape. Hitler held back his armor to let Hermann Goering and his Luftwaffe finish the job, and they weren't up to it. A scratch flotilla of small boats and excursion steamers began an increasingly effective rescue operation. By June 4, 225,000 British and 113,000 French soldiers had been taken off the beaches—albeit with no piece of equipment larger than a rifle.

We remember those fishing smacks and excursion boats, but destroyers did the heaviest work in the evacuation. At Boulogne, the ships came in so close to shore to take off the Welsh Guards that they fought gun duels with German tanks. A third of the troops carried to safety reached it on destroyers.

This tremendous result came at a tremendous cost. On May 10 the British Home Fleet had ninety-four seaworthy destroyers; after Dunkirk, forty-three were still fit for service.

In the House of Commons Churchill gave one of the most famous of the speeches that would bolster British resolve and strengthen American sympathy for his cause: "Even though large tracts of Europe and many old and famous states have fallen or may fall into the grip of the Gestapo and all the odious apparatus of Nazi rule, we shall not flag or fail. We shall go on to the end. We shall fight in France, we shall fight in the seas and oceans, we shall fight with growing confidence and growing strength in the air; we shall defend our island whatever the cost may be. We shall fight on the beaches, we shall fight on the landing grounds, we shall fight in the fields and in the streets, we shall fight in the hills; we shall never surrender."

As Churchill knew, this magnificent defiance perversely contained within it an impediment to the ceaseless struggle it promised. So long as England carried on, its fleet stood between America and Germany. And given his pledge to keep up the fight no matter what, America would always have the protection of that fleet one way or the other. As Churchill wrote the prime minister of Canada, where the Royal Navy would go if a German invasion succeeded, "We must be careful not to let Americans view too complacently the prospect of a British collapse, out of which they could get the British Fleet and the guardianship of the British Empire, minus Great Britain. . . . Although the President is our best friend, no practical help has [come] from the United States yet."

Churchill was in the highly tricky position of having to maintain two contradictory stances before America: we're indomitable, whatever may befall us (in which case no reason for the United States to hurry up with the destroyers); we might be driven down (in which case the destroyers should certainly not leave home). If the former was as well articulated as human speech could make it in his "fight on the beaches" peroration, the latter was succinctly expressed in one of his private messages to Roosevelt (which the prime minister was now signing "Former Naval Person"): "If members of this administration were finished and others came to parley amid the ruins, you must not be blind to the fact that the sole remaining bargaining counter with Germany would be the fleet, and if this country was left by the United States to its fate no one would have the right to blame those then responsible if they made the best terms they could for the surviving inhabitants."

The "deliverance" of Dunkirk, as Churchill called it, could not save France. Italy made the jackal's pounce the prime minister had predicted and declared war on June 10. France gave up a week later.

"The whole fury and might of the enemy must very soon be turned upon us," Churchill told the House. "Hitler knows that he will have to break us in this island or lose the war." A couple of days later Churchill gave a speech in a secret session of the House. It was not recorded, but his notes for it include "If we get through next three months, we get through the next three years," and, looking to America, "It depends upon our resolute bearing and holding out until Election issues are settled there."

In fact, the election was shaping up well from Churchill's point of view. The Republican National Convention met in Philadelphia that June and drafted, amid much fractious uncertainty, the party's foreign-policy plank. The result, said H. L. Mencken, that unfailing fount of promiscuous scorn, "is so written that it will fit both the triumph of democracy and the collapse of democracy and approve both sending of arms and sending of flowers."

What was significant, though, was that the Republicans did not oppose outright all aid to Britain. And when they nominated Wendell Willkie, they chose an internationalist who was as much in favor as FDR of helping England. So in the coming campaign, whatever assaults Republicans might mount on New Deal policies, they would not be attacking the Democratic nominee (Roosevelt had not yet revealed whether he would be running for a third term) as an interventionist.

In the meantime, while the mockingly gorgeous summer strengthened English fields of hops and rye, contrails began to appear in the skies above them as the German air force fought to open the way for invasion. English onlookers tried to read their future in the momentous white scribbles six miles up, and Americans watched almost as closely. England's fighter planes went down; England's cities burned; but England held.

The current of American sympathy flowed more and more strongly toward Britain. Nevertheless, a rider to the June 1940 naval appropriations bill had made it illegal to sell the destroyers—or any such "surplus military material"—unless the chief of naval operations said the ships were not necessary to defend American shores. This put Admiral Stark in a most uncomfortable position. How could a man in the midst of a struggle to build up a navy threatened in two oceans say he didn't need fifty destroyers?

Eventually Roosevelt raised the possibility of a trade: the destroyers for British bases in the western hemisphere. This would allow him to say that the ships had been exchanged for something of greater military value to the United States. He explained the idea in a letter to a recalcitrant senator in which he describes a not wholly credible encounter between himself and the sort of canny rustic who had been a fixture on the American stage for at least a century. "Here is the real meat in the coconut as expressed to me by a Dutchess County farmer yesterday morning. I told him the gist of the proposal, which is, in effect, to buy ninety-nine year leases from Great Britain for at least seven naval and air bases in British Colonial possessions. . . . The farmer replied somewhat as follows:

"'Say, ain't you the Commander-in-Chief? If you are and you own fifty muzzle-loadin' rifles of the Civil War period, you would be a chump if you declined to exchange them for seven modern machine guns—wouldn't you?'"

Through July and August negotiations went on with Britain. At one point Churchill's amour propre got ruffled. At such a time, he said, a quid pro quo deal seemed sordid and ungenerous of the United States. Speaking on the phone to FDR's attorney general, Robert Jackson, Churchill snapped, "Empires just don't bargain."

"Republics do," said Jackson.

In the end a bargain was struck. Britain would get the destroyers, and America the right to operate out of eight British colonies stretching from Newfoundland down to Guiana. As far as the obstacle of Congress well, several distinguished lawyers felt that although the neutrality laws made it illegal for the United States to build and deliver warships to belligerent powers, in this case the ships had been built years ago by the government for its own purposes and could thus be turned over to a private contractor for sale to the British. No need for Congress to get involved.

The president announced the deal on September 3, and despite some fussing, nothing like the crisis FDR half expected developed. A public opinion poll taken two weeks earlier had apparently been quite right in its conclusion: over 60 percent of the American people were for the deal.

The navy was not caught by surprise, but the four-stackers were proving hard to resuscitate. Decades of caked grease had to be chipped away from machinery whose purpose was often incomprehensible, the plans of its ship having been lost. Many of the vessels had been cannibalized for basic parts; others had mysterious capillaries of piping that needed to be deciphered like the hieroglyphics on a tomb. Everything had to be coaxed back to life, from boilers with corroded tubing to treacherous galley stoves that might light up compliantly or might blow off their burner grates.

When, on September 3, the order came, "Proceed with project to turn over fifty destroyers to appropriate British authorities at Halifax," the Atlantic Squadron was ready. The destroyers would arrive in groups of eight, with two weeks between each transfer.

When the first flotilla reached Halifax, the old ships looked every bit as smart as their fellows had at the World's Fair opening. They were freshly painted, fully armed, and their larders were stocked with food. This last made the greatest impression on the British who were waiting to take them over. In Britain a year of war had brought shortages in even the most common foodstuffs, and here were such splendors as fruit cocktail and cocoa.

Captain Taprell Dorling wrote of this bounty, "The ships had been refitted throughout. They were scrupulously clean and fully supplied . . . paint and cordage; messtraps, silver and china, all marked with the anchor and U.S.N.; towels, sheets, blankets, mattresses and pillows. Sextant, chronometer watch, high-powered binoculars for the use of officers and look-outs, parallel rulers and instruments for navigation were not forgotten. A typewriter, paper, envelopes, patent pencil sharpeners, pencils, ink—everything and anything one could imagine, even to books and magazines, an electric coffee machine in the wardroom, were all provided. Storerooms were fully stocked with provisions, including spiced tinned ham and tinned sausages, and canned fruit and corn which do not normally find a place in the dietary of British bluejackets."

The Halifax authorities immediately did their best to get their own hands on the food, ordering that it be replaced at once with standard provisions. Many ships complied, and one commander complained that afterward "during our crossing of the Atlantic our Wardroom lived exclusively on a diet of Stilton cheese and sheeps' hearts (the only dish the steward could make)." The reason so many of the officers stood still for this extortion is that they were green. It was no easy thing to come up with the crews for fifty ships in the middle of a war.

Green or not, they began learning about the four-stackers right away. On the morning of September 9 the American crews mustered on the dock in front of their ships for the last time. The captains remained aboard the eight destroyers while a bugle called "Attention" and "To the Colors." The American flags came down, the skippers came ashore and marched with their men to where trains waited to carry them south to other commands. The navy wanted no photographs of English and American crews fraternizing, so only then did the British sailors appear and board the ships and recommission them under new names (in a graceful conceit typical of the man, Churchill had directed that they be christened after cities in America, Canada, and England that bore the same names). Waiting for the newcomers belowdecks were American indoctrination crews of about twenty men.

Not much except the larders pleased the new tenants. They'd been leery to begin with—an American naval officer had widely been quoted after explaining that the hulls of the four-stackers "were just thick enough to keep out the water and small fish"—and now they discovered a host of unwinning eccentricities. The destroyers were not nimble; they had the turning radius of a battleship. The steering engine that swung the big rudder was connected to the wheel on the bridge by cables that ran unsheathed aft through the engine and boiler rooms, begging to snag something. The vessels proved full of surprises; for instance, when the four-inch guns were raised to their full elevation, they liked to fire themselves.

The British got a couple of weeks to learn these crotchets. Captain Guy Sayer wasn't one of the neophyte officers—he knew enough not to surrender so much as a single can of spiced ham—but he still found "this fortnight was indeed a hectic period and must constitute a record for taking over an entirely unknown, foreign, elderly, and somewhat decrepit warship after twenty-two years laid up in reserve."

Captain Sayer's new command—born the USS *Stockton,* now HMS *Ludlow*—had made it across the Atlantic in the last war, but had gotten in so severe a collision there with a troopship that she had to be partially rebuilt in a Portsmouth dockyard. Sayer was told about this "within a few minutes of my arrival on board by the commanding officer—Lieut. Cdr. Lewis R. Miller, U.S.N.,—who greeted me with, 'Say, Cap'n, d'you know your ship has got a British bow!'"

Sayer immediately took to his American counterpart, and all his colleagues. "No one could have been more friendly, frank and helpful than the American naval authorities. They were completely honest about the ships, pointing out all the defects and weak spots."

These were numerous. The *Ludlow*'s steering engines twice went crazy (although not because of the problematic cables) "and jammed the helm hard over, causing the ship to steer out of control through an East Coast convoy, to be pulled up only just in time to avoid a sandbank, by an anchor hastily dropped!"

Each time the *Ludlow* revealed one of her flaws, Captain Miller, referring to the peccant part, would sympathetically tell Sayer, "That installation stinks to high heaven!"

The crew's quarters "were very cramped by our standards," said Sayer, ". . . and the wardroom austere and unhomely, mainly due to the fixed tables, chairs and settees all in steel frames." Surprisingly, given that the lavishness of American bathrooms was the object of amused envy throughout the British Isles, "The sanitary and bathing arrangements for the crew were rugged and archaic in the extreme, the former consisting of a spar over the top of an open trough into which a branch of the fire main was fed, and over which men were expected to perch like hens roosting!"*

Moreover, the ship was "short legged"—had no great cruising range—and, by Admiralty standards, carried weaponry far too heavy for her slim hull. Sayer was actually worried about the *Ludlow*'s ability to get to England. He expressed this to Miller time after time, always to be told, "She's done it once, and she'll do it again."

And sure enough, "when we did finally arrive, and after experiencing a certain amount of trouble with the engines and auxiliary machinery, I sent Lewis Miller a telegram: 'She stinks to high heaven, but she's done it again!'"

Once across the Atlantic, Sayer discovered that the infamous mock-reassurance about the small-fish-proof hull was a slander. "*Ludlow* was . . . made of remarkably tough steel. . . . We were rammed on the port quarter by another ship at night in heavy weather off Kinnairds Head. The damage, which in a modern ship would have been far more serious, was restricted to bad denting, and when the plates had to be removed in Rosyth Dockyard, much difficulty was experienced due to tools being continually blunted."

A number of the four-stackers had more trouble than the *Ludlow* did in getting across the ocean. In the first group of destroyers, HMS *Chesterfield* twice in quick succession rammed HMS *Churchill* (the only one of the ships not to be named after a town), hurting both badly enough to keep them from sailing

---

*Nor were the facilities sumptuous for the officers. One four-stacker veteran, an American, recalled, "The twelve officers, not counting the captain, who had one of each in his cabin, shared one toilet bowl and one shower. At sea, the saltwater in the head erupted with pulse-beat regularity and made a foot-high geyser inside the bowl. Six navy yards had failed to fix it. We called it, variously, the Fountain of Youth, Old Faithful, and the Douche Bowl."

for England. HMS *Cameron* got to sea without hitting anything, but then had to limp back with generator trouble. The *Newark* broke her nose against a seawall and, that damage repaired, had to abort her crossing when a blizzard carried away two depth charges that then exploded near her hull. In all, twelve of the fifty destroyers were involved in collisions, and during the last three months of 1940 the original eight spent a total of 218 days taking up precious space in British dockyards.

In time, though, they all went to work. Some sank U-boats (not a great many, but any single U-boat kill seemed like a lot when it happened), and some were sunk by them. One was a spectacular suicide. Early in 1942 the *Campbeltown*, shorn of two stacks to disguise herself as a German destroyer, ran through a murderous crevasse of fire—"her sides seemed to be alive with shells," said one of the commandos on the raid—to pile herself up against the lock gate at the port of St.-Nazaire, which held the only drydock on the French coast large enough to accommodate the German battleship *Tirpitz*. The next morning the German intelligence officer interrogating the *Campbeltown*'s captain told his captive how foolish it had been to try to attack that formidable gate "with a flimsy destroyer." But the hull of the flimsy destroyer was packed with depth charges so cunningly hidden by concrete and steel baffles that they escaped the notice of the men examining the ship. When the timers tripped, the explosion killed some 150 Germans aboard the *Campbeltown* and put the lock gates and the drydock they shielded beyond repair until 1947.

Of all FDR's four-stackers, the *Campbeltown* did the most obvious and dramatic damage to the enemy. But their real effect was one of increment, which would count for so much in the long battle. All through 1941, the four-stackers made up nearly a quarter of Britain's antisubmarine force.

They worked hard. In 1943, HMS *Burnham* went into drydock after a year of uninterrupted Atlantic steaming. One of her engineers walked beneath her bottom with a hammer to make a routine test on the rivets. As he tapped each one, it dropped from the hull to his feet amid a little puff of rust.

By then newer ships were doing the job begun by the old-timers. But the four-stackers had stood in the gap when there was nothing else to plug it. When they began struggling their way to England, Churchill told the House, "The fifty American destroyers are rapidly coming into service just when they are most needed." Admiral of the Fleet Sir James Somerville went much further: "Had there been no American 'four stacker' destroyers available and had they not gone into service escorting trade convoys when they did, the outcome of the struggle against the U-boat and the subsequent outcome of the European War itself might have been vastly different."

There was more to it than that. When the deal was concluded, Hanson W. Baldwin, already embarked on his thirty-year career as a military correspondent for the *New York Times*, wrote, "A new chapter of world history was written last week. . . . The destroyers steaming towards Halifax were not only symbols of an ever-closer Anglo-American *rapprochement*, but in the opinions of some observers, sealed what in effect was an unofficial alliance between the English-speaking nations and brought the United States far closer than ever before to entry into the war."

Baldwin was right. The old destroyers had carried America and Britain to the beginning of a road the two nations would walk together for all the hard years ahead.

Long after the transfer, when the war had come to us and burning freighters were brightening the night skies off Boston and Charleston and Key West, one of Stark's admirals told him how much he missed those fifty four-stackers, what a difference it would have made if they'd never been handed over to the Royal Navy. Stark wouldn't have any of that. "Those ships," he said, "have already been fighting for us for more than a year."

Doenitz Goes to France

Germany builds her Biscay U-boat bases, 1940

The German Foreign Office dismissed the destroyer deal: "Germany takes note of the fact that Great Britain has sold out valuable areas of its empire to the United States for fifty old destroyers." The German press took the same tone. "Like the Jew Esau," the English were selling their birthright for "some poor naval leftovers with scarcely any naval value."

But of course Hitler understood what the transaction meant. Less than a month after the first of the four-stackers sailed for Halifax, his foreign minister, Joachim von Ribbentrop, signed a document that began, "The governments of Germany, Italy, and Japan, considering it as a condition precedent of any lasting peace that all nations of the world be given each its own proper place, have decided to stand by and cooperate with one another in regard to their efforts in greater East Asia and regions of Europe respectively wherein it is their prime purpose to establish and maintain a new order of things calculated to promote the mutual prosperity and welfare of the peoples concerned." Article Three had each of the nations going to war when "one of the three contracting powers is attacked by a power at present not involved in the European war or in the Chinese-Japanese conflict."

Admiral Raeder would never get his aircraft carriers, but Hitler had seen a way to bring a great many carriers against a potential opponent in an ocean ten thousand miles away.

"Done in triplicate at Berlin," the pact concluded, "the 27th day of September, 1940, in the 19th year of the fascist era, corresponding to the 27th day of the ninth month of the 15th year of Showa (the reign of Emperor Hirohito)."

Germany had last signed a treaty of high significance just four months earlier. It allowed the French to quit fighting in return for two-thirds of their country, including the coast that ran south by east from Brest down to the Spanish border and embraced the Bay of Biscay. The bay's size and relatively shallow floor gave it some of the fiercest of the fierce Atlantic weather. Yet Doenitz looked toward it with longing. "From the moment that it had started in May 1940," he wrote, "the advance of the German army in the campaign against France had been watched with close attention by U-boat command. If the army succeeded in defeating France, we would be given the advantage of having bases on the Channel and Biscay coasts for our naval operations . . . ; it would mean that we should now have an exit from our 'backyard' in the southeastern corner of the North Sea and be on the shores of the Atlantic, the ocean in which the war at sea . . . must be finally decided."

Throughout the fighting, "U-boat command had a train standing by, which, laden with torpedoes and carrying all the personnel and matériel necessary for the maintenance of U-boats, was dispatched to the Biscay ports on the day after the signing of the armistice." Doenitz found his tour of the Biscay bases more than satisfactory. Any one of them would cut some 450 miles off the journey his boats had to make to reach the Western Approaches. The effect was the same as if the size of his fleet had just been increased by something like a fifth: a shorter turnaround between patrols, and repair facilities infinitely more accessible than the overtaxed German ones.

Doenitz chose Lorient as the most promising of the ports he saw, and outside the town at Kernaval, he found a steep-roofed château that he picked as his future headquarters.

Not long after the admiral's reconnoitering visit the first U-boat put into Lorient: Captain Lemp's *U-30,* looking to take on torpedoes. For the rest of the war, Germany would wage its Atlantic campaign largely from Biscay ports.

Not long after Lemp paid his inaugural visit, construction crews began to arrive in Lorient. They were from the German state's construction company, Organization Todt, named for the man who ran it, Fritz Todt. "Our dear Master Builder," as Hitler once called him, had been in charge of the autobahn system. His position was more analogous to a general's than an engineer's because he had three hundred thousand men working for him. Now his job was to build bases where the U-boats could be refitted before being sent back on patrol. The result is the only vestige of the Thousand Year Reich that may really last a thousand years. As oppressively magnificent as the pyramids—and, like the pyramids, built mostly by slave labor—horizontal bunkers a third of a mile long began to take shape at Lorient and four other towns on the Biscay coast: Brest, La Pallice, St.-Nazaire, and Bordeaux. Before they were done, they would absorb a million tons of steel and 14 million cubic feet of concrete (the Hoover Dam, perhaps America's closest equivalent in monumentality, contains 4.4 million). All the pens differed slightly, but the effect is uniform: U-boat garages in whose impregnable slots the craft could ride with thirty feet of water beneath them and thirty feet of working space overhead. Cranes that, according to their size, could lift out a periscope or a conning tower, ran up and down above the docked boats, and metal blast doors a yard thick protected them once they'd made their way inside.

The great dank, echoing pens were far more than parking space; they also enclosed repair facilities, barracks for up to a thousand men, fuel dumps, mess halls, all beneath a roof perhaps twenty-five feet thick, itself bearing another roof—or series of roofs—that would ensnare and explode and diffuse the blast of any bomb that might find them. The Royal Air Force tried to destroy the bunkers—at Lorient, with three hundred raids and twelve-thousand-pound Tallboy bombs designed specifically for the task. The town of Lorient disappeared. Only three houses were left standing by 1945 (one of them Doenitz's château), but the submarine base was never put out of action and protected and serviced as many as twenty-eight boats simultaneously under the worst of the hammering.

None of the bases suffered any serious harm. When, in 1987, filmmakers needed a set for the popular submarine movie *Das Boot,* they simply moved into La Pallice, where the old machinery stood intact and dim Gothic lettering still proclaimed its exhortations and prohibitions from the unmarred walls.

Germany First

Planning America's naval war, 1940

At the end of June 1940, Admiral Doenitz could claim the destruction of fifty-eight ships—the highest monthly tally of the war thus far. By early fall he had gotten his group tactics to work the way he had envisioned them, and his skippers entered the period they would remember as "the happy time." In mid-October one of his boats, *U-48*, spotted a convoy, radioed its position, and attacked. The submarine sank two ships before being driven off, and the next day *U-38* picked up the convoy, shadowed it until darkness, then sank one ship and nearly got another. *U-38* had also radioed its position, and by the next night Doenitz had five boats waiting. This *wolf pack*—a term that would hold for the rest of the war (and possibly forever after)—came in on the surface, fast. Aided by a moon only three days past full, and later by burning vessels, the pack kept up an assault that began at nine and lasted eight hours straight. The next night, with the moon still helping, another wolf pack found another convoy. At the battle's end, Doenitz reported, "By joint attack . . . over three days seven U-boats with 300 men have sunk 47 ships totaling about 310,000 tons—a tremendous success."

If not quite as tremendous as he thought—it's not easy to

keep a precise accounting during a night action, and the actual number of ships sunk was thirty-two—it was big enough. Doenitz had not lost a single boat. And what must have been just as gratifying to him, he believed he had ratified the tactical theory that he had been working out for more than twenty years.

THE U.S. ELECTION WAS only three weeks away during those calamitous moonlit nights, and Britain was awaiting it with far greater interest than the nation had ever before shown in an American presidential contest. The English hoped that once it was over, America would join them in the fight against Germany.

That wasn't going to be. President Roosevelt knew his country generally favored helping England—the mild response to his destroyer deal had shown that—but sending matériel and sending men were two very different propositions. FDR remained convinced that the nation was far from ready to go to war.

He had, however, been assembling a war cabinet of sorts. While the French army was disintegrating, the president had asked two prominent Republicans to come work for him.

Frank Knox, the publisher of Chicago's *Daily News,* had served in the Rough Riders under Theodore Roosevelt during the war with Spain and had run for vice president on the Republican ticket in 1936. Roosevelt approached him to be secretary of the navy, and he accepted.

Henry Stimson had been just about everything: secretary of war under Taft, an artillery colonel in World War I, governorgeneral of the Philippines, Hoover's secretary of state, chairman of the U.S. delegation to the London naval conference. He was seventy-three years old, he had absolutely nothing to prove, and he was rich. Roosevelt asked him to be secretary of war. Stimson, who had served four Republican administrations, thought about working for this Democratic one. If you'll give me a free hand picking my subordinates, he said, I'll do it.

A man wholly unintimidated by capable assistants, Stimson made good choices. Among the first was John McCloy, the incarnation of brusque and tireless energy, and in a few months to be promoted to associate secretary of war. Then Robert A. Lovett arrived. The son of the president of the Union Pacific Railroad, he had joined the navy in the last war and come out a lieutenant commander in charge of a naval air squadron. Although, like McCloy, he had spent many prosperous years on Wall Street, his interest in flight never waned, and he became assistant secretary for air.

Like Stimson, these men didn't scare easily. One morning Lovett stopped in at his boss's office while the secretary of war was growing increasingly infuriated by the opacity of some report he was going over. Stimson's many admirable qualities did not include a tranquil disposition, and when Lovett interrupted him, he started yelling. His privacy had been violated for no reason; the intrusion was unbearably insolent and only added to the awful pressures on him. This sort of tirade had often brought law clerks to tears. Not Lovett, who merely backed out of the office, quietly closing the door behind him. As he did, he saw McCloy coming past on his way in to work. "Good morning, Jack," said Lovett. "The secretary wants to see you right away."

Another time, McCloy, at the White House with Knox's undersecretary, James Forrestal, got an urgent phone call from his boss: "Where are my goddamn papers?"

"I haven't got your goddamn papers," said McCloy, and hung up. Forrestal took in the exchange and remarked that things certainly were not the same in the Navy Department.

Things weren't the same anywhere in the government. Stimson, who would replace Harry Woodring, a firm isolationist, made his position clear in his confirmation hearing. At the very opening, he said he "did not believe that we shall be safe from invasion if we sit down and wait for the enemy to attack our shores."

Roosevelt had the confidence to pick confident subordinates, and in choosing Stimson and Knox for their posts he had stolen a march on the Republicans as the election drew nearer. But there was more to it than that. Speaking to his secretary of the treasury, Henry Morgenthau, about America's joining the war, Roosevelt said, "I am waiting to be pushed into this situation."

With Stimson and Knox, he had brought aboard two men who were willing to push him hard.

NOT THAT FRANKLIN ROOSEVELT was so easy to push. His affable evasiveness once provoked his secretary of war into a complaint that ended in something approaching poetry. "Conferences with the President are difficult matters," Stimson wrote. "His mind does not follow easily a consecutive chain of thought but he is full of stories and incidents and hops about in his discussions from suggestion to suggestion and it is very much like chasing a vagrant beam of sunlight around a vacant room."

The thicket of jokes, irrelevant anecdotes, and deflections that the president inhabited was particularly vexing to Harold Stark, the new chief of naval operations. Ships were finite things—they could not be counted on to respond to an optimistic inspiration caught on the fly. Stark had spent his entire career dealing with unforgiving technical specifics that were a world apart from FDR's hummingbird dart and glitter.

A Pennsylvanian who had graduated from the U.S. Naval Academy in 1903, Stark was direct and friendly, a man eager to dispense compliments whenever he could. This, coupled with what might be described as a slightly matronly appearance, led some to believe him too mild for high command. Not FDR, though, who appointed Stark over fifty officers senior to him. He had been sworn into his new post the same month the European war began, and he knew the navy was not prepared to play any useful part in it. The freshly minted CNO had a great many concerns that required immediate attention, and a boss who had a genius for avoiding decisions.

On the other hand, at least he had regular access to the president, for the two men were genuinely close. They had first met in 1914, when Stark was a lieutenant commanding the destroyer *Patterson* and Roosevelt was assistant secretary of the navy. Stark had been ordered to take Roosevelt up to his New Brunswick summer home on Campobello Island. As they approached their destination and headed into a difficult channel, the assistant secretary appeared on the bridge and, never timid in maritime matters, told Stark he'd sailed these waters for years and asked to take the conn. "No, sir," said the skipper. "This ship is my command, and I doubt your authority to relieve me." Then, in a brave show of competence, Stark poured on twenty-eight knots and dashed safely through the tricky waters. A quarter century later, when he was made CNO, he wrote Roosevelt recalling the incident. He looked forward to sailing with him again, he said, and this time he would acknowledge his passenger's right to command.

Stark knew his first job was to persuade the president to make the navy bigger. When he became CNO, 116,000 men were in the service. Roosevelt stingily suggested enlarging it by 6,000 more. By the end of the year, Stark had got him to agree to 54,000.

Then there was the question of ships to put them on. Stark asked for a 25 percent increase in the size of the fleet, which translated into three aircraft carriers, eight cruisers, fifty-two destroyers, and thirty-two submarines, along with a host of auxiliary vessels to feed and fix them. (Eight battleships were already in various stages of their four-year gestation.)

In the early months of 1940 Stark testified before the House Naval Affairs Committee. These ships had to be built *now*, he said: "Navies cannot be improvised. For the most part wars are fought and won or lost with the navies that exist at the outbreak of hostilities."

Actually, Stark thought 25 percent wasn't enough, but the president had refused to let him seek more. FDR's instincts were sound, for by the time the naval expansion bill reached the Senate, the increase had been whittled away to 11 percent. When Stark bridled at that, the president assured him he would hold firm on the original figure. FDR held firm for several hours. The very next day he explained that in fact he, too, favored the 11 percent expansion. Stark kept his temper—he almost always did—and spent April patiently explaining the virtues of an 11 percent expansion to Congress.

Then came May and, with it, Hitler's battalions. June, and the French fleet was no longer a dependable buffer between America and continental embroilments. It might even join the German fleet, giving the Third Reich the benefit in minutes at no cost of an extravagant twenty-year building program.

President Roosevelt signed the 11 percent expansion bill on June 15, a Saturday. Stark had spent Friday drafting another bill. In light of the catastrophe that had befallen Western Europe, he had, he said, decided to "go the whole hog" and ask for an American navy that could hold its own in two oceans at the same time.

What followed must have seemed dreamlike to Stark. He was back before the committee the next Tuesday asking for a 70 percent increase on top of the three-day-old 11 percent one.

This would cost $4 billion. The committee only wanted to know if Stark was sure that would be enough. The CNO was not quite certain about the particulars—things were moving fast, and the Naval Affairs Committee approved the bill a week after he'd begun writing it—but he guessed he was talking about 7 new battleships, 7 aircraft carriers, 43 submarines, 29 cruisers, and 115 destroyers.

President Roosevelt signed the bill into law on July 19 and thus gave birth to the fleet with which America would fight the war.

★ ★ ★

So the ships were coming. Now Stark began figuring out what to do with them. When planning theoretical operations, the navy far preferred the Pacific to the Atlantic. Those immense blue distances meant that a war fought there would have to be a proper naval one, with fleets meeting in decisive, clear-cut battles. What was shaping up in the Atlantic was messy and ill defined. But it was in the Atlantic that an immediate threat to America was gathering, and Stark had the discipline to turn his mind from the war he would prefer to fight to the one on offer at the moment.

If it became a shooting war before a strategy had been devised, decisions would be made in reaction to events; if a plan was in place, perhaps the decisions could affect the events, rather than the other way around.

On a morning in late October Stark sat down at his desk and started writing. He worked straight through until two o'clock the next morning and spent the following week going over the result with Frank Knox and the army chief of staff, George Marshall. Then he returned to his desk, hoping to produce a final draft that would persuade the president to decide on a course to take the country through the crisis. What he came up with may be the single most important document of the American effort in World War II.

In it, Stark set down what he saw as the four significant options open to the U.S. forces, assigning each a letter of the alphabet. (A) was to protect our own shores while continuing to send material aid to Britain, but generally keeping out of the fight itself. (B) had us going on the defensive in the Atlantic while attacking the Pacific. (C) was to join Great Britain to the full extent of our ability in both oceans; and (D) was to hang on in the Pacific while attacking in the Atlantic.

Stark assessed each of these choices with brisk vigor—no

military passive voice in this memorandum—and concluded, "I believe that the continued existence of the British Empire, combined with building up a strong protection in our home areas, will do best to ensure the status quo in the Western Hemisphere, and to promote our principal interests." He said why he thought so at the outset: "If Britain wins decisively against Germany, we could win everywhere; but . . . if she loses the problem confronting us would be very great; and while we might not *lose everywhere*, we might possibly not win *anywhere*."

Despite all the lures of the Pacific, Stark favored (D): "The United States could eventually develop a strong offensive as an ally and maintain a defensive in the Pacific."

Knox and Marshall backed the plan; Stimson backed it, too. The president, though as usual not eager to commit himself on paper, backed it. Despite Pearl Harbor, despite the terrible island fighting that followed it for years, the American high command would never abandon what came to be called the "Germany first" strategy.

In the system of military phonetics worked out to ensure clarity in communications, the letter *d* is "dog," and Stark's recommendation took its place in the high annals of the world under the homely name of Plan Dog.

A Length of Garden Hose

FDR sells Lend-Lease, 1940

The ships were on the way and we knew how we were going to use them. But America was not in the war yet, and so Plan Dog's strategy to bulwark Britain was purely theoretical. Although the cash-and-carry improvisation had been getting England matériel, it would not keep doing so for long. Lord Lothian, the British ambassador to Washington, summarized the problem with startling directness when he returned from a brief trip to confer with Churchill in November. To the waiting reporters, he said, "Well, boys, Britain's broke; it's your money we want."

A few days later, Frank Knox, talking with Henry Morgenthau, said, "We are going to pay for the war, are we?" FDR had just authorized $2 billion to outfit ten British divisions, and the treasury secretary asked if this should be allowed to go through. It turned out Knox had been speaking rhetorically. "Got to," he went on, "no question about it."

But the law was clear: no credit for Britain. This was not a problem Knox or Morgenthau could solve; it had to be addressed on the highest level.

The highest level had gone fishing. The 1940 election had finally come, bringing Roosevelt a third term. Understandably worn down by the last few months, the president had slipped away for two weeks on the USS *Tuscaloosa*—he loved a cruiser—but Churchill tracked him down there with a four-thousand-word cable. Mostly it was a magisterial survey of the current state of the war, and a look toward the year ahead: "The decision for 1941 lies upon the seas. It is therefore in shipping and in the power to transport across the ocean, particularly the Atlantic Ocean, that in 1941 the crunch of the whole war will be found." One paragraph, though, dealt with Britain's financial situation almost as bluntly as Lord Lothian had: "The moment approaches when we will no longer be able to pay cash for shipping and other supplies."

The president's fishing wasn't very productive. Despite his following Ernest Hemingway's advice that big stuff was to be had in the Mona Passage between Puerto Rico and the Dominican Republic if it was offered a feathered hook baited with pork rind, the prize of the voyage was a twenty-pound grouper, caught not by FDR but by his aide Harry Hopkins.

Only when the party was homeward bound, said Hopkins, did he realize the president had more on his mind than fish. "I didn't know for quite awhile what he was thinking about, if anything. But then—I began to get the idea that he was refueling, the way he so often does when he seems to be resting and carefree. So I didn't ask him any questions. Then, one evening, he came out with it—the whole program. He didn't seem to have any clear idea how it could be done legally. But there wasn't a doubt in his mind that he'd find a way to do it."

The "whole program" was Lend-Lease. The playwright Robert Sherwood, who composed speeches for FDR, said, "Roosevelt, a creative artist in politics, had put in his time on this cruise evolving the pattern of a masterpiece, and once he could see it clearly in his own mind's eye, he made it quickly and very simply clear to all."

He did that at a press conference on December 17, the day

after he returned to Washington. He liked to start these events with the transparently disingenuous phrase "I don't think there is any particular news . . ." That out of the way, he turned to foreign affairs, saying that he wanted to "get rid of" what he called with fond, avuncular impatience "the silly, foolish old dollar sign."

He gave an example. "Suppose my neighbor's home catches fire, and I have a length of garden hose four or five hundred feet away. If he can take my garden hose and connect it up with his hydrant, I may help him put out his fire. Now, what do I do? I don't say to him before that operation, 'Neighbor, my garden hose cost me fifteen dollars; you have to pay me fifteen dollars for it.' What is the transaction that goes on? I don't want fifteen dollars, I want my garden hose back after the fire is over. All right. If it goes through the fire all right, intact, without any damage to it, he gives it back to me and thanks me very much for the use of it. But suppose it gets smashed up—holes in it—during the fire; we don't have to have too much formality about it, but I say to him, 'I was glad to lend you that hose; I see I can't use it anymore, it's all smashed up.' He says, 'How many feet of it were there?' I tell him, 'There were one hundred and fifty feet of it.' He says, 'All right, I will replace it.' Now, if I get a nice garden hose back, I am in pretty good shape."

Looking back across the fierce debates that followed, Sherwood wrote, "I believe it may accurately be said that with that neighborly analogy, Roosevelt won the fight for Lend-Lease." It was in some ways a preposterous analogy. If your neighbor's house is on fire, you not only lend him your garden hose, you help him use it. Nevertheless, it stuck in people's minds.

Two weeks later, Roosevelt deployed a phrase that had just as much sticking power and considerably more grandeur. Three-fourths of the American people heard it on December 29 when they tuned in Roosevelt's fireside chat. In it, the president called for greater military production—"We must have more ships, more guns, more planes—more of everything"—stating that the surest path to American security was to help keep Britain in the war. He concluded by saying, "We must be the great arsenal of democracy."

Polls showed 60 percent of the president's listeners agreed with him. When the time came, two-thirds of the public supported Lend-Lease, but the debate was more heated than the one over the destroyer deal. The conservative senator Robert Taft was not buying the hose metaphor: "Lending arms is like lending chewing gum—you don't want it back." Senator Burton Wheeler of Montana took the discussion far beyond garden hoses and gum with his declaration that Lend-Lease "will plow under every fourth American boy." Many Americans less furiously engaged with the issue than Wheeler worried that giving the president a free hand to supply arms to another country was crossing a perilous boundary.

Nevertheless, the bill passed on March 11, 1941. Hours afterward it was undergirded by an appropriation of $7 billion. America was going to be arsenal and factory, too.

New ships, new strategy, new matériel—everything was in place. Yet Stark was moving into some of the most frustrating weeks of his life.

The reason is suggested in a press conference the president held on April 15. FDR had long since set a standard for these gatherings that his successors could only hope to emulate. Relaxed, cheerful, confident, amused, and amusing, he was always in control of a pack of those most unherdable creatures, newspaper reporters.

He began with his "I don't think I have anything" rubric, then amended it to admit to one "little human-interest thing." He had just looked at the first Lend-Lease lists of nonmilitary equipment that the British Purchasing Committee wanted, and "there are a number of different items like tar, kettles, and road rollers, and pumps, and graders. The last three items are for nine hundred thousand feet of garden hose!"

The reporters laughed, and FDR went on, "Not garden hose but fire hose—actually fire hose—at a final cost of three hundred thousand dollars. I thought it was a rather nice coincidence."

One of the reporters asked a shrewd question: "Mr. President, do you have any oceangoing fire hose?"

That is, how is the hose going to get there? On the most mercenary level, the question was noting that under cash and carry, the British had already bought the goods they were bringing home, and best of luck getting them there. With Lend-Lease, these were our goods, and the garden hose wouldn't come back if it was at the bottom of the sea. The president didn't answer, and there was some genial back-and-forth about other matters.

"Mr. President, the press reports from Europe indicate that the situation looks rather gloomy for the British at the moment."

"Do they?" Roosevelt asked innocently.

"Would you care to comment?"

"No, no. No. I don't look that way, do I?"

Further laughter, but the question returned, more sharply.

"Mr. President, could you tell whether you feel there is an increasing demand toward the use of American naval power?"

"No, I couldn't tell you that." No longer so amiable, he rode over another question and went on, "I would also—let me put it this way—there has been more nonsense written, more printer's ink spilled, more oratory orated over that subject by people who don't know a hill of beans about it than any other subject in modern times."

This was diversionary bluster. Roosevelt knew what his audience was asking—will American warships escort and protect vessels carrying Lend-Lease goods?—and he squirmed and dodged to avoid giving an answer.

Committing his ships to guard belligerents was an act of

war. He may have wanted the war, but he didn't want to start it. He certainly didn't want to be perceived by the American people as calling for military action so close on the heels of Lend-Lease. The loss, of, say, a cruiser would perhaps have been sufficient provocation to bring the country in, but Hitler wasn't cooperating. He had given strict orders to his U-boat commanders to keep out of the way of American ships, and none had been harmed.

Two days before his press conference the president had extended the "security zone" to Greenland, but the ships patrolling it were merely to report the presence of submarines, not engage them.

Stark believed this a meaningless order, and when he pressed his boss, he got only the same vagrant beam of sunlight that bedeviled Stimson. The secretary of war was also badgering FDR to ask Congress for the power "to use naval, air, and military forces of the United States" in the Atlantic. Feeding Britain supplies wasn't enough: "The men who suffered at Valley Forge and won at Yorktown gave more than money to the cause of freedom."

Roosevelt complained, "I simply have not got enough navy to go around." All his lieutenants were prickly and sour that season. As the humid spring ripened into one of the hottest Washington summers on record, Stimson made what he called his "only wholly pessimistic diary entry in five years." It began, "Altogether, tonight I feel more up against it than ever before. It is a problem whether the country has it in itself to meet such an emergency, whether we are really powerful enough and sincere enough and devoted enough to meet the Germans." Secretary of State Cordell Hull went about muttering, "Everything is going hellward." Eventually Roosevelt took to his bed with what he said was a severe cold. Robert Sherwood didn't see much sign of the ailment, and when he said so to the president's private secretary, Marguerite LeHand, she smiled and explained that the patient was down with "a case of pure exasperation."

* * *

MY PARENTS HAD A much better spring than the president. Nearly a decade had passed since my maternal grandparents had forbidden Emma Folger to marry an architect in the precarious Depression economy. It was late in the day to have taken this step: the invitations had already gone out. I remember my mother telling me that after she'd bent to her parents' wishes, she'd gone weeping to her room with a pair of pinking shears and cut her wedding dress into long white rags.

The prohibition had evidently gone the way of the London naval accords when, one evening in 1940, my mother, riding out from Grand Central Terminal to Bronxville, where she still lived with her parents, saw my father waiting for a train on the platform of the 125th Street Station. She got up from her seat, hurried down the aisle and out of the car, and confronted him.

In later years the two of them remembered only one thing about the conversation that followed. "Then she pinched me in the stomach," my father would say, still surprised and amused half a century afterward. "Then I pinched his stomach," my mother would tell me, still surprised at herself, "and I said, Dick, are you going to marry me or not?"

He was. He did, in the April of FDR's discontent, at the Riverside Church in Manhattan, where Emma worked as an assistant to the Reverend Harry Emerson Fosdick. There was no parental interference this time; the country was awash in Lend-Lease money, and any competent architect had as much work as he could handle.

Fishing Trip
Churchill and Roosevelt meet, 1941

Admiral Stark kept pushing the president to take more force-ful action in the Atlantic. Things were going badly for the British, he insisted—and they certainly were, with U-boats sinking merchant ships at three times the rate English yards could replace them. But Roosevelt still held back on escorting convoys. Instead, the president took a new tack that was bolder than the patrols, yet less provocative than convoy escorts. On June 7, 1941, he announced that America would relieve the British troops garrisoning Iceland.

The three-hundred-mile-long island between Greenland and Norway had been a dependency of Denmark when the war began. Hitler planned to occupy it, but Britain got the jump on him. It was not to prove a popular posting. Though touching the arctic circle, the country is not quite as inhospitable as its name suggests because it is warmed by the Gulf Stream—or at least made habitable. But only a quarter of it *is* habitable, the rest treeless volcanic mountains along whose stony flanks fogs and storms are perpetually brewed by the collision of Gulf and polar waters.

The Germans had thought that any American movement would be to the south, and the occupation took them completely by surprise. The marines arrived, in early July, without difficulty but with little joy. After only a few hours in Reykjavik most of them were calling the port "Rinky-dink." Hvalfjordhur, twenty-five miles up the coast, they just as quickly christened Valley Forge. There followed a great deal of muddy unloading, and the Sixth Marines began sourly to refer to themselves as the Sixth Labor Regiment. The carrier *Wasp* risked a voyage through U-boat waters to ferry in thirty P-40 fighter planes, and the new-comers settled down to their monotonous business.

When Captain Daniel V. Gallery was ordered to command the Fleet Air Base at Reykjavik he found "the situation was grim. Our boys were eking out a miserable existence knee-deep in mud. . . . The wind howled through our broken down Nissen huts with arctic glee. The well-dressed man-about-camp wore two sets of long flannel drawers and without our eider-down sleeping bags we would have frozen. Our galley was equipped with salvaged junk, and the food was terrible."

Griffith Baily Coale arrived in Iceland late in the year. Coale was a successful muralist who believed that the navy should recruit artists to record its doings, and he made his point so per-suasively that he was commissioned a lieutenant commander in the Naval Reserve and sent to sea aboard a destroyer. As his ship approached the island, Coale heard the lookout shout, "Land ho!" and came out on deck. "Soon with the naked eye we see a great mountain rising straight out of the sea, shaped like a sperm whale's tooth. Presently the coast opens up, a great bleak jagged contour of mountains topped by a volcanic cone two thousand feet high and covered with snow. . . . We salt-caked destroyers swing hard left and in a straight column proceed at fifteen knots up the amazing corridor of Hvalfjorhdur, carpeted with dark-green water and walled by sheer chocolate-colored precipices capped with a strangely white icing of snow. . . . The scale is so vast that one is convinced that the scattered houses and church yonder are tiny scale buildings built by the Icelanders for their children."

Coale found a place to bunk with the marines tending an antiaircraft battery. "This is rugged, simple life. My furniture consists of two packing boxes; my wash basin is the bottom of a gasoline can, cunningly lipped over; my drinking water is in a peanut jar, the top of which is my ashtray." Thus berthed, Coale sat and sketched and watched the sentries "driving Icelandic ponies from the camp garbage cans. They trot away and hide behind a hut, peeping like bad boys around the corner at a cop."

Emory Jernigan, now at home aboard his battleship, got shore leave when the *Washington* anchored at Reykjavik. "The people were pretty nice looking," he said. "Most of them were blonde. However, they were the most unfriendly people I ever ran across anywhere in the world. As a general rule, they had bad teeth and very rude manners." The best Jernigan could find to say about Reykjavik was that the bakeries there sold good pastries.

To be fair, the Icelanders were under the occupation of a foreign power, and they'd had little say in the matter. Stimson and Stark might chafe about how slowly things were moving, but America had garrisoned a European nation and was flying regular patrols from its airfields. The garrison had to be supplied, of course, and that meant merchant ships. They would need protecting.

ON JUNE 22, WHILE the marines were on their way to Iceland, Hitler attacked Russia along a fifteen-hundred-mile front. President Roosevelt had known that this was coming (and had sent warnings to the Soviet Union, which Stalin chose to disbelieve) and was thus confident that the heavily engaged Germans wouldn't contest the Iceland occupation.

Not surprisingly, the drastically changed European situation spurred Stark and Stimson and Knox to press once again for convoy escorts. On July 2, Roosevelt agreed. A few days later, with the Japanese making trouble in Indochina, he again changed his mind, saying that "every little episode in the Pacific means fewer ships in the Atlantic." Stark kept his peace, and his stoicism was rewarded late in the month when FDR finally gave the permission Stark had been seeking for months.

Then, having sent his navy to war, the president said it was time for another fishing trip. On August 3, a Sunday, Roosevelt went by train to New London, Connecticut, and there got aboard the presidential yacht *Potomac*. He spent Monday close enough inshore for newspaper reporters to see him fishing. Once darkness had fallen, the *Potomac* made for Martha's Vineyard, where the president's previous fishing boat, the *Tuscaloosa*, was waiting in company with its fellow heavy cruiser *Augusta* and several destroyers. The president and his party boarded the *Augusta*. Admiral Stark was there, fully enjoying himself for the first time in quite a while.

The warships headed north, while the *Potomac* took up her earlier station. On Tuesday, shorebound correspondents could again watch the president—or someone dressed like him—fishing off the yacht's stern.

The actual president was bound for Placentia Bay, Newfoundland. Saturday, August 9, dawned cool there, with mist lying white on the water. The American sailors watching—from the *Tuscaloosa*, the *Augusta*, the old (launched in 1911) *Arkansas*, the destroyers—saw a shape form in the fog and resolve itself into the *Prince of Wales*. The British battleship steamed out into clear daylight. Her band was playing "The Star-Spangled Banner"; the band aboard the *Augusta* answered with "God Save the King."

All the difference between war and peace was visible in the two ships. The *Augusta* was immaculate, her paint clean and as bright as gray can reasonably get. The *Prince of Wales* was new, but she had already seen hard service. A couple of months earlier she'd had to hurry to sea with some civilian technicians still aboard when the *Bismarck,* the most powerful battleship in the world, broke out into the convoy lanes of the open Atlantic. In company with the battle cruiser *Hood* she had found the *Bismarck* and got so badly hurt that she had to retire from the action that followed. The *Hood* fared worse. When a single salvo hit her, she simply disappeared; of the fourteen hundred men aboard, three survived. But the brief action had doomed the *Bismarck,* too. Bleeding oil, she was tracked down by sea and by air.* So that morning in Placentia Bay the *Prince of Wales* bore on its flank the *Bismarck*'s guns on her upperworks, and on her sides the disorienting scythes and daggers of camouflage paint.

Soon boats were crossing between the ships. From the *Augusta* to the *Prince of Wales* came fifteen hundred packages, each containing an orange, half a pound of American cheese, a carton of cigarettes, and a card: "The President of the US of A sends his compliments and best wishes." From the *Prince of Wales* to the *Augusta* came Winston Churchill.

The prime minister climbed aboard and walked beneath the eight-inch guns to where Franklin Roosevelt was standing, braced on the arm of an air force officer, his son Elliott. Churchill bowed and handed FDR a letter from King George VI: "My dear President Roosevelt, This is just a note to bring you my best wishes, and to say how glad I am that you have an opportunity at last of getting to know my Prime Minister. I am sure that you will agree that he is a very remarkable man, and I have no doubt that your meeting will prove of great benefit to our two countries in the pursuit of

---

*It says something about American neutrality that the plane that spotted the German ship and gave away her position to her pursuers was carrying as "adviser" pilot Leonard B. Smith, U.S. Navy.

our common goal." The bow and the letter were more than pleasantries. Robert Sherwood wrote that Churchill never lost sight "of the fact that Roosevelt was his superior in rank—the President being the Head of State, on the level with the King, whereas the Prime Minister is Head of Government. To the average American this may seem a rather academic distinction, but it was of great importance in the relationship of the two men."

The genesis of the meeting went back months, perhaps to a conversation the president had with Harry Hopkins at Christmastime. "You know," said FDR, "a lot of this could be settled if Churchill and I could just sit down together for a while."

"What's stopping you?" Hopkins asked.

The idea had a most urgent appeal to Churchill, who was not only curious to see Roosevelt, but who thought that the invitation to do so surely indicated that the United States was ready to join Britain in the war.

The prime minister was mistaken, and that was not the only misunderstanding during what came to be called the Atlantic Conference. It is pleasing to think that an instant affinity sparked there beneath the cruiser's guns, one that would grow into a deep friendship—"the partnership," as the historian Joseph P. Lash subtitled his study of the two men, "that saved the West." And to a degree this is true; certainly they would preside over what became perhaps the closest and most successful national alliance in history.

But president and prime minister were, as Harry Hopkins put it, "two prima donnas." Roosevelt was jealous of Churchill's oratorical brilliance; Churchill occasionally grew bitter and petulant about his role of suitor. On a deeper level, the prime minister must have felt something close to grief as it became increasingly clear that the ally Britain needed to save her would inevitably surpass her power. Tremendous as the partnership might be, Churchill was the junior partner.

As for the frets of petulance, FDR felt them early in the encounter, when Churchill made it evident (strangely, since the prime minister prepared for this meeting with the most obsessive first-date meticulousness, saying at one point, "I wonder if he will like me") that he did not remember having met Roosevelt at a dinner in England in 1918. "It would be an exaggeration," wrote Sherwood, "to say that Roosevelt and Churchill became chums at the Conference or at any other time. They established an easy intimacy, a joking informality and a moratorium on pomposity and cant—and also a degree of frankness of intercourse which, if not quite complete, was remarkably close to it.

The next day, Sunday, the president went over to the *Prince of Wales*. As the American destroyer that ferried him across from the *Augusta* came alongside, a chief noticed a guy in a peacoat standing around on the battleship's deck doing nothing. The American threw over a line, barking at the loafer to make it fast.

Winston Churchill complied with amiable alacrity, and FDR came aboard for Sunday services. These were held on the wide quarterdeck, with hundreds of sailors, American and British mixed together, looking on. They sang hymns that could have been heard that same Sunday in the churches of both countries—"O God, Our Help in Ages Past," "For Those in Peril on the Sea"—while off in the distance Argentia (a city given, not leased, to the United States by Britain) could be seen coming to life. It was still in the ramshackle shape that reminded a British viewer of a Klondike mining town, but it would become one of the great staging areas for the reconquest of a continent.

The next day was meetings, and these didn't go the way the British had hoped. No declaration of war from America; rather, the promulgation of the Atlantic Charter, a statement of irreproachable ideals—nations' right to self-determination, freedom of the seas, and so forth—to go into effect once victory had been gained in a war that America had not yet entered and that was at the moment being lost.

Churchill left disappointed—although with the "Marines' Hymn" firmly lodged in his head—as were the British people, though he put the best face he could on the proceedings in a broadcast to them: "And so we came back across the waves, uplifted in spirit and fortified in resolve."

The prime minister was to meet one more famous American during the voyage. On his way home, he was shown his first Donald Duck cartoon. He described it as "a gay but inconsequent entertainment." In the lively and all-but-omniscient book that he tartly titled *Mr. Roosevelt's Navy: The Private War of the U.S. Atlantic Fleet, 1939–1942,* the historian Patrick Abbazia adds that Churchill "might have said the same of the meeting at Argentia."

This seems a little too dismissive. Perhaps Abbazia's close study of FDR's cautious increments of engagement gave him a twinge of the same frustration that Stimson felt. Felix Frankfurter thought the meeting far from inconsequent. "We live by symbols," he wrote the president, "and you two in the open ocean . . . in the setting of that Sunday service, gave meaning to the conflict between civilization and arrogant, brute challenge; and gave promise more powerful and binding than any formal treaty could, that civilization has brains and resources that tyranny will not be able to overcome."

And Admiral Stark came away much more satisfied than Churchill. He had discussed convoying with his British counterpart, Admiral Sir Dudley Pound. It was really going to happen.

The Moving Square Mile

Learning and relearning the lessons of convoy,
1917–41

Stark's anxiety about convoying might have come not only from FDR's reluctance, but from that of almost everyone involved in the decision. The convoy system looks so rational from our undisturbed perspective of the world wars of the last century that it seems the inevitable product of those conflicts. In fact, it very nearly never happened at all.

In 1915, a year into the First World War, a U-boat sank the British liner *Lusitania,* killing 128 American passengers and so infuriating their countrymen that Germany eventually drew in her claws and left neutral shipping unmolested. Many months and many, many lives later, with victory no closer than it had been, Germany declared an unrestricted submarine campaign. This brought America into the war in April 1917, and William S. Sims was put in charge of the naval part of it.

Sims was loyal, energetic, a born raconteur (without the repellent qualities that phrase so often signals), and, something that rarely harms a career, uncommonly handsome. He was also a controversialist, inescapably because in the early years of the last century he was a visionary in the truest sense of the word. He knew what needed to be done to change the designs of the ships that had recently evolved during the tremendous, painful transition from wood to steel and sail to steam. In the historian Elting Morison's phrase, "he remembered Pearl Harbor before it happened." That is, in a service nourished by its past and necessarily bound by tradition, Sims could see the future, and he worked all his life to bring his navy into it. By the time we entered World War I he was known throughout the service as "the man who taught the U.S. navy how to shoot."

But shrewd and effective though Sims was, he had no idea what was going on with the British merchant fleet when America entered the war, and finding out was one of the greatest shocks of his life. Sent across the Atlantic to coordinate the American naval effort with the British, he called on John Jellicoe, the first sea lord.

Jellicoe, quiet, cheerful, the least dramatizing of men, took a piece of paper from his desk and gave it to his new ally. Sims read it with growing astonishment. "It was a record of tonnage losses for the last few months," he wrote. "This showed that the total sinkings, British and neutral, had reached 536,000 tons in February, and 603,000 in March; it further disclosed that sinkings were taking place in April which indicated the destruction of nearly 900,000 tons."

Sims said, "I had never imagined anything so terrible."

"Yes." Speaking "as quietly," Sims remembered, "as though he were discussing the weather and not the future of the British Empire," Jellicoe said, "It is impossible for us to go on with the war if losses like this continue."

England would go down—perhaps as early as August, certainly by the end of October. The country had six weeks' worth of grain on hand.

"Is there no solution to the problem?" Sims asked.

"Absolutely none that we can see."

Sims tackled the crisis with all his hectoring tenacity.

What had Britain been doing to avert it? "Everything," Jellicoe said. Tens of thousands of mines laid, forty thousand antisubmarine inventions submitted to the patent office, and most important, Sims wrote, "all the destroyers, yachts, trawlers, sea-going tugs, and other light vessels which could possibly be assembled. Almost any craft which could carry a wireless [radio], a gun, and depth charge was boldly sent out to sea."

The British battle fleet had immobilized the German battle fleet. In any naval war waged from the time guns first went to sea, this would have meant victory. The submarine had changed the scheme of things. Now the big warship could be done in by a small one. But that small vessel could be harried and destroyed by other small vessels, ones designed for the purpose that were agile enough to keep on top of the submarine, drop explosives on it, fire guns at it when it had to come up.

Destroyers were best suited for this job, and Britain had hundreds of them. But while the British were scratching up tugs and trawlers to send against U-boats, they had to keep many of their destroyers tied close to the Grand Fleet, guarding its big warships from submarine attack.

Sims took this in and saw something that only a few recognized. Those dreadnoughts were being convoyed.

The merchant ships were not.

Unlike the challenges involved in getting guns big as factory chimneys seaborne, there was nothing new about convoying, which is gathering defenseless ships together in a herd to escort them with armed ones. Julius Caesar had sent his invading legionnaries to Britain under convoy. During the Napoleonic wars convoys had proved so effective that England made it illegal for merchantmen to leave port without an escort.

Why hadn't this been tried in the present war? Sims wanted to know.

It had been considered, he learned, but the Admiralty was opposed to it. The vast scale of the shipping required to keep Britain fed and armed made it all but impossible. Moreover, a convoy presented a far larger target than a single ship. Finally, convoy was merely a defensive measure; centuries of naval tradition mandated offense always.

Sims certainly believed in the offensive, too. But what sort of offense did those vessels going out on patrol hunting submarines really amount to? The ships would cover an assigned square of ocean thirty miles on a side, which meant that lookouts were hoping to discover an object a couple of hundred feet long, lying close to the surface, somewhere in nine hundred square miles of sea.

On the other hand, when the U-boat sights a convoy—and this was Sims's crucial insight—it must attack if the captain wants to do his job. In attacking, the submarine will bring down upon itself the convoy's warships. Because the convoy is far more likely than any patrol to foment a battle, it was actually an offensive weapon after all.

So Sims once again found himself embroiled in a controversy. He was not alone; some in the Admiralty had long favored convoying. Sims, though, represented a powerful new ally and, having spent his professional life persuading people against their wills, may well have had the decisive word. In any event, nobody could have given a clearer explanation of why he believed what he did.

He pointed out that since the opening of the war in 1914, troops and supplies had been shuttled across the narrow strait between Britain and France in an "immune zone, which was constantly patrolled by destroyers and other anti-submarine craft," without the loss of so much as a stirrup or a can of rations, let alone a life. "If we could arrange our ships in compact convoys and protect them with destroyers we would really create another immune zone of this kind and this would be different from the one established across the Channel only in that it would be a movable one. In this way we should establish about a square mile of the surface of the ocean in which submarines could not operate without great danger, and then we could move that square mile along until port was reached."

In mid-May a convoy assembled in the Mediterranean and sent to England arrived intact on the twentieth, a date that, Sims said, "marked one of the great turning points of the war. That critical voyage meant nothing less than that the Allies had found the way of defeating the German submarine."

They had. But like so many great messages, this one took a long time to sink in: years—decades—would be spent learning, applying, forgetting, perverting, relearning, and applying it once again.

The Allies applied it now, and it took hold. When Sims had arrived in London, the U-boats were sinking an average of more than one merchant ship every two days. A little over a year later, it was one every fourteen days. In the awful spring of 1917, nearly 900,000 tons of Allied shipping went down in April. The Germans sank 302,000 tons in January 1918, and just 112,427 the following October. Halfway through the next month, the war was over.

Sims wrote that "the American navy had been privileged to play a part" in "one of the greatest victories against the organized forces of evil in all history," but he was exhausted, and uncharacteristically melancholy. Speaking of the navy, he said, "I have never liked it. I would rather have been in a productive occupation. There has never been a time when I have not been uncomfortable in a uniform."

Later, brightening a little, Sims wrote, "However, the festive Hun is now down and out for all time, so that nothing else really matters."

★ ★ ★

Now the festivities had resumed, and so had the convoys.

As in Sims's day, the Royal Navy, which again wanted to pursue rather than to lure, and the skippers of the merchantmen, who feared it would be both too tricky and too slow to sail in close company, had been recalcitrant. But as before, the numbers won the argument, and by the time Roosevelt and Churchill met in Placentia Bay, the system had been up and running smoothly for months.

A transatlantic convoy of the time would be made up of forty-five to sixty merchantmen, steaming nine hundred yards apart, deployed in nine to twelve columns with a thousand yards separating each file. Here was Sims's moving square mile—actually a box perhaps two miles long and four wide, guarded by escort vessels. In the beginning these often included a battleship, there to counter heavy surface raiders such as the one that had captured Captain Gainard. But by 1941 these were scarce, and the battleships went about other business. Smaller ships kept watch over the convoys: destroyers, of which there were never enough, and corvettes, tough little British craft buoyant as champagne corks, wonderfully seaworthy and damnably uncomfortable for their crews. The warships were in the charge of the escort commander; a convoy commodore was responsible for keeping order among the merchant ships and sailed aboard one of them.

As the U.S. navy prepared to take its part in these caravans, support vessels and destroyers began to congregate in the wide, chill waters of Casco Bay, Maine.

On September 16, HX 150, the war's first transatlantic convoy to be partly shepherded by an American escort, set sail from Nova Scotia (*HX* meant "Halifax to Great Britain"). Its merchantmen left port in the charge of the Canadian navy, a prodigy that in two years had managed to grow itself from almost nothing into an armada of four hundred ships. The next day the Canadians were relieved by five American destroyers: *Upshur, Ericsson, Eberle, Ellis,* and *Dallas,* Captain Morton L. Deyo commanding. Captain Deyo had a great many inexperienced sailors in his division. The newly minted communications men who had to take down the messages from the convoy's commander flashed out in Morse code by signal lamp were swamped by the commodore's goodwill. No cool British taciturnity from Rear Admiral Manners: he greeted the newcomers with "I am very delighted to have all of you to guard this convoy for the next few days," and followed this with "Very many thanks for your complete list of ships. Yes, we are taking the Iceland ships. When relief escort arrives, I will pass the papers to him. Will you please direct ships for Iceland to form on the port side well clear and we will take them on.' I presume they have no one experienced in signals so would it not be better to put them in one column and follow the leader? Will appreciate your advice."

The Americans turned up no U-boats, which was probably just as well, but the convoy was not dull. Some of the freighters, worn to near ruin by two years of war steaming, flagged astern and had to be harried back into line. The SS *Nigaristan* opted out of the war by bursting into flames without German assistance, and the *Eberle* stood by her through a midnight gale and managed to bring off the entire crew.

The genial Manners did not fail to notice this. When, south of Iceland, the convoy reached the momp (a dismal word confected from "midocean meeting place," where the Americans turned over their charges to the Royal Navy), he sent a final garrulous message that nobody resented having to take down: "Comconvoy to Comescort: Please accept my best congratulations on the brand of work and efficiencies of all your ships in looking after us so very well, and my very grateful thanks for all your kindly advice and help. Wish you all success with best of luck and good hunting. If you come across Admiral Nimitz, give him my love. We were great friends some years ago out in China."

By the end of the next month, American destroyers had taken nearly seven hundred ships safely across.

The Rattlesnakes of the Atlantic

America's first lesson, 1941

★ ★ ★

A third of the way into *The Cruel Sea,* his justly celebrated novel about the Battle of the Atlantic, Nicholas Monsarrat's hero, Keith Lockhart—as his creator was, an officer aboard one of the too lively corvettes—takes stock of the new presence. "There were, as yet, no Americans officially upon the scene; their two years' profitable neutrality had not yet been ended by the galvanic shot-in-the-arm of Pearl Harbour. But here and there they were to be met: flyers relaxing at Liverpool between trans-ocean trips, and sailors in the anonymous middle reaches of the Atlantic. For they were now escorting some of the convoys, from American ports to a point where they could be taken over by the British escort: strange-looking escorts, with long names often beginning with 'Jacob' or 'Ephraim,' would appear from the mist, and spell out morse messages very slowly and gently, for the dull British to assimilate as best they could. [It evidently did not occur to these veterans that they were being treated to inexperience rather than condescension.] 'They must think we're a lot of kids,' said Leading-Signalman Wells disgustedly one day, when an exceptionally prudent American operator had tried his patience to the limit. 'It's like Lesson Number One back in barracks. And what a bloody ignorant way to spell "harbour."' . . . But the main reaction was a pleasant sense of comradeship; it was good to have some more ships lending a hand, at this time of strain, and the fact that the trans-Atlantic link was being completed in this natural way, American handing over to British, gave the latter a grateful and brotherly satisfaction. The Americans were still out of the war; but between Lend-Lease, and this unobtrusive naval effort, they were certainly doing their best round the edges."

Those edges were drawing closer. Five days before HX-150 set out, President Roosevelt had come on the radio with a fierce speech. A U-boat had attacked an American destroyer, the *Greer*. "We have sought no shooting war with Hitler. We do not seek it now. But neither do we want peace so much that we are willing to pay for it by permitting him to attack our naval and merchant ships. . . . When you see a rattlesnake poised to strike, you do not wait until he has struck before you crush him. These Nazi raiders are the rattlesnakes of the Atlantic."

What had actually happened was a wan provocation for such vehement rhetoric.

On September 4 the USS *Greer*, one of the old four-stackers that hadn't been handed over to Britain, was making for Iceland. A hundred miles or so south of Reykjavik, a British patrol bomber sloped overhead to report, "Enemy U-boat submerging about ten miles northeast."

The captain of the *Greer*, Lawrence H. Frost, who had had her for just a little over a month, swung to follow the submarine. He called his crew to battle stations and tracked the boat while broadcasting its position. He signaled the bomber, which asked if Frost intended to attack. The American said he did not, and the Briton, low on fuel, tossed four depth charges into the sea and headed landward.

Meanwhile Captain Frost kept dogging the German. After several hours the U-boat's skipper, George-Werner Fraatz, came to the surface and fired a torpedo. Once shot at, the *Greer* attacked with depth charges, but Captain Fraatz had been in this game longer than Captain Frost and had little trouble getting away. The most significant thing to emerge from this bloodless first battle between the Kriegsmarine and the U.S. navy was FDR's speech. Toward its end, the president, after making his rattlesnake metaphor, declared, "In the waters we deem necessary for our defense, American naval vessels and American planes will no longer wait until Axis submarines lurking under the waters . . . strike their deadly blow—first . . . our patrolling vessels and planes will protect all merchant ships—not only American ships but ships of any flag—engaged in commerce in our defensive waters."

Winston Churchill knew what this meant: "Hitler will have to choose between losing the Battle of the Atlantic or coming into frequent conflict with United States ships."

Admiral Raeder put it more bluntly. He told Hitler that the president of the United States had declared war on Germany: "There is no longer any difference between British and American ships!"

But still Hitler stayed his hand against the Americans.

Nevertheless, as Churchill had said, convoy meant "frequent conflict."

At this time theory, not long enough tested, held that the escorts should stand in close to the ships they were protecting—one thousand to fifteen hundred yards. This was comforting to the merchantmen, but was an inflexible and hampering arrangement against U-boat attacks. And so it proved on the night of October 15.

Convoy SC 48, some fifty merchantmen heading east from Canada, was heavily escorted—seven destroyers and seven corvettes at one point—but it was having a bad night. Doenitz's group tactics were working as well as even that exacting commander could wish. Half a dozen merchantmen had been destroyed since sundown. Each foundered beneath the light of flares, red distress rockets and livid star shells, cold, fuming, and transient. The flares were sent up in hopes of illuminating the attackers, but they only dazzled the lookouts while offering them nothing but glimpses of the tormented convoy. At midnight a Norwegian tanker exploded and, burning, lit the scene more brightly and steadily than any flare could. A Canadian corvette hurried down the convoy to find survivors, while the destroyer USS *Kearny* came forward at fifteen knots. The American ship saw the corvette in time to avoid a collision, but backing her engines left the destroyer all but motionless and silhouetted by the blazing tanker. The *U-568* fired a spread of three torpedoes. Two missed; the one that didn't instantly killed seven men in the No. 1 fireroom. In his history of this long, peculiar quasi-war, Patrick Abbazia thought it worth setting down their names—Luther Curtis, George Calvert, Russell Wade, Sidney Larraviere, Herman Gateway, Louis Dobnikar, Iral Stoltz—because "they were the first to die under their own flag in World War II."

Their ship didn't die. The *Kearny* was new—built at a cost of $5 million and launched just the year before—and she had a strong double hull. She also had a No. 2 fireroom; that is, each of her two engines was served from separate compartments that could be sealed off and made watertight. The *Kearny* was under way just minutes after being struck, and dawn found her making for Iceland at ten knots. The old *Greer* came up to give her a hand, and so they came safely home together, the first U.S. navy ship of the war to be fired on and the first to be hit.

The president's response was his strongest statement yet on the Atlantic struggle: "We have wished to avoid shooting. But the shooting has started. And history has recorded who fired the first shot. In the long run, however, all that will matter is who fires the last shot.

"America has been attacked. The USS *Kearny* is not just a navy ship. She belongs to every man, woman, and child in this nation."

Not every citizen felt the warmth of that common ownership. After the newspapers reported that George Calvert's mother had collapsed upon learning of her son's death, the Calvert family received a mocking letter telling them, "Your dear son was sent to his death by the murdering imbecile head of our Government." But despite this bit of malevolence, the public seemed largely undisturbed by what was going on in the Atlantic. Robert Sherwood thought that a fatalistic torpor had settled on his country. "The American people," he wrote later, "always have considered the men in their regular armed forces—Navy, Army and, most of all, Marine Corps—as rugged mercenaries who signed up voluntarily, as do policemen or firemen, for hazardous service. There was little or no self-identification of the normal American civilian with the professional American soldier or sailor. In the case of drafted men, however, the attitude was entirely different. They were 'our boys' who must be kept out of harm's way at all costs. Since there were no drafted men in the Navy at the time, there was no great popular indignation against Hitler for the attacks on the destroyers; but what is most important is that neither was there any serious popular indignation against Roosevelt for his responsibility in thus exposing our ships."

FDR made his tough speech on Navy Day (October 27, the birthday of that vigorous supporter of the service Theodore Roosevelt). Four days later, an American destroyer whose name may have amused Nicholas Monsarrat, the USS *Reuben James,* was helping see HX 156 into a cold Halloween morning when a lookout on Captain Erich Topp's *U-552* made out the convoy. Dawn was still distant enough for the merchantmen to seem little more than patches of deeper blackness in the general black, but as Topp followed the convoy, a stratum of dim gray silhouetted one of the destroyers that was guarding it.

Topp's job was to sink tankers, not destroyers. He knew, though, that the same faint glow that showed him the warship would soon strengthen enough to reveal his boat to its lookouts; if he took the time to go around it and get at the convoy, he would surely be seen. Well, better a destroyer than nothing. Topp fired two torpedoes. One hit the ship in nearly the same spot on her port side where the *Kearny* had been struck on her starboard. But the *Reuben James* was not a new ship; she was a four-stacker, older than many of the men who crewed her. She had no double hull, and fewer watertight compartments. The torpedo ignited her forward magazine. The *Reuben James* split in two just in front of her fourth stack, and the forward part was gone in seconds, taking with it every officer and the captain, Tex Edwards. The stern stayed afloat for perhaps five minutes, giving some of the men there the chance to escape into the winter sea.

Griffith Baily Coale, the painter, was with the convoy aboard the destroyer *Hilary P. Jones*. "A sudden loud explosion brings me upright. Know instantly that is a torpedo and not a depth charge. Spring from my bunk, jump for the bulkhead door, spin the wheel releasing the dogs, and land on the deck in a split second, with General Quarters still rasping. It is not us. A mile ahead a rising cloud of dark smoke hangs over the black loom of a ship. With a terrific roar, a column of orange flame towers high into the night air as her magazines go up, subsides, leaving a great black pall of smoke licked by moving tongues of orange." The destroyer *Niblack* came up to keep watch over the *Hilary P. Jones* while she picked up survivors. "Before we know it, we hear the cursing, praying, and hoarse shouts for help, and we are all among her men, like black shiny seals in the oily water . . . blown up and choking with oil and water, they are like small animals caught in molasses."

The crewmen of the *Jones* hung cargo nets over the side, threw lines, went into the sea themselves to help. "It is a lengthy and desperately hard job to get these men aboard. Our men are working feverishly, but less than half have come over the rail and thirty-eight minutes have passed."

Still, many would live. More would have if the soundman on the *Niblack* hadn't got a contact. The *Hilary P. Jones* confirmed it. Now came the wrenching decision that would have to be made so many times in the years ahead, that would be forced on my father's destroyer division in the very last days of the war. Was the contact firm? Was it really a U-boat? If the chances were good it was, the decision was made.

The two destroyers put on speed and dropped depth charges. It was day now, bright enough for Coale to see that the heart of each white explosion was "tinged with blood color in the dawning."

The destroyers killed some of their own with those depth charges; they never got Topp; but they did, in the end, rescue forty-five men from the *Reuben James,* something of a triumph considering the circumstances. One hundred and fifteen died with the first American fighting ship sunk in the war.

The folksinger Woody Guthrie read of the sinking in the New York City newspapers and wrote a song about it. He began with the honorable intention of mentioning every dead sailor by name—

> *There's Harold Hammer Beasley, a first rate man at sea*
> *From Hinton, West Virginia, he had his first degree.*
> *There's Jim Franklin Benson, a good machinist's mate*
> *Come up from North Carolina, to sail the Reuben James.*

—but was eventually persuaded that this was too unwieldy. The chorus, as it finally worked itself out, distills all the names into a question we remember today:

> *Tell me what were their names, tell me what were their names,*
> *Did you have a friend on the good Reuben James?*

Most Americans did not. "Among the general public," Sherwood wrote, "there seemed to be more interest in the Army–Notre Dame football game."

Roosevelt did nothing. There was nothing he could do. Earlier in the month he had harried through Congress an amendment to the Neutrality Law that allowed the arming of merchant ships and permitted them to sail in war zones. He had not done it easily, and now, Sherwood said, "He had no more tricks left. The hat from which he had pulled so many rabbits was empty."

The status quo may have been exasperating for the president; it was worse for the men out in the Atlantic. They were there on duty they were forbidden to even talk about during their infrequent shore leave, and the duty was severe. No North Atlantic winter is mild, and this one was proving harder than most. The ceaseless wind occasionally sent up waves powerful enough to punch in a gun shield, or blast the glass in the wheelhouse windows into a helmsman's face.

In a way, the people protecting the convoys lived the life of the very, very old. The simplest tasks were daunting in prospect, dangerous in performance. Everything was exhausting: going from the wardroom to the bridge was to navigate a hellish fun house where the floor might drop forty feet, and steel doorframes swivel sixty degrees in a deft, prankish attempt to break your spine. The seasick made themselves choke down food only because it was so much more painful to vomit on an empty stomach.

Every normal fixture became a peril. On the destroyer *Lea*, which had just lost two men washed overboard in a single day, the violent seas so agitated the deck-mounted torpedo tubes that one launched itself. The torpedo did not explode, but before it rolled overboard it clattered around the deck for five minutes and took off Electrician's Mate Alfred Buck's foot. When the *Lea*'s pharmacist's mate knelt down to help Buck, the same seas that had knocked loose the torpedo broke one of his arms and one of his legs.

A sailor weary beyond enduring of the gyrating fireroom of the four-stacker *Decatur* cut his wrists with a razor blade. But not skillfully enough: his pragmatic shipmates bound the wounds and sent him back to his post.

Others sought less drastic ways to get out of it. There were desertions—so many that some ships had to put to sea badly shorthanded. In November, President Roosevelt, with the greatest reluctance, allowed draftees to be sent into the navy.

For the most part, though, the seamen stuck it out, gale after gale. In perpendicular seas, the escort captains endlessly badgered the merchant skippers to bring their ships nearer together, and the merchantmen endlessly protested that they couldn't steer well enough in fifty-foot waves to keep close company. Do it anyway, the escorts said, and they tried, a freighter sometimes pitching so heavily forward that its propeller would rise clear of the water, a hazy, clamorous circle churning thin air while the ship shuddered though a series of train-wreck jolts. Seawater got into the fuel lines; pieces of ship continually disappeared into the wailing murk; on one destroyer the watch couldn't be relieved for twelve hours because nobody would have been able to reach them alive, which condemned the lookouts to sixteen straight hours of excruciating vigilance.

Nobody sank a U-boat. Nobody *saw* a U-boat. Nevertheless, the American ships got fourteen convoys through safely during the five weeks between the sinking of the *Reuben James* on October 31 and the first Sunday in December 1941, which was the seventh.

A Present in the Führer's Lap
Hitler declares war, 1941

★ ★ ★

The news from Pearl Harbor was big, and the men keeping watch over the convoys understood that. However, it struck them quite differently from how it did their civilian counterparts back in the States. Many shared the bleak gleam of pleasure a sailor in HX 156 expressed: "We'll now give three silent cheers for the bastards who jumped ship to join the Pacific Fleet."

Sailors who had made sure that even during empty, exhausted gray days at anchor in Hvalfjordhur between patrols they could get their guns manned and firing within five minutes wondered what the hell the battleship sailors lazing on their sunny atoll had been thinking. A lot of Atlantic seamen believed they would finally have the chance to get warm, and they were right. Ships would begin steaming west to take the ghostly place of vessels the Japanese navy had stricken from our roster. Seaman Jernigan would happily leave Iceland and its unwelcoming inhabitants and, eventually, his battleship for destroyer duty on the other side of the world. Before too long the Canadian navy would be doing 49 percent of the Atlantic convoying, and the British 50 percent.

That American 1 percent who kept working the frigid convoy lanes had learned a great deal. Not quickly enough—nobody learns quickly enough in war—and not well enough yet. But they had survived a trying, lonely ordeal, and what they knew would be both strength and reassurance to the hundreds of thousands of Americans who were about to come join them.

WORD OF PEARL HARBOR reached the cruiser *Vincennes* during an Atlantic storm that had, earlier in the day, torn the ship's Curtiss float plane from its moorings and flung it over the side. "It will be good," said one of the officers, "to be fighting a declared war for a change."

But it wasn't a declared war, not for the Atlantic forces, not yet.

Germany had damaged one new American destroyer and sunk one old one and killed some 130 sailors. Japan had destroyed our main battle line in the Pacific and killed 2,500 men. The United States declared war the next day on the Empire of Japan, but not on Germany. Despite Admiral Stark's careful formulation of the Germany First plan and our military's acceptance of its principles, FDR didn't see how he could go before Congress and ask for two declarations of war.

Years afterward, Winston Churchill wrote of his feelings when he heard about the Pearl Harbor attack. "No American will think it wrong of me if I proclaim that to have the United States at our side was the greatest joy. I could not foretell the course of events. I do not pretend to have measured accurately the martial might of Japan, but now at this very moment I knew the United States was in the war, up to the neck and in to the death. So we had won after all! Yes, after Dunkirk; after the fall of France . . . after the deadly struggle of the U-boat war . . . after seventeen months of lonely fighting and nineteen months of my responsibility in dire stress, we had won the war."

Churchill had been having dinner with several guests at Chequers, the prime minister's country retreat. He was gloomy and distracted that evening, and paid little attention when his valet came in with a $15 portable radio (a gift from Harry Hopkins) so the company could hear the nine-o'clock news. It took a moment for the import to register on Churchill, then he jumped up, slammed shut the lid of the radio, and started from the room saying, "We shall declare war on Japan." John Winant, the American ambassador, hurried after him, saying, "Good God, you can't declare war on a radio announcement." Winant persuaded the prime minister instead to call America, and soon Churchill was speaking with Roosevelt, who told him, "It's quite true. They have attacked us at Pearl Harbor. We are all in the same boat now."

Not quite the same boat, though. Boiling with plans for the new alliance, Churchill said he was going to leave for Washington at once. His foreign secretary, Anthony Eden, cautioned against it, saying "he was not sure that the Americans would want him so soon."

Eden saw the possible problems that might be raised by the arrival of this ebullient man who had worked so hard to bring America into a European war when it was Asia that had struck the grievous blow. The foreign secretary had read the situation correctly. In the whirling days that followed the seventh, Roosevelt found the time to write two letters asking Churchill not to come—and the tact to send neither of them.

In a radio address two days after the air raid, FDR linked the dictatorships of Germany and Japan—"We must realize, for example, that the Japanese successes against the United States in the Pacific are helpful to German operatives in Libya"—but one of them had attacked America, and one of them hadn't. On the evening of the seventh, Admiral Stark began to get the full picture of the calamity over the phone from Rear Admiral Claude C. Bloch, commandant of the naval district in Hawaii: the battleships *Nevada, California,* and *West Virginia* were on fire;

the *Oklahoma* and the *Arizona* were gone. "Did our patrol planes get them before they hit us?" Stark asked. "No," said Bloch. "The first word that we had was that a destroyer was torpedoed by a sub, and ten minutes later the Japs came in a flock and that is what did the damage." Then Stark asked a revealing question: was the submarine German?

It most certainly wasn't. The Japanese attack came as much of a surprise to Hitler as it had to Roosevelt and Churchill. Like Roosevelt and Churchill, Hitler had believed war between America and Japan was imminent, but had no sense of where or when it would begin. He had also assumed since as early as the 1920s that Germany would again fight the United States. On the eve of his invasion of Russia he met with the Japanese foreign minister, Yosuke Matsuoka, to urge on him the advantages of attacking Singapore at once. It would devastate the British and keep America out of the war until Germany was finished with Russia. Hitler was at his most stridently persuasive, but Matsuoka was cool to the idea.* Hitler left the talk not only dissatisfied but disgusted; Matsuoka, he said, combined "the hypocrisy of an American Bible missionary with the cunning of a Japanese Asiatic."

So Singapore got a few more months of peace while the German armies advanced into Russia, quickly at first, then more slowly, and then, on December 2, with the towers of Moscow in sight and the temperature standing at thirty-two degrees below zero, not at all. Three days later a hundred Soviet divisions counterattacked, and two days after *that* the reports of Pearl Harbor reached Hitler.

He was delighted. This, he said, "drops like a present into our

---

*Tokyo thought exactly the opposite of what Hitler did: that an attack on Singapore would bring America into the war, on the side of Britain, immediately.

lap." He told his generals, "We can't lose the war at all. We now have an ally which has never been conquered in three thousand years."

For ally she would be. Although the Tri-Partite Act mandated that Germany support Japan only if the nation was attacked, Hitler wanted this war. "I don't see much future for the Americans," he said shortly afterward. "It's a decayed country. And they have their racial problems, and the problem of social inequalities. . . . My feelings against Americanism are feelings of hatred and deep repugnance. . . . Everything about the behavior of American society reveals that it's half Judaized, and the other half Negrified. How can one expect a state like that to hold together—a country where everything is built on the dollar."

The muzzle Hitler had placed on his submarines in the Atlantic had been meant to keep America out of the war until Russia was defeated. Now there was no further need for such restraint. "Through the outbreak of war between Japan and the USA," said his lieutenant Joseph Goebbels, "a complete shift in the general world picture has taken place. The United States will scarcely now be in a position to transport worthwhile matériel to England, let alone the Soviet Union."

On December 9 Hitler ordered his U-boats to attack all American shipping, but he did not immediately declare war. He wanted time to prepare a speech that would put the business in the best possible light for the German people.

On the afternoon of Thursday, December 11, Hitler went before the Reichstag and spoke for an hour and a half, declaring the assault against Russia a triumph, then moving on to a long denunciation of Roosevelt, who was set on destroying the Third Reich, and sustained in his determination by the "entire satanic insidiousness" of the Jews. Now was the time to act. Any hesitation would only allow the American enemy to grow in strength and malice. Hours before, he had given the American chargé d'affaires a formal declaration of war.

Churchill started out for America at once. So did the German navy. Not, however, nearly as much of the German navy as Admiral Doenitz would have liked.

Five Boats against America

The East Coast submarine offensive, 1942

Doenitz had been eager to attack the eastern United States for months. He knew and respected the increasing strength of the Atlantic convoys that were putting to use all the hard-won lessons of the naval war. He also knew that there had been no lessons, hard-won or otherwise, along some of the world's richest sea-lanes.

The national arsenal and factory that had prospered so spectacularly supplying his enemies needed every kind of raw matériel, and a great deal of it came by sea—bauxite, from which airplane aluminum was conjured, from Brazil; sugar and coffee and rubber. Even products mined or grown on American soil moved by water: oil from the Gulf ports, lumber and coal and iron ore—the rail and highway systems could carry only a fraction of it. By 1941, 95 percent of the oil sent to the East Coast from the fields of Louisiana and Texas got there aboard tankers plying routes where shipping had never been disturbed and where, Doenitz strongly suspected, nobody had the least idea how to protect it.

As far back as September he had asked Hitler that, should the Führer ever decide to lift his prohibition against attacking American ships, "I should like to be given timely warning, in order to have my forces in position off the American coast before war was actually declared."

Because the Japanese and not Hitler set the agenda for America's entry into the war, Doenitz didn't get his timely warning. On December 7, 1941, he wrote, "There was not a single German U-boat in American waters."

Taking stock of what he had at his disposal, he again had occasion to resent the hegemony of the battleship. "We had, all told, ninety-one operational U-boats. Of these, twenty-three . . . were in the Mediterranean and three more were under orders from Naval High Command to proceed there; six were stationed west of Gibraltar, and four were deployed along the Norwegian coast. Of the remaining fifty-five available, 60 percent were in dockyard hands. . . .

"There were only twenty-two boats at sea and about half of these were en route to or from their operational base areas. Thus . . . after two and a half years of war there were never more than ten or twelve boats actively and simultaneously engaged in our most important task, the war on shipping."

Planning his foray to a distant coast, he wanted to use Type IX boats, considerably larger than the dependable VIIs, and thus with more fuel to burn in American waters; they had a cruising range of eighty-seven hundred miles. On December 9 he asked for twelve of them. High Command told him he could have six, and one of these wouldn't be ready to sail for weeks.

So, five boats against America. He weighed how to use them to greatest effect. Not in one of his wolf packs this time, yet working in close enough concert as to seem a more formidable force than they in fact were. He would deploy them along the coast between the St. Lawrence and Cape Hatteras, and then "the five boats would receive from me by radio the time and date at which they could simultaneously go into action." He named his operation *Paukenschlag*, a word meaning "drumbeat" or "drumroll," but which has harsher connotations to it, something like "thunderbolt."

As the last days of 1941 ran out, the five boats crossed the Bay of Biscay.

One of the first to sail was *U-123—Ein Zwei Drei* to her crew— under Reinhard Hardegan. He was vain and enough of a braggart to annoy his fellow U-boat skippers, but superbly competent. He was tough, too. He'd been a naval aviator before he joined the boats and had in 1936 come out of a crash with a shortened right leg and intermittent stomach bleeding. The injuries were severe enough to get him declared "unfit for further U-boat service." Yet he had always contrived to keep a jump ahead of his medical records, and here he was, in command of *U-123*, heading toward the new American war.

He didn't know that, though. His orders were sealed and not to be opened until the boat reached twenty degrees west longitude. In the meantime, Christmas came. Hardegan had smuggled a fir tree aboard, and it went up in the control room; no candles, but the boat's electricians had improvised passable substitutes, and although Hardegan ran a strictly dry ship, this one time his men had wine punch.

Two days later *123* crossed twenty degrees west, which was satisfying for everyone aboard for more than one reason. The sailors would find out what their mission was, and they were now on a *Frontboot*—that is, a warship officially operating in enemy waters—and thus entitled to combat pay. Hardegan broke the seals on his orders and learned that he was part of Operation Paukenschlag, then was briefly mystified to find a guidebook to the 1939 New York World's Fair. War had come so quickly that this was the best High Command could provide in the way of New York City Harbor charts.

It wasn't bad. It showed the busy shoreline in considerable detail. The orders mandated that when Hardegan got the word, he would begin operations off New York, then range four hundred miles south to Cape Hatteras. He was to go only after big targets, ten thousand tons or more.

On January 9 the signal came through: commence attacking on the thirteenth. On the eleventh, though, late in the afternoon, *U-123*'s lookouts spotted a steamer. Hardegan had come up on the bridge at the first sighting and now called for the *Groener*, a book by a maritime expert of that name containing the profiles of every known merchant vessel. This one, with its near-vertical stack higher than its masts, belonged to the Alfred Holt Shipping Company, the Blue Funnel line. British.

Hardegan swung his boat around and ran beside the ship, slowly closing with her. He asked for the UZO, and up to the bridge came the *Uboot-Zieloptik*, huge-eyed, fourteen-pound Zeiss binoculars that, once locked to the bridge's UZO post not only showed the target but allowed the user to draw a bead on it, controlling the torpedo settings as the glasses moved. The captain edged his boat forward until the range had narrowed sufficiently, turned over the UZO to Rudolf Hoffmann, his first watch officer (the IWO; on an American warship, the executive officer), and ordered one of the four forward torpedo tubes flooded.

"Folgen?" called Hoffmann, asking if all the calculations necessary for one moving object to put a missile into another hundreds of yards away—bearing, range, angle—were being properly transmitted from the UZO to the calculator in the conning tower, thence to the forward torpedo room. Hoffmann decided on a depth setting and pressed the launch button. *"Los!"* he yelled, and the torpedo was on its way.

It had nearly a mile to run—a greater range than Hardegan liked—and he and Hoffmann began counting the seconds. They had reached ninety-seven when yellow flame bloomed just aft of the target's funnel.

The U-boat's radioman reported that the freighter immediately began signaling "S-S-S"—"I am struck by a torpedo"—and Hardegan circled until he was standing off the ship's port bow, then fired a second torpedo from a stern tube. This one took only thirty-one seconds to reach its goal. Five minutes later the ship was gone.

Hardegan turned and headed for New York; he'd have to push to get there on time.

He left behind him, three hundred miles off Cape Cod, fragments of the thirty-eight-year-old, twin screw steamer *Cyclops,* out of Liverpool. She had been heading from Panama to Halifax with 101 people aboard. At 9,076 tons she was smaller than Dönitz's preferred targets, but not by much. In the last moments of her life, *Cyclops*'s radioman had raised Thomaston, Maine, which alerted Halifax, which sent two minesweepers to help.

They couldn't get there quickly enough to spare the survivors a night in the winter Atlantic. *U-123*'s attack had killed only two men outright—the ship's doctor and a gunner—but by the time the minesweeper *Red Deer* arrived, only 83 were left to save.

Early on the morning of the fourteenth the *123*'s lookouts saw the white pulse of the Montauk Point light on the tip of the south shore of Long Island. Mariners had known for three centuries that this coast was perilous—strong, tricky currents, abrupt shallows—and Hardegan made his way along it with care, although close enough in that at least one of his officers worried someone ashore would hear the engines and catch the blunt, hollow smell of diesel exhaust and know what it meant. For his part, the captain watched with growing wonder. Running on the surface, he saw automobile headlights pass and bright geometries of streetlights behind them. Closer to him, marker buoys dipped and shone. Didn't the creators of this smug efflorescence know they were at war?

Dawn put an end to the show, and Hardegan took *U-123* down to the seabed for the day to rest on the rich mulch of crockery and tires and gun carriages and pipestems and rum bottles and bones that all the generations of commerce had sown there.

At dusk the boat rose and continued west, into the bottom of New York Harbor. The lookouts stopped their ceaseless scanning to gape. A couple of months later German movie houses would be showing newsreels of dancing couples and elevated trains purportedly taken from the deck of *123*. They were frauds, but the truth was striking enough: a great pleated, silver sail of light, shining and shifting like the aurora borealis, stoked by Rockefeller Center and the Empire State Building and a million cars, lifted halfway up the sky. In the distance, the lamps of the Rockaways added a horizontal counterpoint. Closer by, off the starboard bow, a low stretch of beach carried a structure Hardegan recognized at once—a large Ferris wheel—and, just to its left, one he would have understood only had he studied the World's Fair guidebook with unusual care: the tall, slender mushroom with umbrella-like ribs of ironwork was the Parachute Jump, a popular attraction moved from Flushing Meadows when the fair closed. January wasn't a big month for Coney Island, but the place was never wholly dark. Hardegan would have seen the bulge of neon-charged haze that, year-round, rode Nathan's long-famous hot dog stand, which was running full tilt even at this dark, late, cold hour.

Hardegan let his men look at the heedless shore for a long time. "I cannot describe the feeling with words," he wrote, "but it was unbelievably beautiful and great. I would have given away a kingdom for this moment if I had had one. We were the first to be here, and for the first time in this war a German soldier looked out on the coast of the USA."

Hardegan headed back east and later that night found the British tanker *Coimbra*, fat with eighty thousand barrels of oil. He fired two torpedoes and split it in three pieces. The captain and thirty-five of the crew burned to death. Long Island citizens called police stations in Quogue and Hampton Bays to report the fire they could see from their homes.

TEN DAYS LATER, HARDEGAN headed home; his colleagues soon followed. They'd used up all their torpedoes and left twenty-five ships dead along the Eastern seabeds. The five boats had been responsible for 70 percent of the Allied shipping sunk that month. Doenitz followed the venerable military axiom of reinforcing success, dispatching more boats as they became available. "The hub of big shipbuilding and the production of armaments lies in the United States," he wrote. "If, therefore, I get there boldly, and particularly the oil supplies, I am getting to the root of the evil." Every day England consumed four tankers' worth of oil and gasoline. The admiral may not have known the exact figure, but he knew what would happen if those tankers didn't get there.

Dozens of merchant ships were lost along American shores, then hundreds, each one representing a blow to the Allied effort equivalent to a successful bombing raid on a manufacturing city.

That dignified, closed phrase *were lost* masks a thousand terrible, small epics of suffering and courage. In March, for instance, *U-71* hit the *Dixie Arrow* off Cape Hatteras. The tanker was carrying ninety-six thousand barrels of crude oil and thirty-three men. She was a happy ship: good captain, good food. Crude oil doesn't burn easily, but a torpedo is more than enough to ignite it, and the ship became a sort of tray for a great liquid-fed torch. Able Seamen Oscar Chappell had the helm. Standing in the furnace heat, he looked about the ship and saw that the crew were huddling at the bow. He told the five other sailors on the bridge to join them, then took the wheel again and turned the *Dixie Arrow* into the wind. This drove the flames away from the bow and toward Seaman Chappell. He had just enough time to lock the wheel before he died beside it. Because of him, twenty-two men of the *Dixie Arrow* survived.

★ ★ ★

ADMIRAL DOENITZ KNEW AS well as anyone alive that U-boat men were determined. But even he was occasionally startled by just *how* determined. While Hardegan was homeward-bound and the Eastern coastal waters still so thick with oil that gloomy fires would spontaneously combust on the breast of confined and sluggish waves, word spread about "the American shooting gallery." The Type VIIs wanted in on this. Doenitz had initially believed that the VIIs didn't have quite enough range to operate off the American coast. But skippers and crews worked out ways. They crossed the Atlantic at low speeds to conserve fuel, and to Doenitz's surprise "they filled some of the drinking- and washing-water tanks with fuel. Of their own free will they sacrificed many of the amenities of their living quarters in order to make room for the larger quantities of stores, spare parts and other expendable articles which an increase in the radius of action demanded."

None was more determined than Captain Peter Cremer. Sailing west in his VII, the *U-333*, he tangled with a tanker, the *British Prestige*, which rammed him and rode over his boat. Seawater jetted into the control room from the periscope well and the ventilation ducts. The cascade suggested the pressure hull had been ruptured, and Cremer surfaced to see what had happened. The conning-tower hatch wouldn't open, so the captain went out the galley hatch and quickly got the picture: "The tanker had first hit us at the bow, twisted our nose to port and then, with the turning of her screws acting like a chopper, shaved off the bridge. . . . The watertight stem was torn open . . . the periscope snapped, the D/F [direction finder] set and torpedo aiming sight destroyed. The bow caps of tubes two and four were jammed and could not be opened."

Time for any prudent skipper to go home: "No one would have reproached me if I had broken off the patrol and turned back." Instead, Cremer entered in *333*'s log, "Intention—ahead into the straits of Florida. Surfaced by day, in no circumstances return home without a steamer."

On May 4 Cremer saw the Bethel Shoal buoy, some twenty miles northeast of Vero Beach, and headed south along the coast. Like Hardegan before him, he was amazed. "We had left a blacked-out Europe behind us. Whether in Stettin, Berlin, Paris, Lorient or La Rochelle—everywhere had been pitch-dark." Here, though, guided by the Jupiter Inlet lighthouse, he stood in close enough to "read the flickering neon signs." Not only that: "from Miami and its luxurious suburbs a mile-wide band of light was being thrown upward to glow like an aureole against the under-sides of the cloud layer, visible from far below the horizon. All this after nearly five months of war!"

He let his men come up on the bridge and have a look. They were enchanted. They forgot their half-destroyed boat with its two dead torpedo tubes. "Against the footlight glare of a carefree new world were passing the silhouettes of ships recognizable in every detail and shape as the outlines in a sales catalog. Here they were formally presented to us on a plate: please help yourselves!"

That first night under the footlights, the *U-333* hit the tanker *Java Arrow*, blew the stern off a Dutch freighter named the *Amazone*, and attacked another tanker, the *Halsey*, which exploded. The lush tropic moon that had been competing with the brilliant shore to light the battlefield began to set. Nobody came to pester *U-333*. Cremer figured his ruin of a ship might have a few more good days of hunting here, and he was right.

"The survivors of sunken steamers and tankers," Cremer wrote of those days, "were often hailed by the men on the conning tower of U-boats and asked for the names of their ship and the cargo. Sometimes they even told."

And why not? Their ship was gone, some, maybe many, of their shipmates dead, their captain likely not there. They weren't military men, most of them, just sailors, who had experienced the worst misfortune that can befall a sailor. Best to placate the owners of the fearsome machine that had brought this about.

So the U-boats would cruise through the wreckage, the men on deck cordial and interested, sometimes indicating to the occupants of the lifeboats the best course toward land, sometimes giving them water or cigarettes or bandages. The German sailors enjoyed a joke during that prosperous season. As they headed away from a sinking ship, from the growing dawn, they liked to call out, "Send the bill to Roosevelt!"

The Most Even-Tempered
Man in the Navy

Admiral King in command, 1942

The president may not have received a bill for the *Cyclops* or the
Java Arrow, but he did feel hounded. When, in March, Churchill
sent Harry Hopkins a stern cable saying, "I am most deeply concerned at the immense sinking of tankers west of the 40th merid-
ian and in the Caribbean Sea. . . . The situation is so serious that
drastic action of some kind is necessary," Roosevelt responded
with a most uncharacteristic testy hauteur: "Your interest in
steps to be taken to combat the Atlantic submarine menace as
indicated by your recent message to Mr. Hopkins on this subject impels me to request your particular consideration of heavy
attacks on submarine bases and building and repair yards, thus
checking submarine activities at their source and where the submarines congregate." In other words, if you don't want tankers
sunk off our shores, do something about it yourself. Churchill
did, sending air raid after futile air raid against the impregnable
Biscay submarine bunkers.

The prime minister knew very well, though, that what the
official historian of the Royal Navy was to call the "holocaust"

taking place off our shores was due to American and not British negligence. This negligence had many causes and there were many excuses for it. The country had, after all, just been flung into a world-girdling sea war with a substantial part of its naval strength vanished. But after months, indeed years, of seeing what was coming, here is what the navy had on hand to protect the "Eastern Sea Frontier" (the U.S. coastline to two hundred miles out) from the St. Lawrence River to North Carolina when Hardegan headed our way: one Coast Guard cutter; four yard patrol boats (these YPs could be pretty much anything assigned the designation—fishing boats, for instance); four subchasers (one hundred feet long, made of wood, crew of thirty); three Eagle boats from World War I (originally produced by Ford with much fanfare, they turned out to be a sort of anti–Model T—costly, inefficient, universally detested); and five airplanes fit for combat duty.

The man in overall charge of this gimcrack armada was Admiral Ernest J. King. Plucked from the brink of retirement after the Pearl Harbor debacle, he is remembered for his summation of this turn in his career: "When they get in trouble, they send for the sons of bitches." He later denied saying this, but added that he regretted he hadn't. What he did say was "Any good naval officer is a son of a bitch" (although nobody ever called the quite adequate Lord Nelson one), and he was certainly the most intimidating person in the American high command. He was also possibly the smartest.

"Not since the Army of Northern Virginia had an American military force depended so much upon a single commander as the United States Navy, in the year 1942, did on Ernest Joseph King," wrote Elting Morison, who was keeping the Eastern Sea Frontier War Diary during the crisis. "If not the only officer who could have retrieved the physical and spiritual disaster that befell his service on December 7, 1941, he was the officer who did.

. . . Behind the bleak and fixed composure some intense spirit burned away, a spirit fed by incalculable devotions to individual concepts of self and the service. Above and beyond all these ran resolution—grim, harsh, ruthless and whatever else it can be made to seem—but above all resolution."

Roosevelt saw this in King, and more besides. "He's a grand navy man," FDR told his son Elliott. "'Wars can only be won by sea power; therefore, the navy's plans must be the best; furthermore, only the Pacific is a naval theater; therefore, only the Pacific is important.'" The president ended his paraphrase with a laugh and said, "That's not exactly his reasoning, but it's close enough."

It was close enough. King saw the shape of the whole war clearly while the smoke was still hanging over Pearl, and it pretty much all went his way. But his heart was in the Pacific operations to come, and perhaps the most controversial part of his career began when Doenitz's boats arrived on the East Coast.

Ernest King was born in Lorain, Ohio, in 1878. His father was a foreman in the railroad repair shops there, and from his earliest days King loved the complexity and precision of machinery. He understood it, too; as soon as he could buy a car, he took apart its engine and, once satisfied to have the theories of internal combustion made concrete, put it back together again.

He graduated from Annapolis in 1901 and just eight years later made a reputation for himself in the service by winning from the Naval Institute's *Proceedings* magazine the considerable prize of $500 for an essay entitled "Some Ideas About Organization Aboard Ship." In 1920 he tossed off—not quite the right phrase, but he did work awfully quickly—an article for *Proceedings* about how naval officers should be educated. It was, to say the least, influential. In 1980 his biographer Thomas Buell could write, "The report's basic ideas have since been refined, but naval training and career management today still conform to the concepts and principles that King set down in one day over half a century ago."

King did everything in his changing service: commanded a destroyer division before the First World War, won the Navy Cross for his work on the staff of the commander of the Atlantic Fleet during it, got interested in submarines and took charge of their New London base, taught himself to fly and commanded the carriers *Lexington* and *Saratoga* in the 1939 fleet exercises. (He was forced to use them in support of the battleships rather than independently, as he wished. Pearl Harbor granted that wish.)

He was good, and he knew it; so good that he saw no reason to practice false bonhomie, or, many of his contemporaries thought, even the most common civility. He drank heavily and expected the same of those around him—he was proud of a cocktail he'd invented and named the King's Peg: champagne and brandy sharing a tall glass with a derisory shard of ice—womanized energetically enough to earn a lifelong reputation for it, and drew on apparently inexhaustible reserves of anger. One of his six spectacularly good-looking daughters said, "He is the most even-tempered man in the navy. He is always in a rage."

He made no effort to conceal his disposition and seems once in a while to have displayed an indulgent fondness toward it, as when he sent one of the women who put oil on his emotional waters a photograph of him leaning back in a chair laughing. "Abby," he wrote, "you see it can be done." It wasn't done often enough, though, for FDR to feel able to make him chief of naval operations in 1939. King wanted the job, thought he deserved it, but was far too proud to try to curry favor with the president. With word due he went ashore looking for news—he was at anchor in Guantánamo Bay at the time—and ran into Harold Stark in a crowd of other admirals. One of them told him that Stark had just been made CNO. Showing no temper at all this time, King walked over to his rival and warmly congratulated him. King, sixty and four years away from mandatory retirement, got a place on the Governing Board.

This august body was made up of senior officers approaching retirement who had risen high but would rise no higher and thus were likely beyond the goads and snares of self-interest. They offered advice on any number of maritime subjects and had no power to see that the advice was taken. It was an honorable way to ease out of a career.

A friend meeting King at a Sunday-afternoon cocktail party was startled to find the admiral in tears. Yet a year later, when a junior officer who barely knew King ran into him in the Navy Department, the admiral told him, "They're not done with me yet. I'll have another chance."

That he got it was largely due to the generous-spirited Stark, one of King's few contemporaries who, beyond acknowledging his competence, actually liked the man. Stark urged FDR to make King commander in chief, U.S. Fleet. That didn't happen, but in the summer of 1940, with the U.S. navy taking responsibility for the defense of the western hemisphere, Ernest King was offered command of the Atlantic Squadron. Once having attained the naval pinnacle of flag rank, admirals fly their personal pennant, and King, as a former vice admiral, had three stars on his. This was a two-star job, a rear admiral's, but King said that didn't matter at all and in mid-December broke his two-star flag in the old battleship *Texas*. He got the vagrant star back soon, and another one besides, making him a full admiral. In February 1941, with its work getting stiffer all the time, the Atlantic Squadron became the Atlantic Fleet, and King took command of it.

A couple of months later the new CINCLANT—Commander in Chief, Atlantic Fleet—issued a statement ("Atlantic Fleet Confidential Memorandum") that both defined the working conditions that would prevail for years to come, and the tenor of the man who wrote it. King took his first point for granted:

"1. If and when the existing emergency becomes intensified—develops into a state of war—all of us will accept cheerfully and willingly the difficulties and discomforts as well as the hazards and the dangers with which we shall then be confronted."

Right now, though, the admiral went on, those dangers were only potential, but the "difficulties and discomforts" were all on hand, and they had to be treated with the "same spirit of cheerfulness and willingness." This meant not being disheartened by a "lack of trained seagoing *personnel,* inadequacies of *matériel,* the necessity to continue *operations* in that area which is strategically central, and the *waiting* for developments over which we have no control."

Personnel: train all we have to fill the needs of our present ships, then give them over to new ships. Matériel: distinguish between what is necessary and what is desirable, and forget about the latter. When in the yard (and here King displays his exasperating predilection for peppering the most straightforward sentences with quotation marks, whose overall effect is to make him sound not nearly as smart as he is), "we must take heed of the fact that overhaul periods . . . longer than those required for urgent items of work not only keep our own ships 'out of service' but affect the availability of labor and matériel for new ships." Operations: accept "the circumstances premised on strategical considerations imposed by the current international situation" and respond to them with "the forces available, even though they are less in number and in power than appear adequate." Waiting: use the time to make yourself better at what you do.

"4. I expect the officers of the Atlantic Fleet to be the leaders in what may be called the 'pioneer spirit'—to lead in the determination that the difficulties and discomforts . . . shall be dealt with as 'enemies' to be overcome by our own efforts. . . . There is *work* in plenty for all hands."

Fifth and last was the dictum that encapsulated it all: the too long patrols, the crews of the rusting four-stackers trying to wring some fun out of Iceland's pallid diversions, the desperate amateurism that was to defend our Eastern seaboard. The italics are most definitely King's:

"We must do all that we can with what we have."

King personally did the most with what he had, working eighteen-hour days. November 23, 1941, found him worn-out and discouraged. It was his sixty-third birthday; just a year left until retirement. One of his friends said, "It was the only time I ever saw him was completely down and out. King wrote a number of letters to us saying that there was nothing more ahead of him."

One of the many things King disliked were the biweekly trips he had to make from the naval base at Newport where he was stationed to Washington "to straighten out those dumb bastards once again." But the meeting with Frank Knox on December 16 was something else. The secretary of the navy wanted King to become CINCUS—Commander in Chief, U.S. Fleet. This shook King, but not so much that he didn't have some conditions. Before accepting the job he asked the president for three things. He did not want to give press conferences. This was fine by FDR. King wanted command over all the bureaus in the Navy Department. That, said the president, would take a change in federal law, but he promised to replace any bureau chief King didn't like. The final request was editorial: in the wake of Pearl Harbor any command that was pronounced "sink us" seemed unfortunate.

Fine. CINCUS would change to the no lovelier but less subversive COMINCH. Two days later Roosevelt signed Executive Order 8984, giving King "supreme command of the operating forces of the several fleets of the United States Navy and the operating forces of the Naval Coastal Frontier Command."

So Ernest King undertook, with unprecedented authority, to run what would become a navy of unprecedented strength.*

At the moment, though, King's navy was not ready for the job that Doenitz gave it. In the first four months of 1942 the U-boats sank 515,000 tons—eighty-seven ships—along the East Coast. This ongoing calamity was a matter of concern to Admiral Royal R. Ingersoll, who had replaced King as commander in chief, Atlantic Fleet, and something more than that to Vice Admiral Adolphus Andrews, who commanded the Eastern Sea Frontier from his headquarters at 90 Church Street in Manhattan. That is, Ingersoll was responsible for what happened in most of the ocean, but it was Andrews who had to cope with the first American action of the new Atlantic war.

Adolphus "Dolly" (there it is again, the four-year-old's nickname cherished by Annapolis men) Andrews was a landlocked Texas boy a year younger than King who first saw a ship when he arrived at the Naval Academy, where he graduated at the head of his class. He had a fine career, serving as an aide to Theodore Roosevelt and Calvin Coolidge, seeing duty on four battleships.

---

*The mandatory retirement continued to rankle. The next October, with the great victory of Midway behind him, he was still nervous enough to write the president a stiff little letter saying, "It appears proper that I should bring to your notice the fact that the record shows I shall attain the age of 64 years on November 23rd next—one month from today.

"I am, as always, at your service."

Back came the letter with this scrawled on the bottom:

E.J.K.—
So what, old top?
I may send you a Birthday present!
                    FDR

Many of his contemporaries thought he had pursued that career too ruthlessly, and some saw him as a humorless politician. Stimson once called him a "terrible old fusspocket of a society man." But he was capable and committed, and he wasn't scared of King. Nor was he sanguine as the New Year dawned.

He hadn't a single ship, he reported, "that an enemy submarine could not outdistance when operating on the surface. In most cases the guns of these vessels would be outranged by those of the submarine." Two weeks after Pearl Harbor he wrote, "It is submitted that should enemy submarines operate off this coast, this command has no forces available to take adequate action against them, either offensive or defensive."

Admiral Andrews was to learn the most extreme meanings of *doing all you can with what you have.*

The effort drew on every kind of ingenuity, from the bait-shop owner's to the theoretical physicist's at MIT, and it reached far beyond the U.S. navy itself. In the beginning it put—for the first time since the War of 1812—untried American militia up against some of the world's most competent professional warriors.

The Hooligan Navy

Yachts and cabin cruisers go to war, 1942

A century and a half earlier Admiral Nelson had written, "Was I to die at this moment, 'Want of Frigates' would be found stamped on my heart." There were never enough of them. A frigate was supple, light, but powerful, useful as scout, courier, and, perhaps most of all, escort.

The East Coast had little that could serve as a plausible escort, and no convoy system whatever. This surprised and vexed the British, who had been running convoys along their coastlines from the earliest days of the war. The system was working across the breadth of the Atlantic, but it failed in the final few miles.

The British, not happy to guard a freighter over two thousand miles of ocean only to see it incinerated within sight of Atlantic City, called for coastal convoys. Admiral King did not much like the British. He suspected them of trying to rig the war to suit their imperial purposes, and he bridled at their assumption, far from unjustified, that they knew more about fighting U-boats than America did. His reputation has suffered some at the hands of those who felt he wouldn't institute convoys off our shores just because the British wanted him to. In fact, he had almost nothing to conduct them with.

Why the lack of escort vessels? Blame began being doled out during the first offshore shipping crisis, and seventy years later it still is. Some held King responsible—too aloof, too resistant to British example, too skeptical of the abilities of escort vessels. President Roosevelt, a small-boat enthusiast, liked to grumble about the navy's indifference to "anything under a thousand tons," but he never pushed hard for smaller ships until the U-boats came. For once, that ever-convenient scapegoat Congress cannot be blamed: nobody had asked for escort funding.

Now the money was there, and smaller ships were being laid down. But unfortunately, a small vessel can no more be willed into existence overnight than can an aircraft carrier.

As early as the summer before, Alfred Stanford had been pointing out to the navy that a great many small ships were at hand. Stanford was a New York newspaperman who had moved profitably into advertising ("Good fun," he said, "if it weren't for the clients") and taken up yachting. Now he was the commodore of the Cruising Club of America, and he believed its members could help. They owned pleasure boats, but they knew the sea and its ways, and they were willing. Not surprisingly, the navy had wanted nothing to do with these well-meaning amateurs.

But things looked quite different in the alarming early months of 1942, when the Eastern Sea Frontier command was happy to accept the help of thirty yachts, fifty to ninety feet long, to go patrolling for U-boats. The Coast Guard Auxiliary Act followed, enlisting small-boat owners and their craft for spans as brief as thirty days.

So the Corsair Fleet put to sea. That was the dashing name the Coast Guard gave the effort, but its members promptly and permanently called it the Hooligan Navy. Some of them were stockbrokers, many were sports fishermen, and some were rum-runners who had learned how to handle boats evading Coast Guard vigilance in Prohibition days. One of them was Ernest

Hemingway, who talked his government out of $32,000 worth of radio direction-finding equipment for his thirty-eight-foot fishing boat *Pilar,* hot with a plan to run aboard a surfaced U-boat in Cuban waters and sink it through some alchemy of gallantry and exhibitionism.

These volunteers took their work seriously. They couldn't sink submarines, but they could spot them and radio for help. They were sentries, pickets, and they came to have the official title of the Coastal Picket Patrol. *Sea Gypsy, Vema, Redhead,* and a clutch of other Bermuda racers, seventy-foot-long ballerinas out of Greenport, Long Island, stood watch for a week at a time in the heaviest weather. The Coast Guard hadn't expected real tenacity from the Picket Patrol, but *Primrose IV,* under the command of a Harvard professor, and a hundred like her, stuck it out when the fierce winter of 1942 came down.

How much good they did remains a matter of debate. Even the fleet's creator had his doubts. "I can't honestly say that the patrol made a significant contribution," Stanford said years later. "In theory, it made a lot of sense. It was probably worthwhile in preparing the younger men for other duties at sea." That seems unquestionable: many of the sailors aboard these boats passed into regular navy service for the duration. But for every submarine they sighted, their dozens of false alarms further distracted and enervated what scant navy protection the United States had. The Picket Patrol rarely intimidated the Germans. One day the crew of a cabin cruiser off the Florida coast stood dumbfounded as the sea boiled beside them and the conning tower of a submarine rose, sheeting water, and rose and rose until, as high above as if he had been standing on the rooftree of a house, the U-boat's skipper called down in what was reported to be "excellent Americanese," "Get the hell out of here, you guys! Do you want to get hurt? Now, scram!"

Captain Peter Cremer said he was delighted to have the

civilians swarming around because their "value was precisely nil," and they "created complete chaos by also seeing U-boats everywhere and sending the few destroyers to chase hither and thither and find nothing."

But those earnest volunteers served another function.

A thirty-foot lapstrake boat lying at the modest end of the scale for anything that might be called a cabin cruiser, the *Kitsis* was a typical unit of the Hooligan Navy. She was christened not for an ancient Egyptian deity, but an amalgam of the nicknames of her owner and his wife, Kit and Sis Johnson. Her master, Clarence Johnson, a Vero Beach, Florida, businessman, had been out on nighttime patrols—"fishing" was his constant, unpersuasive explanation—for four months running without encountering anything unusual. But soon after May 5 turned to May 6, and Johnson's friend Ottie Roach relieved him at the wheel, the men saw a fiery speck rising like a meteor drawn back from the earth to the heavens. It brightened in silent explosion and floated down the sky. Kit took over—it was his boat, after all—and headed toward the flare.

After a while Roach yelled and pointed off the port bow. Johnson turned on his searchlight and lit up a lifeboat so full that it was barely afloat. They had found survivors from Captain Cremer's first victim, the *Java Arrow*.

The *Kitsis* didn't have the power to tow the boat, so one by one the occupants struggled aboard, burned, bleeding, vomiting, twenty-two of them. This was far more people than the *Kitsis* had been designed to carry, and Ottie Roach was standing in the bilge handing up buckets of oily water to be emptied over the side when, at five twenty in the morning, Johnson put his boat alongside the Coast Guard pier at Fort Pierce.

Kit Johnson came home full of febrile energy; Sis made him scrambled eggs and sent him up to bed. Then she took a bucket of rags, a can of Old Dutch Cleanser, and a mop, drove the family

Studebaker to the pier at Fort Pierce, and found the *Kitsis*. After breathing in as much as she could of the morning breeze, she went below to scrub the blood out of the mattresses and hose the decks free of what she called "slime."

She was back home by the time her eight-year-old son, Rody, came in from school. "Is Dad going fishing tonight?" he asked.

"Yes," she said.

All along the coast, from Maine to the Keys, boats like the *Kitsis* were pulling from the water men and women who for the rest of their lives would be grateful the Hooligan Navy had been there.

Panic Party

The "mystery ship" fiasco, 1942

While the yachts and powerboats sought the telltale white V of water that followed a periscope and often found it whether it was there or not, Admiral Andrews begged Admiral King to give him some destroyers. King did, but only in the small chinks of time between transatlantic convoy duty, often for just a few days. Even then, they were deployed on submarine-hunting patrols that were as irresistible to navy men as they were ineffectual.

The British told us so. Only convoys worked. King said he agreed, but hadn't enough ships for coastal convoys.

Doing all you can with what you have meant backing long shots such as the Picket Patrol. None was longer than Project LQ, the "mystery ships," a sort of Boys' True Adventure fantasy that had to be paid for in the real world.

The project came straight from FDR and appealed to his sense of panache. The British had tried the same thing in the last war with mixed success, and in this one with none. They'd abandoned it by the time—February 4, 1942—Kenneth M. Beyer, an ensign on the new battleship *North Carolina,* just back from gunnery practice and at anchor in the Brooklyn Navy Yard, was summoned by his captain, who said, "I have a set of orders for you. I don't know why the urgency, but you are to be in Washington today. It's eleven o'clock, you don't have much time. I know you must be as surprised as I am."

Beyer was, but of course he packed and left the *"Carie"* immediately. The next morning he and another ensign met Commander W. J. Carter, who was coordinating the project. Carter invited them to take a seat and offered them coffee. Beyer thought that if this was how ensigns were treated in Washington, things were going to be pretty good. Then Carter told them they had been selected for a highly secret project that was considered hazardous sea duty. It was all strictly volunteer, and if either of them wanted to turn it down, he must feel free to stop the commander at any point and leave. "There will be two heavily armed merchant-type ships," Carter went on. "They will be freighter configuration and have sizable navy crews. All personnel will be specially selected. The ships will operate as disguised merchantmen, U-boat decoys, or Q-ships as the British called them."

Beyer did not stop the commander and leave. He took the train to Portsmouth, New Hampshire, where his ship was being refitted. There he met his executive officer, Lawrence Neville, who had also just arrived. Over lunch Neville handed him a sheet of paper: "USS *Asterion* (AK100)—USS *Atik* (AK101): Tonnage Gross 3209, Length 318'6", Beam 46'. Cruising radius 9600 at 9.5 knots." Small and slow, thought Beyer, but he was impressed by their armament: "Four—4"/50 cal. main battery; four—.50 cal machine guns; six—single depth charge throwers; five—Lewis .30 cal. machine guns." Beyer and Neville walked through a freezing-cold afternoon to the drydock to see the ships. They were still wearing their old names, *Evelyn* and *Carolyn*. The volunteers stood in silence staring at the *Evelyn*. After a while Neville said, "Oh, my God!" Neither man knew, though neither man would have been surprised, that the navy expected the ships to last no more than a month.

The two decrepit, thirty-year-old freighters had been bought from the A. H. Bull Steamship Company, paid for with cash carried in a suitcase by a doubtless uncomfortable Admiral Andrews, dressed in civilian clothes to transport the covertly assembled money. Everything about the project was like that. Beyer was to become the treasurer of a bogus company drawing on a revolving account at a Washington bank. He would use part of the funds to outfit his ship's crew with merchant-sailor clothes. He was forbidden, of course, to tell his family why he had gone from being an ensign on a battleship to being an ensign on a freighter.

The secrecy was complete, save that the ships were being converted by scores of navy-yard workers, and it was said to be the talk of the Portsmouth boardinghouses. The conversion involved getting the guns in place, then building an elaborate set of stage-set baffles to hide them, and stuffing the cargo holds with buoyant wood pulp.

The plan was for the two ships to go loitering out to sea singly and dawdle around until they attracted the notice of a submarine. Once a torpedo hit, a "panic party" would take to the lifeboats and make a show of abandoning ship. Then the U-boat, not wishing to spend another torpedo, would surface and prepare to finish off the still-floating freighter with gunfire. At that moment the falsework would drop, and the rest of the crew would leap from hiding to open up with the four-inch guns and demolish the ambushed submarine.

The two secret vessels went through strange, surreptitious commissioning ceremonies on March 5, a month and a day after Beyer had received his summons.

The *Carolyn/Atik* and the *Evelyn/Asterion* sailed from Portsmouth on March 23. The next morning they went through some perfunctory combat drill—the *Atik* fired a single round from each of her four cannon—and shot off the .50-caliber machine guns. Beyer remembered that "the light red tracers" provided "a display of morbid celebration."

Then, after just thirty-six hours of such exercises, the ships went their separate ways, generating as much smoke as they could, hoping to hook a German submarine captain with their lure. It took the *Atik* only four days. The captain was Reinhard Hardegan, back in his *123* for a second swipe at the apparently helpless East Coast. Hardegan saw the freighter toward dusk, followed it through rising seas for several hours, and fired a torpedo. It hit just forward of the bridge, but the explosion seemed curiously weak and muffled to Hardegan. The freighter lost way and signaled "SS CAROLYN TORPEDO ATTACK BURNING FORWARD REQUIRD SSISTANCE." Hardegan unknowingly played his proper role by moving in to sink the ship with his deck gun, while boat crews abandoned it with what seemed to him unusual haste.

The steamer turned toward him and gathered speed. Its plywood bulkheads fell away, and a four-inch gun started firing. The shells fell wide, but two machine guns found their target, the .50-caliber bullets flashing and clattering against the conning tower. Midshipman Rudolf Holzer took a wound between hip and knee that left his right leg joined to his body by only a strip of skin.

Hardegan backed away at flank speed—he had no trouble outdistancing the *Atik*—while his midshipman died and his men, furious at being tricked and at the trap itself, debated killing the *Atik*'s entire crew. This proved unnecessary. The sea was rough now. Hardegan fired a second torpedo that struck the engine room.

Only the *Asterion* answered the *Atik*'s signal. It was picked up, but the sea was loud with distress calls that night, and those who heard thought it was just another tanker. The *Asterion* was 150 miles away; she came as quickly as she could, but a full gale was blowing, and her captain wrote that his ship "made good about two knots over the ground. No signs seen of *Atik*."

No signs were ever seen, and 139 officers and men disappeared. Their families didn't find out how or why until 1946. The *Asterion* nearly thrashed herself to pieces in her haste to aid her sister, and after her fruitless search had to limp to Hampton Roads, Virginia, for repairs.

There were three other Q-ships. The trawler *Eagle* never once sighted a submarine, and a three-masted schooner was well disguised but withdrawn from the service when she almost foundered in a gale. Largest of them all was the tanker *Gulf Dawn*, armed and given the fake trappings of a fleet oiler and renamed *Big Horn*. Joe Gainard, around whom storm clouds always seemed to gather, and who was back in the navy now, got command of her. The *Big Horn* went to the Caribbean, setting up as a convoy straggler. Unfortunately—but not for Gainard, given the odds—the wolf pack was having easy enough going with the convoy itself and didn't need to go looking for singletons.

A disgusted King called off Project LQ late in 1943. Before that Gainard had been ordered to the Pacific in command of an attack transport. The years had worn on him, though, and he fell ill and was sent to the navy hospital in San Diego. He died there on December 23, 1943. He had survived his former command the *City of Flint* by a little less than a year; a U-boat had put an end to the sturdy old workhorse the previous January.

Dan van der Vat, a British historian of the Atlantic campaign, wrote that Project LQ "was in its small way the most self-destructive operation undertaken by the US Navy in the war." A quarter of the men who volunteered for it died. The Germans lost Midshipman Holzer.

Cadet O'Hara's Last Fight

*The Naval Armed Guard and the ordeal
of the* Stephen Hopkins, 1942

"Do you want to go to sea immediately?" During the weeks following Pearl Harbor this question drew bold affirmatives in recruiting stations across the country. The recruiters were as good as their word; the eager respondents were often at sea in days. But not, to their dismay, on a destroyer or a cruiser. Rather, they shipped out aboard a freighter—or, worse yet, a tanker—as part of a service they had never heard of: the Naval Armed Guard.

Plans to arm merchant ships had been going on for nearly a year before America entered the war. At first the training of the men who were to work the guns was scattered and haphazard, some of it taking place in a small, ramshackle camp in Little Creek, Virginia. In September 1941, Little Creek got orders to train two hundred officers and a thousand enlisted men by early January. The first class contained 207 men, 27 of them officers, and most of them leery of the assignment they had drawn. The officers established a club and painted the motto they'd worked up on a sign that went in the bar: READY!—AIM!—ABANDON SHIP!

A Virginian named Floyd Jones arrived at Little Creek a month later. "All we did was train on a .30-caliber machine gun, that was all we had at the time. We didn't know what we were training for, but a few days later they called us to the flagpole and told us we were training for armed guard duty on merchant ships in case of war."

The machine gun might have seemed a feeble tool for the job it had to do, but it was appropriate because in the beginning that was the best the navy could come up with. In the early days of the arming program, some merchant ships put to sea carrying on their main gun mount a creosote log, a promissory token of a cannon yet to be forged.

It was the same story with the men. Pushed through brief courses, they were token sailors. Some went to war with a single week's training in "seamanship," followed by another week learning gunnery, which culminated in watching a gun being fired. One recruit summed up his month of training, which included squeezing off a brief burst from one of the .30-calibers, saying, "We knew two things for sure when we got finished there: do not stand in front of the gun when it is being fired, and don't salute doormen."

Out of such scrabbled-together ingredients the navy made Armed Guard crews and put them aboard merchant ships, with the social effects one might imagine. The novelist Robert Ruark, who served in the Armed Guard, described the situation in a *Saturday Evening Post* article that ran under the vivid title "They Called 'Em Fish Food." "The big bugaboo in our business has been, and always will be, the maintenance of cordial relationships with the merchant personnel. Although the master is boss of the ship, he has no jurisdiction over the Navy detachment, and in time of combat is actually ranked by the ensign or lieutenant. . . . During the early days of the war . . . we were resented, and with some justice." Not only did the Armed Guard members have to adapt themselves to a wholly alien community; they were to take charge of it whenever action was possible. A ship captain's job rarely inculcates a spirit of cooperative egalitarianism in its holder, and few merchant skippers liked the idea of handing over their command to adolescents fresh from a few courses in seafaring.

Nor did the weaponry entrusted to these neophytes inspire confidence. One newly fledged lieutenant came aboard his ship to find workers busy installing a Mark VII four-inch gun from the chromolithograph days of the Spanish-American War.

Surprisingly, the gun worked. Equally surprising, so did the Naval Armed Guard. Beverley Britten, who served in it, wrote after the war about having been one of what he called the "Navy's step-children." He well understood why the Armed Guard "quickly became known as the least-desired duty in the Navy. The AG was physically separated from his fellow Navymen, placed in a small group aboard a ship run by civilians." The public didn't know what he did, and the navy tended to forget about him. "He was not only out of sight of the 'brass' but pretty much out of mind, unless something bad happened." Nevertheless, Britten concluded, almost everyone in it "came to love armed guard service, and the old 'S.S. Rustpot.'"

That turned out to be a lot of people—145,000 by the time the war ended. It is not the least achievement of a hard-pressed democracy that this peculiar martial arrangement, which depended entirely on a thousand hermetic societies cooperating with small cadres of arbitrarily empowered outsiders, should produce in the first months of the war the ship's company aboard the *Stephen Hopkins*.

The *Stephen Hopkins* was not the "S.S. Rustpot," nor was she armed with a creosote log. The freighter was brand-new, launched in April 1942 and ready for service by May. When Robert Ruark published his article, in the spring of 1944, he could write that the average freighter "carries two semiautomatic, dual-purpose, 3-inch guns or a 4 or 5 inch gun aft and a 3-incher forward, and eight 20-mms., which fire explosive shells with appalling rapidity." Looking back, though, he remembered, "There was a time when, if you had a ten-man gun crew, a 4-inch gun and a couple of .50 caliber machine guns, you were considered a very lucky guy." That's about what the *Stephen Hopkins* got: a four-inch gun, mounted on the stern, two 37mms forward, and four .50-caliber Browning machine guns. The main gun was an old-timer from World War I, but it was a considerable weapon. It fired a shell half as tall as a man, throwing a thirty-three-pound projectile upward of nine miles. It could easily cripple a surfaced U-boat if it got one in its sights. A U-boat, however, was not what the *Stephen Hopkins* was destined to encounter.

The *Stier* didn't look any more like a warship than did the *Atik*. Born in 1936 as the five-thousand-ton German freighter *Cairo*, she had been taken by her government when the war started. After spending a couple of years sowing mines in the Bay of Biscay, she steamed up to conquered Poland and, hidden in the port of Gdynia, received six 5.9-inch guns with a modern fire-control system to train them, along with eight smaller guns, torpedo tubes, and two seaplanes. These riches were concealed behind a superstructure painted a dingy gray and here and there bleeding red lead. The *Stier* was meant to deceive but, unlike the Q-ships, she was no decoy. Her job was not to lure an enemy into attacking, but to look innocuous for as long as possible before attacking the enemy. The *Stier*'s role was the same as a U-boat's—destroy commerce—but on the surface, and for month after month. The raider could stay at sea for half a year without refueling.

Under Captain Horst Gerlach, the *Stier* left Gdynia in May 1942, made her way through the Kiel Canal from the Baltic to the North Sea, took on fuel in the Netherlands at the prettily named port of Petroleumhaven, fought her way down through the Channel to the French coast, then broke out, headed for the South Atlantic.

Once there, the routine was as simple as it was effective. The *Stier* would sidle innocently up to another merchantman, then show her teeth and order it to surrender. When Gerlach tried this on the big ten-thousand-ton American tanker *Stanvac Calcutta*, his victim fought until her captain was killed and the ship took a torpedo in the stern. The British steamer *Gemstone* gave up without a fight, and this is more than understandable. The *Stier* was classified as an "auxiliary cruiser," and she had the punch of any conventional cruiser. Half a year earlier the *Koroman*, *Stier*'s identical sister ship, drew the Australian cruiser *Sydney* close to her with a flurry of baffling signals. The German opened fire at point-blank range, and the *Sydney* was lost along with every one of her 645-man crew, the largest Allied ship to go down with all hands during the war.

Captain Gerlach had done so well that on September 1, the third anniversary of the outbreak of the war, he was expecting at least a message of congratulations from Germany, and possibly some medals for himself and his crew. He was miffed when no such word came, but at least a few days later he was told to rendezvous with the *Tannenfels* to receive supplies and give over some of the prisoners that had been crowding his ship (surface raiders, unlike U-boats, had the room to take on prisoners and did). The *Tannenfels* was a blockade runner, much larger than the *Stier* but more lightly armed. The two ships met on September 25 and for the next two days drifted in company while Gerlach took advantage of the good weather to have his men go over the side and chip away at the impasto of marine growth the *Stier*'s hull had acquired during the long cruise. On the morning of the twenty-seventh the wind and sea rose, and rain came on. The job was all but finished anyway, and Gerlach had called in most of his working parties when, he reported later, "I heard the call 'Vessel in sight to starboard, direction thirty degrees . . .' Then followed an immediate alarm, calling the ship, and the realization that it was not one of our own, nor a neutral vessel, but definitely a large enemy steamer.

"A flag signal 'stop at once' was set."

If the *Stephen Hopkins* was lucky in its armament, according to Robert Ruark's assessment, it was also lucky in its fifteen-strong Armed Guard contingent, half again as large as the "ten-man crew" Ruark said was impressive at that time. The *Hopkins*'s Armed Guard was under the command of Kenneth M. Willett, who, like Beyer of the *Asterion*, had left battleship duty—the *California*—for service of a very different kind. He came aboard the *Hopkins* as an ensign and was promoted to lieutenant (j.g.) at sea in June. For a man just recently into his twenties—he had been born in 1919—given charge of other young men largely new to the sea and a gun that was older than he was, he had been sent out with pretty stiff instructions. "There shall be no surrender and no abandoning ship so long as the guns can be fought. In case of casualty to members of the gun crew the remaining men shall continue to serve the gun."

His captain had got the same message more directly:

March 30, 1942
From: The Secretary of the Navy
To: Master SS Stephen Hopkins,
              7184 Gross Tons

1. It is the policy of the United States Government that no U.S. Flag merchant ship be permitted to fall into the hands of the enemy.

2. The ship shall be defended by her armament, by maneuver, and by every available means as long as possible. When, in the judgment of the Master, capture is inevitable, he shall scuttle the ship.

The master of the *Stephen Hopkins* was Paul Buck, a thirty-nine-year-old Massachusetts man who had first gone to sea when he was sixteen, and whose previous command had been a United Fruit Company steamer. Ordinary Seaman Rodger Piercy remembered him as "a quiet, likeable type, but a strict disciplinarian and his officers were much the same. They were friendly, helpful and yet aloof, as officers should be."

But unlike many merchant skippers, Captain Buck wasn't aloof from his Armed Guard contingent. Soon after the *Hopkins* left San Pedro on her maiden voyage, carrying supplies to the South Pacific, Buck called his officers together, along with Willett, and told them they must cooperate. He went on to make sure that they did. There were frequent abandon-ship and fire drills, which the merchant sailors were used to, but, Piercy wrote, "now we were divided into crews under navy personnel and assigned gun positions and duties. We were instructed in ammunition handling, how to take the guns apart and reassemble them, how to load them, oil them, and keep them covered in the weather. . . . It was intensely interesting and everyone aboard was serious about doing their jobs well."

The sailors and the Armed Guard were easy with one another long before the ship reached Bora-Bora. Willett became friends with the youngest man aboard, Edwin O'Hara, an eighteen-year-old cadet midshipman—that is, a student at the Merchant Marine Academy receiving sea training. O'Hara was fascinated by machinery and liked to help serve the four-inch gun even when he was off duty.

The *Stephen Hopkins* went from Bora-Bora to Wellington, New Zealand, then on to Melbourne and down the Australian coast to Port Lincoln, where it picked up sixty-four thousand bags of wheat bound for South Africa.

The *Hopkins* set sail for Durban on August 3. The voyage

across the Indian Ocean should have taken a little over two weeks, but a hurricane so badly punished the ship that she didn't arrive until September 2, struggling into port with lifeboats smashed, the deckhouse wrenched loose from its pinnings, the forward gun mounts ruined, an ammunition hold flooded, and the bow stove in. In a letter home Arthur Chamberlain, the *Hopkins*'s other cadet midshipman, added a note to his brother: "Robert, don't ever go to sea!"

The crew got leave, the ship got repaired, and the *Hopkins* went down to Cape Town to unload two thousand tons of sugar. There the men learned that they were to go to Paramaribo, on the northeast shoulder of South America, fill up with bauxite, and take it to New Orleans. Captain Buck had been warned that raiders were active in their path and kept up the drills. But the ship was homeward bound, even though it still had half the world to go, and the crew was full of good cheer as they rounded the Cape of Good Hope and entered the South Atlantic. Some of the off-duty men had left breakfast to shoot craps when the lookouts sighted two ships, not all that far off, over a rough, smoky sea.

Captain Buck was on the bridge with Lieutenant Willett when the smaller of the two ships signaled the *Hopkins* to stop.

Captain Buck did not obey Captain Gerlach's order. He had the U.S. ensign run up into the rainy morning and told the helmsman hard left rudder, swinging his ship to port and putting her stern toward the *Stier*. This made the *Hopkins* a smaller target and let her main gun bear, pointing its muzzle at the six German guns that, although their bore was less than two inches wider, fired a projectile three times as heavy.

The first shots came from the raider's lighter guns, the twenties and the 37mms. Buck's second-in-command, Chief Mate Richard Moczkowski, was hit early, in the chest and arm. It was a bad wound, as the ship's chief steward, Ford Stilson, charged with giving medical help, discovered when he got to the bridge with an armful of bandages. Stilson made a tourniquet and applied it. Moczkowski waved him off. The mate had been lying on the deck, but he got Rodger Piercy to help him to his feet. He was hit again, in the leg, and again Stilson bandaged him. "All this time," Stilson said, "shells had been riddling the superstructure and our own four-inch had started at a rapid rate about the time I was bandaging the mate."

When the stern gun opened up, Edwin O'Hara was commanding its crew. Willett had given the order, but he was still on the bridge. "Fire!" called O'Hara, and "we immediately let go," Piercy wrote. "We knew we hit her but did not know to what extent." They fired again, and Willett arrived to take over. Piercy had seen him making his way aft: "He got hit in the stomach with shrapnel which sliced him open and knocked him down. He got up and came to the stern with part of his intestines hanging out."

The shells from the *Stier*'s big guns were beginning to arrive. Even the largest ship is infinitesimal once it gets out onto the ocean, but to those aboard it any sizable vessel is a whole town, with its concourses and alleys and back lots and crossroads. The *Hopkins* had forty-one men in her merchant crew, but she was 441 feet long, which is roughly the equivalent of a forty-story office building laid on its side, with one occupant per floor. When the shells began to find it, the ship would have grown larger around its tenants, for they could have no idea what was going on just a few yards away. Each was in his own unending car accident.

George Cronk, the second assistant engineer, was asleep after standing the midnight watch when the general-quarters alarm woke him. Before he could get into his clothes the ship had already been hit several times. Nevertheless the cables of maritime routine pulled the chief engineer, Rudolph Rutz, into Cronk's quarters holding a rack of three test tubes for the daily analysis of boiler water. "Here's your test tubes," said Rutz over the jackhammer noise, "but I don't think you'll need them."

The deck was already ruined when Cronk went out on it. Below him, a shell burst the main boiler, about the worst thing that can happen to an engine-room crew. Cronk and Rutz carried out those who had escaped being scalded to death.

"We were taking an awful beating," said Piercy. "The shrapnel was heavy, and the boys handling the aiming mechanism were being blown off their seats about every second or third round." But they got back on their seats, the ones still conscious, and Chief Moczkowski kept the stern to the enemy, and Willett, hand pressed hard against the long gash in his abdomen, kept directing the fire. In the three-foot-high circle of steel armor that surrounded the four-inch gun, men kept dropping. "We knew they had terrific gun power," Piercy said, "because when they would catch us with a unified salvo, our ship would almost jump out of the water from stem to stern." One of those shots from one of those salvos found the ammunition locker. "We could not get another shell from the locker, but still had some on deck. O'Hara ran to the gun and climbed on a seat to aim. . . . Willett was firing." Then O'Hara was down on the deck.

They ran out of shells. Seaman Second Class Moses Barker saw a few more in the ready box kept near the gun. But they'd been at the ready for too long, since before the hurricane, and were welded together by rust. Barker pulled at them until the skin came off his fingers. He got one final shell into the breech and crouched away from the sluice of machine-gun bullets. "They were coming so hard overhead I hollered, 'Fire.' I had my face right against the breech. If he had pulled the trigger my head would have been a block down the street. But he was already dead. They were all dead except me. So I ran and pulled the trigger. I didn't even look to see what I was shooting or anything. I just pulled the trigger and got behind the gun again."

Barker gave up. There was nothing else he could do. "We had .50-caliber machine guns; two on each side. I went over there to try to shoot one of them. I didn't know how to. The only thing I knew how to do was the four-inch. . . . I got off the gun and went amidship." Away from his post, he realized he didn't have a life jacket and was going to need one. When he arrived at the passageway that led to where he knew some were stored, he found the ship's sole passenger blocking the way. Barker started past him, into a now unfamiliar tunnel full of crushed metal and gouting steam. The man wouldn't let him by: "Son, you don't want to go in there. Everyone is dead." Barker explained why he had to go in. The passenger pulled off the life jacket he was wearing, put it on the gunner, tied it shut, and told him to go save himself.

Who *was* this passenger who handed his life to another man and then, as Barker said, "just stayed there on the ship"? All we know is his name: George Townsend. Barker thought he had come aboard at Cape Town; Piercy, at Durban. He was listed as working for an oil company. Barker said he was a "soldier of fortune." If so, he showed himself to be quite a soldier when fortune turned against him.

Although some who survived it thought the battle lasted three hours, in twenty minutes the *Hopkins* was a floating junkyard, and not going to float much longer. But while she floated, she fought. Willett kept exhorting his crew to aim for the hull, their efforts rewarded by an occasional brief glow that might have marked a hit on their tormentor. Then one of the *Stier*'s shells blew up the four-inch gun's magazine.

The main gun was done for, one of the thirty-sevens had vanished with its crew, leaving a scorched hole, and beneath the blazing upperworks hot little clusters of electrical fire hissed and sparked everywhere. The *Hopkins* was crawling along at one knot. Captain Buck gave the order to abandon ship. Almost every steam line had been cut, and the whistle could give out only a weak slobber.

Sailors made their way around blades of ruptured plating

seeking an intact lifeboat. Salvos kept coming in, two and three a minute, and then there was a different sort of concussion. The four-inch gun was in action again. The shells in the ready box that Barker had torn his hands on had been knocked loose by the magazine explosion, and Deck Cadet O'Hara, back on his feet, was spending the last minutes of his short life firing them.

Three lifeboats had been completely shot away, but the No. 1 starboard boat still hung in its davits. Chief Moczkowski ordered it lowered. Rodger Piercy helped free it and it jerked downward. Moczkowski himself refused to leave the ship.

George Cronk, who had received the foot column delivery from Rudolph Rutz twenty minutes earlier, found him putting life jackets on wounded men. The chief engineer told him to help out on the boat deck. Cronk never saw him again.

As the *Hopkins* settled lower, some of the crew jumped. Wallace Breck, of the Armed Guard, saw Captain Buck and Cadet Midshipman Arthur Chamberlain, who had urged his brother not to go to sea, coming down from the bridge. Buck was hit and fell. He handed Chamberlain something—the ship's log, Breck thought. There were no boats, and Chamberlain went off the stern and was pulled in by the still-turning propeller.

Piercy came upon Lieutenant Willett, still alive and trying to cut away life rafts. "We offered to drop [him] over the side and help him to the raft, but he declined. He was too far gone, and he knew it. He didn't want to cause anyone to lose precious time when he couldn't make it." Willett gave his last order: throw the rafts overboard and go after them. Get away from the ship.

Piercy did, but once in the sea—"I felt like I had suddenly become a Popsicle! Oh, that water was cold"—he couldn't see any rafts. After a while he spotted the No. 1 lifeboat and struggled toward it. He got aboard, and a little later helped pick up George Cronk. The boat found Ford Stilson on a raft, and as soon as he climbed in, he started tending the wounded. They looked for more survivors. Someone had seen Captain Buck on a raft; nobody saw him again. The sea grew higher and visibility lower. One of the German ships nosed around and went away. The other one looked as if it might be on fire. They saw a doughnut raft "with at least five men on it," Cronk said. "We rowed for two hours until our hands were blistered and still could not pick up the men." The wind rose. They put two corpses out of the boat.

The next morning they found wreckage but no people. Second Engineer Cronk was the senior man aboard the boat and thus in charge of the other survivors. It was not a job he wanted, but he went ahead and had them take stock: twenty-four gallons of water, and perhaps a month's worth of malted-milk tablets, C rations, and chocolate. Piercy remembered, "Captain Buck had told someone not to try to go to Africa as the wind and tide would be against you, but take the longer route and try for Brazil." Cronk put Stilson in charge of all the food and water, set the sail, and headed west.

Cronk kept a log.

OCTOBER 1st . . . Cut water to 6 ounces per day per man, so as to give more to the wounded men.

OCTOBER 7th. McDaniels, and Cook, died at 6:30 P.M. . . . .

OCTOBER 8th . . . Romero died at about 2:30. Buried at sunset. . . . .

OCTOBER 11th. Good breeze until 9 A.M., ran into rain squall caught 1 gallon water.

OCTOBER 12th. George Gelogotes, fireman, died this morning. . . .

OCTOBER 19th. High winds and seas, shipping lots of water, bailing all night, everybody wet from rain and spray. Most everyone has sores that won't heal.

OCTOBER 23rd . . . Cut food ration in half 4 days ago. . . .

On October 25, a frill of motion above the hideously familiar gunwale: "a yellow moth." The bug was a messenger of life. It had to have come from land.

Two days later, the only note of emotion in the log: "Hurrah, sighted land 4AM. Landed at the small Brazilian village of Barra de Itabapoana."

The village was indeed small, perhaps one hundred inhabitants, and poor. But it seemed paradisiacal to the fifteen survivors who'd just spent thirty-one days in an open boat. "They fed us boiled rice, chicken, fish, bananas, and a pudding made from mandioca," wrote Piercy. "Wow! What a feast! Women, men, and children were all over the place and all trying to help us. It was wonderful."

Word of their arrival reached the port city of Victoria, and the navy immediately dispatched an officer by Piper Cub, from which he had to transfer to a locomotive, and then a taxi when that ran out of track. Sixteen and a half hours after he set out, he was with the men of the *Hopkins* and reported, "The survivors were in wonderful condition. After thirty days of being battered together on a cramped lifeboat, they were lavishing praise on one another, helping one another, and best of all, wanting to go back again. You were made to realize how small your own troubles were, and how big [and] good humans can be."

They were sent to Rio de Janeiro, mended some there, and then it was north, to New York City (where, despite all he'd been through, Rodger Piercy was alarmed by the inhabitants of Greenwich Village), and eventually back to sea.

Not until the war was over did the survivors of the *Stephen Hopkins* learn what they'd managed to do.

Five minutes after the freighter opened fire, Captain Gerlach had thought he was fighting a cruiser. One shell made his torpedo tubes useless; another came into the engine room and knocked out the *Stier*'s electrical system. Between them, Willett and O'Hara fired thirty-five rounds and scored fifteen hits. One of them started a fire that the Germans couldn't douse. At 10:42, Gerlach wrote, "The entire crew on the boat deck began to hear my speech of the resolution that we had to give up the ship. 'Sieg-heil auf Fuehrer . . . Victory to our leader. . . .' A spontaneous singing of the national anthem."

The *Tannenfels* took off the crew, the captain last of all. "As the stern of the ship began to dip our crew watched from *Tannenfels*'s foredeck as she began to sink faster and faster. . . . We repeated Sieg-Heil after my beautiful ship reared up and went down stern first and bow showing in dead silence."

The *Stier* and the *Stephen Hopkins* lie a couple of thousand yards apart two miles down on the South Atlantic seabed. The *Stier* was the last German raider to break free of the tightening Allied cordon. She is the only German surface warship destroyed by an American vessel in World War II. It is perhaps not necessary to say that she is the only cruiser ever sunk by a freighter.

"Start Swinging, Lady"
The Liberty ships, 1941–45

The *Stephen Hopkins* was a Liberty ship, one of the firstborn of a family that would grow to more than twenty-seven hundred.

In 1936, with Europe on the simmer, Congress had established the U.S. Maritime Commission "to provide the nation with a modern merchant marine, which would also serve as a naval auxiliary in time of war." The commission mandated an ambitious program, one that would create as many as five hundred ships by 1946. Naturally the commission sought standardized dimensions for its cargo ships, but the design for the one most copiously produced was brought us by Britain.

In September 1940 a British Shipbuilding Mission arrived in America eager to make good some of the losses inflicted by German submarines. They ordered sixty "Ocean-class" ships for transatlantic service. These were needed quickly, which meant they had to be simple. No innovations, no features that hadn't been well tried. The result would be powered by a triple expansion engine, whose connecting rods reached down from its three cylinders to turn the propeller shaft with a dignified stolidity that suggested the big, slow-breathing steam engines of the Victorian era. In fact, the entire ship was Victorian. After the war was over, the American Society of Mechanical Engineers saluted the Liberty ship as "an 1879 steamer sailing across the oceans of the world to 20th century triumph." American industry did not pride itself on copying sixty-year-old machinery developed by another country, but these were stringent times, and the congressional committee weighing the proposal for what was called a "five-year vessel" (to make clear that longevity was not expected of it) issued a glum endorsement: "It is slow and seaworthy . . . but for the demands of modern commerce in foreign trade it would not compare in speed, equipment and general serviceability with up-to-date cargo vessels. The design is the best that can be devised for an emergency product to be quickly, cheaply and simply built." As for the future, "they will be constructed for the emergency and whether they have any utility afterward will be determined then." This was followed by the tepid prospect that "the coastal trade may offer some possibilities in those directions."

In the end, the vessels proved hardy enough to far outlive their five-year expiration date. One that we'd given to Russia when the Germans were in the suburbs of Stalingrad turned up running supplies to Fidel Castro during the Cuban missile crisis. But the ship delighted nobody, least of all President Roosevelt, who, although not denying the need for it, took to referring to it as the Ugly Duckling. This caught on with the public, which irritated Admiral Emory Scott Land, an academy man who had been naval attaché in London and had taken early retirement from the navy to become head of the Maritime Commission.

Land had a first-rate advertising man's facility with the language. In 1943 he produced the following for a short-lived quasi-holiday called National Maritime Day:

God gave us two ends to use.
One to think with!

One to sit with!
The war depends on which we choose.
Heads we win!
Tails we lose!

LAND PUT THE COGNOMEN *Liberty ship* into the ring against *Ugly Duckling*, and it won.

The ships were 441'6" long, 57 feet wide, and could carry 9,000 tons of cargo in their 5 holds, which is to say 440 light tanks packed in along with 2,840 jeeps as well as food, ammunition, and troops. With such a capacity, getting safely through a single voyage would pay for the $1.5 million ship.

The first, *Patrick Henry*, was laid down in Baltimore on the final day of April 1941, at the Bethlehem-Fairfield shipyard, which Bethlehem Steel had built in nine months. The *Patrick Henry* took shape on one of the yard's sixteen ways and went into the water on September 27. This was fast work, but out on the West Coast the second Liberty, the *Star of Oregon*, which had been laid down much later, was ready for service only one day after the *Patrick Henry*.

She had been built in the Portland yard of Henry Kaiser, who would come to dominate the largest shipbuilding program in history. A stocky, energetic man just shy of sixty, Kaiser didn't know anything about ships when he started making them, but he knew a great deal about organizing huge projects, and no prospective job seems ever to have daunted him.

Above all he was a salesman. Jesse Jones, head of Roosevelt's Reconstruction Finance Corporation, once told him, "I don't want you to deal with anyone around here but me. You'd talk them out of their watches, and when I'd ask them about it, they'd say, 'See, he talked me out of my watch, isn't that wonderful?'" He'd been talking people out of watches since he was a teenager in upstate New York. He owned his own photography business by the time he was twenty, but left it when his prospective father-in-law demanded that his daughter's suitor earn $125 per week. Kaiser went west. He got involved in a Seattle hardware concern, then took up what he modestly termed "the sand and gravel business," which meant building highways. By 1931 he was so solidly established that he bid in one of the main contracts for building the Boulder Dam, then went on to do the same with the Grand Coulee Dam and the San Francisco–Oakland Bay Bridge. Kaiser had a shipyard up and running in Seattle by the time the British Shipbuilding Mission arrived. It was relatively small, but that he had built it and got it working in eleven months impressed the commission members. So did Kaiser's bluster, or what would have been bluster if he hadn't had real muscle behind it. "Give me the backing," he told Cyril Thompson, the commission's head, "and I'll build you two hundred ships during 1942."

"Kaiser went about the task in a big way," Thompson wrote later. "First he hired a vast flood of workers; there were 12,000,000 unemployed in America in the early days. Many of the newcomers not only had a high degree of intelligence, but had mechanical aptitude as well. That explains why Americans were able to build up a vast shipbuilding industry in such a short time, practically from nothing. . . . By 1942 two of Kaiser's yards alone employed more workers than the whole of Britain's shipbuilding industry." Kaiser acquired his workforce and their tools with a swashbuckling, high-hearted rapacity. At a time when established industry managers had not quite grasped the scope of what was being asked them and moved cautiously, Kaiser waded right in—it was cost plus, after all—and seized every derrick and bulldozer he could find. He infuriated competitors by paying wages high enough to lure skilled workers away to fill unskilled slots. He hired people before he had anything to put them to work on. It was all terribly extravagant, but as one of FDR's economic advisers, Eliot Janeway, put it, Kaiser succeeded by "instinctively grasping Roosevelt's rule that energy was more efficient than efficiency."

Eighteen different yards built Liberty ships, but Kaiser's were by far the most productive. Since the first European settlement, the East Coast had been the heart of American shipbuilding, and even in 1941 it was responsible for more than two-thirds of the ships produced in the United States. Two years later the West Coast was launching more tonnage than any other region. Henry Kaiser was largely responsible for the shift.

He set up an assembly line that imitated an automaking plant on a statewide level. Chunks of ships were fabricated hundreds of miles apart, brought together at the yard on flatcars, and swung into place at the last minute. As important, Kaiser welded his hulls rather than riveting them, which was how ships had been built ever since metal hulls replaced wooden ones. But trained riveters were scarce, and welding was much faster. He built ships in months, then weeks, and finally days. The *Robert E. Peary* was laid down in Kaiser's No. 2 Yard, in Richmond, California, on November 8, 1942, and the hull assembled from 250-ton prefabricated sections that same day. On the ninth the upperworks and deck went in, and on the tenth the masts and booms were planted and the wiring strung. The ship was launched on the twelfth: four days, fifteen hours, and twenty-nine minutes. This was something of a stunt, but the *Peary* saw a war's worth of service and stayed afloat until she was scrapped in 1963.

In 1944 Warner Bros. put out a cartoon called "The Weakly Report." It is a drearily mild parody of newsreels about wartime conditions (food rationing: a customer in a butcher shop orders a porterhouse, then pays to sniff it before it's whisked back into the meat locker), but one scene has a bit of snap. It shows a bunting-draped platform on which a woman waits holding a bottle of champagne next to an official in a top hat. Clearly a ship is to be launched, but no ship is there, nothing but sky and sea beyond the empty ways. The woman mentions this, and the official shakes his head impatiently. "Just start swinging, lady." She does, and the ship has materialized in time for the bottle to break against its bow.

ONCE LAUNCHED, A LIBERTY ship was turned over to a private shipping company, which oversaw its loading, while the seaman's union hiring hall supplied the crew.

This simply stated arrangement was infinitely complex in its ramifications. When the popular New York City sports reporter Tom O'Reilly sought duty as a purser aboard a Liberty, he was introduced to a shipping-line official who explained it to him: "'O'Reilly, the shipping business is very simple. It runs smoothly—in jerks.' He then pointed out that the Liberty ship I was to join would be owned by the War Shipping Administration, operated by the American South African Line, Inc., carry a cargo for the United States Army, sail under strict control of the United States Navy, while at the same time being governed by the rules of the Maritime Commission, the United States Customs Authority, the National Maritime Union, the Masters, Mates, and Pilots Association, the Marine Engineers' Beneficial Society, and other unions."

In the very rarefaction of his profession, O'Reilly might be said to be a typical member of a merchant crew. The men came aboard the ships from everywhere, and for every reason, some of them valuable old hands, many, like O'Reilly, new to the sea.

After December 7, he said, "slowly, but inexorably, the sports figures began to disappear and I found myself feeling somewhat superfluous." Unlike most merchant mariners, O'Reilly was able to deplore his situation with "Mr. John J. Farrell, a sportsman who also happens to be one of the owners of the American South African Steamship Line, Inc." Farrell asked him if he could add, and "since I once got the result of a Washington, D.C., football game that had ended in a 73-0 score into the paper correctly, I replied in the affirmative." When O'Reilly nodded yes to the only other question in this job interview—"Can you typewrite?"—Farrell said that was all O'Reilly needed to know to be a purser.

O'Reilly reported to the Bureau of Marine Inspection and Navigation, where "I was sworn in and given a certificate of registry as a staff officer on vessels of the United States Merchant Marine. This sounded absolutely wonderful until I looked at my title. I was listed as a 'junior assistant purser,' an appellation that couldn't have sounded any lower if they had called me 'subnovice orderly.'" Nevertheless, even though in the steamship offices his job—managing payroll and paperwork—was referred to as "ship's clerk," he was an officer. After all, "John Paul Jones had started his sea career as a ship's clerk. Who knows? Ships have been named after him."

O'Reilly picked up his ship in a Baltimore drydock. Censorship regulations prevented him from mentioning her name in his account, but of course she looked like every other Liberty ship, which was, as the president had pointed out, not much. Also, this one had already paid for herself: built six months earlier, she had completed a voyage and grime from the cargo of coal she'd carried still streaked her sides. Welders on her deck crouched in their Aztec masks over the crackling blue-white flames of acetylene torches.

O'Reilly got a perfectly representative first glimpse of a Liberty ship and, when the men assembled in the officers' mess to sign the ship's articles, of its crew: "There were serious sailors and screwballs, gay buckos and dullards, veteran 'shellbacks who'd turned the Horn in sail' and kids fresh from the plow. Some would have been here even if the world were at peace. Others were making a pretty tough decision." Later, after a liberty down in the Canal Zone, the captain said that in fact his company was a little out of the ordinary. "You know, O'Reilly, we've got a damned good crew on here. They spent eight hundred in ten hours and didn't pull a single knife."

The merchant seamen would have had more to spend than their navy counterparts. Years later an Armed Guard veteran still remembered the difference. In 1942, he said, a seaman on a merchant ship got "$100 a month, 100% bonus, war zone $15 per day, and an air raid allowance of $150 for each port." A navy sailor "received $56 a month and 10% sea pay." Yet the navy offered things the merchant service didn't: retirement benefits, free uniforms and medical care, and all the intangibles conferred by being part of a highly ordered tradition that went back to the birth of the republic.

As against that, the merchant service had a strain of democracy that would not extend to the navy for some years. There, black sailors were almost always eligible solely for mess duty. In the merchant marine, they held every job right up to captain. This was obliquely reflected by eighteen Liberty ships being named for African-Americans. At least two of them were manned by all-black crews. When the *Frederick Douglass,* westbound to New York, was torpedoed and sunk, every man aboard got off safely, and so did one woman, the twenty-three-year-old Domillie James, of 23 Oxford Street, Bristol, England, who was said to be "very pretty." A British rescue ship took the survivors to Halifax, where the Royal Canadian Navy report mentioned that Domillie James was "coloured," and that "she said she boarded the ship on Sunday 12 September whilst the [gangway] watch 'was seeking shelter from the rain.' Alleged that the ship's bosun Jerome Davis [who can scarcely have believed his luck], had aided and abetted her hiding on board." The report concluded, "It may be of interest to note that the majority of the ship's crew including the master, are coloured."

Black, white, navy, merchant, they ran the same risks, and, they felt, more of them on the Liberty ships. That swift, thrifty welding sometimes failed in small ways, and sometimes in large ones. Robert Ruark remembered a fellow Armed Guard lieutenant telling him, "And when my coxswain woke me up, he said, 'Excuse me for bothering you, sir, but the ship just broke in two.'"

It didn't happen often, but it didn't have to in order to make a strong impression on the men whose lives depended on those welds holding. They talked about it a lot on O'Reilly's ship. "There is the theory that a welded ship, once broken, gets a tear in her side, like the run in a lady's silk stocking." During a meal, one of the officers inquired whether the meat had been "cooked or welded."

Welding failures tended to happen in the chill of far northern waters, where the Liberties had to go to bring supplies to the Russian ports of Murmansk, Archangel, and Molotovsk. The Murmansk run, up around Norway to the arctic circle, exposed the convoys to every German war machine save trench mortars: planes out of occupied Norway, surface ships (and not just raiders; the battleship *Tirpitz* was in one of those fjords), lots of submarines.

The ships putting out from Reykjavik on the fifteen-hundred-mile journey to Murmansk got the worst of a wilderness where every drop of spray had a blade in it and the ice could form on the upperworks so thickly that the ship capsized.

There was a wild unreality to those arctic voyages. The fully laden ships were given another tier of cargo, and their decks became a Hooverville of wooden crates, some of them eight feet high and ten long. Ships' carpenters knocked together ladders and bridges between them, over which the Armed Guard would slip and scramble on their way to the guns. Sometimes their antiaircraft fire would be joined by the machine guns mounted on the turrets of tanks lashed down amid the jumble of crating. Sometimes it was always dark, sometimes it never was. The sea was always cold, but in the winter it was as quickly lethal as burning oil to anyone cast into it.

Arctic service may have been the grimmest sea duty the war had to offer, but the Liberties went everywhere. Tom O'Reilly ended up steaming thirty-six thousand miles, around both capes and through the Suez Canal to Cairo before he got home to Wee-hawken.

There was danger to spare in any sea, but Atlantic duty was different. The Japanese believed the targets of their warships should be other warships. Doenitz aimed for commerce and only commerce. His captains avoided destroyers whenever they could, but were willing to give their lives going after a freighter and especially a tanker.

American sailors called tankers "floating firecrackers," but they went out on them all through the war. So, too, with the Liberty ships, and all the rest of the merchant fleet. However abundantly America built the freighters and tankers, there were always enough sailors to man them: fifty-five thousand in 1941, and close on a quarter million in 1945.

Coming back from one of the arctic voyages, Lieutenant (j.g.) Blake Hughes, commanding the Armed Guard on the inaugural Liberty ship *Patrick Henry,* sent this in to headquarters: "I want to preface this report of our return voyage from Archangel with a tribute to the 23 men under my command, none of whom, with the exception of the coxswain, had even been to sea before, and none of whom had previously been in action. . . . At the close of the first day of attack . . . when 25 per cent of our ships had been destroyed by submarines and 60 to 70 Heinkel and Focke-Wulf planes, and while we were still at general quarters, I received the following message by phone at my station on the flying bridge: *All the men would like you to know, sir, that their spirits are high and that they are ready for the enemy.* With the picture of a near-by ship completely pulverized in a horrible explosion a few minutes before still before me, I thought these were the most courageous words I ever heard."

Lieutenant Hughes was speaking officially, and for the record. On the eve of his world tour, O'Reilly heard the same story, less formally expressed. He'd been talking with Savannah, the ship's chief cook, and asked him the name of the last ship that had paid him off.

"I wasn't paid off," Savannah said, "I was knocked off. A light we thought was on the Baltimore lightship was on a sub. Eight of us got into a lifeboat an' they all died but me. It was January, an' cold. I swore I'd never go out again, but here I am."

A Visit to the Ship Cemetery

Desperate times on the Eastern seaboard, 1943

One day in June 1942, Lieutenant Carl Ossman, training for Armed Guard duty, was standing in the chow line when a classmate came up waving a copy of the local newspaper. It contained the text of Roosevelt's most recent fireside chat, in which the president happily reported that Americans were now building ships faster than the Germans could sink them. "You can imagine," said Ossman, "the feelings of us who were getting ready to report to those sinkable merchant ships."

If Lieutenant Ossman did not love this strategy, neither did Admiral King. A month before FDR's broadcast, King had issued a memorandum throughout the Navy Department:

> Subject: Combatting the Submarine Menace—
> Building Merchant Ships vs Building Anti-Submarine Craft.

1. It is desired that "all hands" take note of the alternatives posed in the following questions:

   "Shall we continue to try to build merchant ships faster than enemy submarines can sink them?

or,

> Shall we build anti-submarine craft of such character and
> in such numbers that we can sink submarines faster than
> the enemy can build them!"

2.   The answer appears obvious . . .

King would prefer to build ships that could sink submarines
rather than supply more targets. But even this determined man
could not force the immediate construction of escorts. Priorities kept shifting: merchantmen got first call, then, later, landing
craft.

Still, new escort vessels were beginning to appear. Among the
first were PCs—patrol craft—173 feet long, and with real teeth: a
three-inch gun and depth charges. They were handsome ships,
but small ("Don't call my friggin' boat a friggin' boat," a sailor
aboard one of them expostulated) and not suited for midocean
work. The historian Richard M. Ketchum, who spent the war on
a PC, remembered, "You didn't want to be shot at with a *rifle*
aboard one of those." Of course they were immediately pressed
into duties beyond their intended capabilities. So were a lot of
other vessels during those harried months.

One of the first of many civilian ships the navy took in was the
yacht *Alva*, built in 1931 by the Krupp works at Kiel for William
K. Vanderbilt II, who gave her to the government a month before
Pearl Harbor. Half a year later she emerged from the Norfolk
Navy Yard as *PG* (patrol gunboat) *57,* the USS *Plymouth*. She had
nothing to do with the Hooligan Navy. Two hundred and seventy feet long, with a crew of 155, *PG-57* mounted a four-inch
and two three-inch guns. The morning after he came aboard,
her first captain, waking up in his stateroom, spotted a cluster
of buttons in the bulkhead next to his bed. Sleepily curious, he
pushed one. Chiming and tinkling, there slid out of the paneling

an emissary from another world: a shelf of shining barware and decanters filled with liquor. Other millionaires gave over their yachts—Henry Ford, Huntington Hartford, Arthur Lehman, Mrs. Jesse Ball duPont—and in the meantime Admiral Andrews was scouring the Eastern seaboard for anything that could possibly inconvenience a submarine.

In early July of 1942 Ensign Ellis Sard, aboard the minesweeper *Fulmar* off Portland, Maine, received a blinker message: he was hereby detached to take command of *YP-438*. Sard, a recent Harvard graduate (who, according to a colleague of mine who knew him, looked "exactly like Robert Mitchum"), had been in the navy for just over a year; he was twenty-five years old. "The braid on my cap was salty green, and in my pocket were orders taking me to Boston and my first command."

Sard found his new command undergoing conversion in a forlorn, third-rate shipyard. She was a 120-foot long, 130-ton fishing boat. Her masts and rigging had been stripped away and lay around her "like the guts of a dead cat." All that remained of her motive power was the Atlas diesel engine that had been born with her, in 1906. A chief in the yard offered some consolation: "She used to be a beautiful two-masted schooner, and when we get through with her, she'll be seaworthy enough." Then he added, "That's what happens when politicians demand ships out of thin air. They wouldn't give us the money when we needed it."

The conversion of the yard-patrol vessel went forward: three 20mm guns came aboard, and depth-charge racks were set up in the stern. They held four depth charges, two each. A crew of eight arrived—one too few to man the twenties.

Sard's ship underwent her dock trials in late September. He found that the *YP-438* could cruise at eight knots with a flank speed of maybe ten. The navy accepted the YP from the yard, and Captain Sard took her out under his command for the first time. A few days later, with four new men bringing his crew to "a grand total of twelve," they ran down the south shore of Boston and put on speed to drop their first depth charge. "We went to general quarters, and the YP shivered and shook with the unaccustomed exertion. The depth charge dropped and went off with a violent thud. As if from fright, the engine broke down immediately, and the heads overflowed."

The motor mechanic (the YP didn't rate anything as lofty as an engineer), a Minnesota Swede named Hansen, explained, "There are things, sir, I'm afraid you can't do if the engine is to keep running."

"Such as."

"Don't drop no more depth charges."

Hansen's repairs got them to Provincetown Harbor, there to be greeted by a full hurricane, which left Sard no choice but to cut the anchor cable (the ship was too fragile to raise its largest anchor) and run before it. Fortunately the engine had recovered from the affront of the depth charge and kept clattering gamely away throughout the ordeal.

The storm bought them a week of repairs in the yard, then *YP-438* was ordered to New York. The engine broke down. Hansen said he could keep it going for three hours at a time. The YP stuttered its way to New York, where Sard was sent to 90 Church Street, headquarters of the Eastern Sea Frontier. A commander told him, "Thirty of these ships have come through New York, and every one of them has come through in miserable condition." Sard said everything was fine except the engine.

"Goddammit, Captain, how do you sail with a ship in that condition? You're the commanding officer, and it's your responsibility to see that things are right." Then the commander relented: "I know you have little choice in the matter, but every damn one of these ships has been a waste of money. This time I'm really going to raise hell and see that you get fixed up."

And he did. The Atlas came apart and every piece was put

to rights, burnished, refurbished, new parts cut when old ones proved beyond repair. At last the engine was reassembled and fired up. It wouldn't start. "Somebody laughed out of sheer discouragement, and Hansen went berserk. He yelled, screamed, and brandished a kitchen cleaver. The crew subdued him and he was led off to a hospital in a straitjacket. This willing and capable man had simply been driven mad by a crazy demon of an old diesel." They got another mechanic.

Now came sailing orders: THERE IS A POSSIBILITY OF ENEMY SUBMARINE AND MINE ACTIVITY ALONG THE ATLANTIC COAST X DESTROY ENEMY FORCES EXCOUNTERED X WHEN FULLY PREPARED FOR SEA PROCEED COASTWISE WITHOUT DELAY TO MIAMI.

"Destroy enemy forces." A couple of months earlier *YP-389*, another Boston fishing boat, had encountered a submarine. Disdaining to squander a torpedo on such a target, the German stood out of range of the YP's 30mms (over its captain's protests, it had put to sea with its three-inch gun broken; orders were orders) and sank it with the U-boat's cannon.

Sard headed south inspirited by a small miracle: after leaving Norfolk "the YP had for the first time in her history run twenty-four hours without a breakdown." But this brought them to a somber place. "There is a buoy south of Hatteras, which we picked up in midmorning. It marked the start of the wreck area," where the U-boats had been busy. "We passed our first wreck . . . then another, then another. Surely a sunken ship is as sad as any of the sad sights of war. It is not spectacular the way a devastated city is, or as gruesome as a pile of corpses, but it brings a melancholy chill. The masts of the wrecks poked above water with maybe one spar bobbing loose; there was no wreckage or oil visible, and only rarely did a hull show above the surface. It was quiet and sad, and a little spooky. If you ever need proof that a ship is a living thing, look at a sunken one."

Now the breakdowns started again, and an ugly cross sea

began to work apart the planks in the hull. Water flowed in, and the YP won several weeks in a yard at Charleston. Then on south, the engine racketing itself toward extinction, which overtook it at Fort Lauderdale. Sard signaled for a tow. A boat came and they passed it a line, only to get pulled onto the rocks of a submerged breakwater. The tide began to run out. Another boat arrived and stood by while Sard and his men handed across the ship's logs and as much equipment as they could: the guns, the depth-charge racks. The cook, seawater sloshing about his ankles, took a roast from the oven and brought it to the bridge. The captain and crew had their last meal aboard. By the next morning, the *YP-438* had disappeared.

So went out Captain Sard's year, and his nation's. Between July, when he got his orders to take over his new command, and December, Doenitz's men had sunk 524 ships.

"Sighted Sub . . ."

A little good news, 1943

During his long, patient courtship of America, Churchill liked to quote the last line of a poem called (after its first line) "Say Not the Struggle Naught Availeth" by Arthur Hugh Clough: "But westward, look, the land is bright."

In the context of 1940 Churchill meant it more literally than the poet had. To the prime minister, the land west across the ocean was bright with factories, money, energy, an inexhaustible supply of potential soldiers. Clough, writing a century earlier, had been speaking of how things can change before our perception of them does. While waves continue what seems their weary, futile nibbling at the shore,

> *Far back, through creeks and inlets making,*
> *Comes silent flooding in, the main,*
> *And not by eastern windows only,*
> *When daylight comes, comes in the light;*
> *In front, the sun climbs slow, how slowly,*
> *But westward, look, the land is bright.*

As the dark year of 1942 waned, even as the disintegrating
YP-438 picked its way through spars and funnels off Hatteras,
the Allied sky was growing imperceptibly brighter. Ten thousand
miles away from the smoking shores of Florida and the Carolinas, navy airmen had broken, for the first time, the Japanese
advance across the Pacific. At Stalingrad, the furnace that consumed two million lives was about to shut down with the capitu-
lation of ninety thousand German troops.

There would be no Midway, no great surrender, in the Atlantic. But little by little, we were learning what to do about U-boats.

In the spring, convoys of a sort began to operate along
the East Coast. Their extemporized nature is suggested in the
name Admiral Andrews gave to them: bucket brigades. Twenty
or thirty ships would assemble at a port and, setting out in the
early morning, scuttle in company, guarded by whatever might
be at hand, to another port a day's steaming away. Much of the
Atlantic coast north of Hatteras is punctuated by good harbors
every hundred miles or so, and the ships would spend the night
in these, protected by booms and netting and minefields.

As the year progressed, the operations got more elaborate,
culminating in the Interlocking Convoy System, which ran from
Guantánamo to Halifax under guidelines laid down by the navy
in April: "As a result of experience in the north Atlantic it now
appears that the minimum strength that will afford reasonable
protection is five escorts per convoy of 40 or 50 ships, of which
all should make 18 knots (the maximum at which sound gear is
usable), and be equipped with sound and depth charges, and two
should be destroyers to permit ranging to the flanks and astern
and rejoining without waste of time."

If there were many good reasons why escort vessels couldn't
be whistled up, there were few to explain what remains one of
the strangest aspects of the U-boat war. Those city lights that
amazed and fascinated Hardegan and Cremer on their first

The peril: one of Admiral Doenitz's "excellent" Type VII U-boats on the prowl during a war patrol in rough North Atlantic waters. The Esso tanker *R. P. Resor* (*below*), her back broken, burns five miles off the New Jersey coast in February 1942, not long after German submarines arrived off American shores. Only two of her crew survived.

The four-stacker destroyer USS *Toucey* puts on speed (*top*). Built for service in World War I, she was identical to the fifty ships Roosevelt turned over to Great Britain in 1940. Two newly created warships of the "Hooligan Navy" (*center*) do their best to look martial. The Oregon Shipbuilding Corporation (*above*)—shown here with nearly twenty Liberty ships in various stages of their swift construction—was part of the tremendous industrial response to the crisis: this Portland yard alone turned out over one thousand ships during the war.

A convoy (*top*) steams east across the Atlantic late in 1942. Soon, destroyer escorts would be helping guard the freighters and tankers. DE 150 (*below*), the USS *Neunzer,* slides down the ways at the Consolidated yards in the spring of 1943.

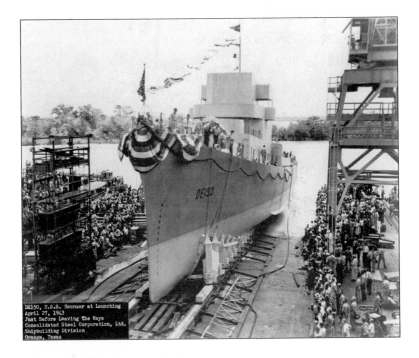

DE150, U.S.S. Neunzer at Launching
April 27, 1943
Just Before Leaving The Ways
Consolidated Steel Corporation, Ltd.
Shipbuilding Division
Orange, Texas

The officers of the *Neunzer*: Lieutenant R. B. Snow sits in the right fore-ground of the photograph, which is surrounded by some of the letters he wrote his wife, Emma. The sketch at the lower right shows the ship's bridge. *(Author's collection.)*

CVEs like the USS *Santee* (*top*) were budget aircraft carriers built on merchant hulls: the *Santee* began life as an Esso tanker. These "baby flattops" helped give the Allies a decisive advantage in the Atlantic. One of their crewmen, Lawrence Britton (*center*) of the USS *Nassau*, embodies the unending vigilance that was at the heart of all war steaming. Among the many technological innovations Germany brought to the fight were acoustic homing torpedoes; Lieutenant Snow offered the suggestion (*above*) on how to distract them from their targets. He was told it reached FDR's desk. (*Author's collection.*)

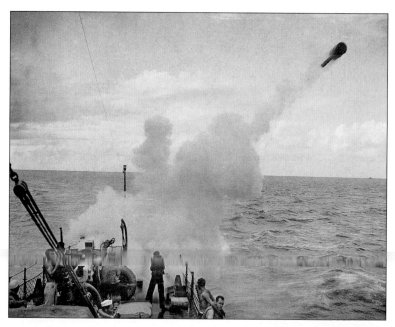

A PC on convoy duty fires a depth charge from one of her K-guns (*top*).
Sailors of the big Treasury-class Coast Guard cutter *Spencer* (*above*) stand
between the depth charge racks at the ship's stern watching one of the first
explosions in an action that destroyed the *U-175* on April 17, 1943.

Casualties: The USS *Fiske,* DE-143, splits in half after being torpedoed off Casablanca on August 2, 1944 (*top*). Crewmen can be seen making their way across the severed bow section, which lies almost on its side. The last moments of the *U-118* (*above*). Planes from the escort carrier *Bogue* sighted the submarine on June 12, 1943, and sank it with depth charges.

Jubilant sailors (*top*) from the destroyer escort *Pillsbury* swarm the deck of the captured *U-505* on June 4, 1944. It is touch and go whether they will be able to keep their prize afloat, but they'll succeed, and the *U-505*'s last voyage will end at the Chicago Museum of Science and Industry. Type XXIs (*above*) lie, battered by incessant air raids, in a shipyard at war's end. The big, fast boats could have made real trouble for the Allies, but they came too late to help Germany.

American voyages just kept burning. In the disorderly process of a democracy going to war, it turned out that nobody had the authority to make the mayor of Atlantic City darken his town. Admiral Andrews begged municipalities to institute blackouts and was told, in effect, fat chance. The town fathers of Miami indignantly stated that it would discourage tourists and be bad for business. Why a darkened marquee on the Frolic Club or the Chez Paree would dispirit vacationers more than morning strolls past oil-sodden corpses on beaches was never explained. In the end, it took a columnist in the *Miami Daily News* to prod his neighbors into doing something about what had become a national disgrace. On July 12 Jack Kofoed's article began, "It seems that no small number of people in our town fail to comprehend that the war is at our doorsteps. There have been ships torpedoed within a few miles of the beach hotels. All of us have seen members of the crews in our streets. It has been pointed out that the lume [a nice word that Kofoed seems to have invented] for the city lights offers an excellent background for predatory submarines. Everyone knows that the ships silhouetted by that lume are vital to our national welfare." Where Admiral Andrews was helpless, Kofoed did the job, and eight months after Pearl Harbor, Miami went dark.

Escort vessels may have been scarce, but for antisubmarine work airplanes were scarcer still. This was largely the result of the severe growing pains that afflicted the flying machine between the wars, which had put the services at one another's throats in an obstreperous rivalry that Congress tried to settle by giving the army and the navy separate and independent air arms.

This meant that the navy was responsible for all planes that flew off ships, the army for all that took off from land. It was simple. It was simplistic. What about that place where land and water meet? The navy wanted its own long-range, land-based aircraft to patrol for submarines. No, the army sulkily replied, if the plane touches solid ground, it belongs to us. If the navy wanted long-range patrols, it should build seaplanes.

The navy started to, but didn't have nearly enough of them by the time Doenitz arrived. King asked the Army Air Force for help. It came, grudgingly of course, in the form of eighty-four—and, eventually, three hundred—medium bombers. The army kept control of them, but the army airmen didn't like the job. They would far rather have been walking on flak over Bremen than spending hour upon hour over the unvarying flatness and almost unvarying eventlessness of the sea. Eventually King's persistence and army boredom worked to transfer the land-based coastal planes to the navy.

An airplane—a navy airplane, a land-based one—got the first U-boat to be sunk by Americans. The plane was a Lockheed Hudson, one of a Lend-Lease order for two hundred light bombers won by the Lockheed Aircraft Corporation. As the Atlantic campaign intensified, the U.S. navy managed to pry loose twenty of them for Patrol Squadron 82, based in Newfoundland.

On March 1, 1942, Ensign William Trepuni, flying out of Argentia, spotted a submarine. It was crash-diving, but Trepuni dove faster and dropped depth charges. Circling the roiled water, he saw a spreading oil slick and fragments of decking. This was enough to justify claiming a kill, and he did. Captured German records confirmed it after the war: *U-656*, on her second voyage, and never having sunk anything, was lost with all her crew.

Two weeks later another pilot in Trepuni's squadron, Donald Francis Mason, came upon *U-503* and destroyed it. Any airman would have been pleased with this outcome, but Mason had a particularly pressing reason to hope for it.

He had been famous for a month and a half. On January 18, patrolling in his PBY—a Catalina flying boat—he had seen something and dropped two bombs on it. He reported this incident in a phrase that the *New York Times* immediately compared to Commodore Perry's on Lake Erie during the War of 1812 ("We have met the enemy, and they are ours"), and which still rattles around in the national consciousness: "Sighted sub. Sank same." (The fatalists of the Naval Armed Guard immediately adopted a paraphrase: "Sighted sub. Glub. Glub.") It soon became clear, though, that whatever Mason may have sighted, he sank nothing.

The navy was so desperate for good news just then that it is still widely reported that the service's propagandists had invented the message. But Mason really did radio his quartet of exultant sibilants.

Now, though, he had actually sunk same, and soon an American ship would be able to make the claim as well. The USS *Roper*, a four-stacker launched in the summer of 1918, was turned over to Admiral Andrews for duty on the Eastern Sea Frontier in early March and had spent an increasingly frustrating month steaming through lakes of oil bled by dying tankers and past the corpses of American sailors kept pointlessly afloat by their life jackets.

The captain, Hamilton W. Howe, had the crew at general quarters almost constantly for five days straight. They were not at their battle stations on the evening of April 13, but those days of wearing vigil added to the volatile brew of ferocity and buck fever that annihilated the crew of *U-85*.

Captain Eberhardt Gregor, on his fourth war patrol, had sunk the Swedish freighter *Christina Knudson* off New Jersey three nights earlier and was waiting in the moonless dark off Cape Hatteras with only a hundred feet of water beneath the keel of his Type VII when the *Roper* found him just after midnight. Knowing his boat would be an easy target at such a shallow depth, Gregor tried to run for deeper water. Despite the darkness, the sea was phosphorescent and the lookouts of the *Roper* could see their quarry's wake from two thousand yards away. Captain Howe followed the cool glow at twenty knots, but he was not convinced that he was closing on a submarine until a torpedo cut past along the destroyer's port side.

Howe ordered general quarters and ten minutes later was close enough to use the twenty-four-inch searchlight on the *Roper*'s flying bridge. There was the *U-85*, three hundred yards away and swinging to starboard. "Open fire!" But nobody did, the crew apparently frozen now that the invisible thing they had been pursuing for so long was there before them, astonishingly tangible in the chalky glare. Finally a chief got one of the fifties working. Men were coming out of the submarine's conning tower, and some fell. Were the others going for the deck gun? The *Roper* carried five three-inch guns, and all of them were dumb. Four of them would remain so: their excited crews had fired before the shells were loaded, producing the same effect as if a dud round had hung fire in the barrel. All four crews, incredibly, followed the prudent peacetime drill of waiting ten minutes before cracking the breach, while their muzzles stayed canted up toward the black sky. Only Boatswain's Mate Harry Heyman, captain of gun No. 5, had not prematurely fired, and now he called, "Ready, sir!" His men loaded an armor-piercing shell and shot it. A flash showed a hit on the conning tower. Heyman fired again, and the submarine was down by the stern, its crew tumbling into the water.

The *Roper* headed toward the struggling men. "Please!" they called as she approached. *"Bitte!"* She was in among them. One of the German sailors scrabbled at her hull, pleading. The destroyer released depth charges where the submarine had been. Eleven of them rolled down the rails into the water, and every German who saw them splash off the stern knew that he had only seconds to live.

The *Roper* stood by until daybreak, dropped more gratuitous depth charges, then set about fishing the German dead—there were no survivors—out of the water. They were piled on deck amidships and a tarpaulin put over them to discourage the souvenir hunting that had begun.

The *Roper* transferred the corpses to a navy tug, which took them to Portsmouth, Virginia. Neither the town nor the naval hospital there had enough coffins, but the Veterans Administration provided twenty-nine at a cost of $1,193.55, and the German sailors were buried with military honors at the National Cemetery in Hampton. Their graves are still there.

An American ship had indisputably sunk a submarine, and of course that was good news. But despite this four-stacker having been taken out of mothballs and put back to work as early as 1930, her victory has a feel of amateurism. It is most obvious in those impotent guns but has more to it than that. The *U-85* went down in water shallow enough for divers to go inside the boat and study mechanical details, perhaps even get coding material. There could have been at least twenty-nine crewmen to interrogate. But the crew was mute, and their boat had been so thoroughly mauled after it ceased to offer any threat that its secrets were forever sealed in it. Today it is a highly popular objective for sports divers, who have paid it thousands of visits over the years. One of them was Homer Hickham, who understood what he was looking at, because he is also a historian and the author of *Torpedo Junction*, a thorough history of Doenitz's East Coast campaign. He had no trouble identifying the G-7 torpedo that still lies on the wreck. But neither Hickham nor the navy divers sent down that spring, or anyone else, has ever been able to venture inside.

Well, sure, there was amateurism. We were amateurs. Doenitz had been training his men to the strictest standards for years in a discipline he had done much to invent. King had to whistle up a whole navy-within-a-navy in a few months. The ships were almost ready. Once launched, though, they'd be set to waging a highly specialized campaign, and they would need a lot of specialists to work them.

In the navy, institutions, like ships, get commissioned, as the Submarine Chasing Training Center was, on March 16, 1942, in Miami. The school, which, despite some carping from the Chamber of Commerce, took over a good stretch of the waterfront along with a dozen Biscayne Boulevard hotels, did far more to help win the war than its defiantly bright municipality had done to lose it.

The school's job was to teach its students how to fight submarines, and to run it a real destroyerman came in from the sea. Samuel Eliot Morison, the foremost historian of America's naval war, said that Commander Eugene F. McDaniel, whom he knew, was a lean, mean, thin-lipped officer whose eyes burned with hatred of the enemy and all his works, and whose heart glowed with devotion to the Navy, especially the antisubmarine part of it. Somewhat of the fanatical zeal of a seventeenth-century Scots Covenanter in his make-up; but a sense of organization and a natural teaching ability were there too."

He brought in some professional educators from the University of Chicago to help him get started, but he made sure that his teachers had, like him, hunted submarines and, after their instructional turn ashore, went back to hunt more. McDaniel's school opened with 50 students, but before long it was taking in 250 officers a week. This was what people have recently (and mercifully) begun to stop calling a 24-7 operation, and a new draft of officers arrived every Monday. Richard B. Snow got there in February 1943, and though he was often overwhelmed and sometimes miserable, my father was impressed and fascinated by Commander McDaniel. No matter how large his administrative duties grew, and the school was soon educating thousands, McDaniel always found time to teach. "Our commanding officer gave a long lecture on convoy duties yesterday," my father wrote my mother, "and he was corking—having seen a great deal of that duty on a fleet destroyer in the North Atlantic before he reluctantly left his ship to head the school here."

My father was a good fifteen years older than most of his classmates, but he had one thing in common with almost every other student in the school: a year or two earlier, the last thing he expected in life was to have Commander McDaniel teaching him how to keep a submarine away from a tanker.

How Lieutenant Snow
Got to Sea

A reserve officer's journey, 1943

★ ★ ★

Not everyone's father was an architect, not everyone's father had a single child long after he thought this an impossibility, not everyone's father remembered to his last days the words of a novelty song that begins "I run the old mill / Over there to Reubensville." But, if you will, take this man as your father, or uncle, or grandfather; or your aunt, or mother; or yourself. A person, that is, finding a path through life that, although thicketed with uncertainties, at least doesn't lead anywhere near gunfire. You may go broke, your best friend may sicken and die, you may be jilted, or fired, or insulted by your dry cleaner. But nobody is going to try to shoot you or drown you or burn you while you sleep. Well, the joke, every generation or so since the contentious world began, is on you.

My father had a yearning for the U.S. navy very early, but he didn't know it. Born in 1905 on the Stanford University campus, where his father was resident physician, one of his first memories was of being frantic with desire to go up to "the city" with his parents and brother to see "the Fleet." But he was too young.

"I was wild. They were leaving me behind! I didn't know what the Fleet was, but I had to get to it. I savored the word. I believe I imagined it as a delicious drink." It was the Great White Fleet, stopping by San Francisco in 1908 on the final leg of the circuit of the globe another navy-minded Roosevelt, Theodore, had ordered to show that the United States was open for business as a world power.

My father didn't get to see it, and that put an end to his naval ambitions for thirty-five years. His family came east; he grew up in Manhattan and entered Columbia College. He learned to play the violin, and during a summer studying the instrument at Fontainebleau in France, he met a tall, slender viola student named Emma Folger. After the decade-long rupture of their engagement, when they at last got married in the spring of 1941, they set up housekeeping in a nice apartment on East Ninety-seventh Street, and all was bright and happy and untroubled for a full nine months while the Great Depression gave its last bow and stepped aside to make way for something worse.

Emma Snow turned thirty-nine on December 7. "We had a very happy day," my father said. But midway through it, "we were sitting in our apartment and we were listening to a beautiful Philharmonic concert." An announcer broke in. "I said, 'Jesus Christ, this is Toscanini and they're interrupting—' That's how much of a naval officer I was. Pearl Harbor? I didn't know what the hell it was." The concert came back on, "but then, as we thought it over, we thought, this is serious."

Serious enough for him to seek out Martha Love, an old girlfriend from his architecture school days. She was now Martha McCagg, having married Louis McCagg, who was running the navy's District Security Office in Manhattan. "Their responsibility was to keep industrial production going, and to keep things from burning up or being dynamited. He needed technically minded people, and so Martha suggested, 'Why don't you go down and talk with Louis? He needs people that can read plans, that can make industrial analyses, that can make plan evaluations.'"

Louis McCagg couldn't have been more accommodating. He invited my father down to 90 Church Street, talked over the work that needed doing, and said that he could start as a civilian agent and then get a commission in the Naval Reserve.

That's just what happened. Before long my father was inspecting shipyards ("I'd never seen a shipyard before"), and when his naval commission came through, he inspected them in uniform. He spent his nights at home, he had time to keep a hand in his architecture practice, and sailors back from the North Atlantic convoy runs saluted him on the street.

He hated it. "In all my professional experience the thing I liked least is inspecting, because you're looking over other people's efforts, and presumably sometimes they knew what they were doing. I learned a lot, I saw a lot, it was serious work. But then when I began to do this work as a naval officer, not as a civilian agent, I began to feel, I'm riding up and down in the subway in a uniform; what kind of a way is this for a man my age to spend his life when we're really engaged in a war?"

He talked it over with his still new wife, who was far from enthusiastic, but who understood. He went back to Louis McCagg, who came from society, and had, as the phrase then went, friends in high places. So it was that among the thousand fleabites of his working day, Henry Stimson got to consider the momentous question of whether a Richard B. Snow, who knew a friend of a cousin or something, should get to go to sea.

First the would-be sailor had to pass a demanding correspondence course. He learned about towropes and spring lines and steam turbines and the rigging of ships from the days of sail. He had always had difficulty with math, and navigation was hard for him, but even in a profession that required good draftsmanship he drew exceptionally well, and he aced every part of the course that required illustration. His rendering of the Baldt Patent anchor was considered a particular masterpiece. He studied the tenth edition of *Knight's Modern Seamanship* until passages like this yielded up their secrets: "When the second anchor is let go 88.38 fathoms on the lee chain must be at the outboard lip of the hawse-pipe. The next shackle in the chain is at 95 fathoms. Therefore measure back (95 – 88.38) or 6.62 fathoms from the outboard lip of the lee hawse-pipe and make the mark on deck."

By early 1943 he knew as much about ships as you could without going on one. In February he was ordered south to Miami and the tutelage of Commander McDaniel.

"Thank you darling," he wrote in his first letter to my mother, on Valentine's Day, "for your patience in allowing me to chase after a new trade." He'd never been south, and he was surprised by everything he found in Florida. "I had foolishly pictured it as barren and sandy—not at all! I have yet to see any really good architecture, and yet everything looks charming because it's dripping with greenery and brilliant color." He passed his blinker-code test and already felt enough of an old salt to write that he was in "a land where junior officers and ensigns swarm. A stripe and a half is quite respectable and anything above that is impressive! As opposed to the Third Naval District where ex-businessmen are running around in 2½ stripes without the faintest idea of what a bollard is."

They lived well down there—the Sub Chaser school became Miami's leading business and my father found himself put up in hotel suites and garden apartments—but McDaniel worked them hard: "I have not been very good about writing but we have been having a hell of a week. Last Tuesday afloat all morning doing practice antisubmarine runs. Wednesday all day piloting and navigation (this was very pleasant—we ran down to Key Largo and back on a YP which used to be somebody's very handsome yacht). All night Wednesday on antisubmarine patrol duty (the real thing, with very little sleep). Friday final examination in mooring board plotting, Saturday final examination in engineering and quizzes in anti sub warfare. Sunday a frightful navigation exam. Monday final exercises in seamanship and tomorrow, final examination in administration—All this, of course, in addition to the regular 8 full hours a day of classes and homework. What a job!" (Although he did find time to notice that "the girls in Miami all seem to have blond hair and sunburned legs on which they wear no stockings—very seductive. I have an idea that by and large they are of easy virtue, but that just may be wishful thinking—and anyway I wouldn't know anything about that.")

In early March he was "sworn in as Lieutenant, USNR (temporary, as all these appointments are, for the duration only) which is a great satisfaction, except for the fact that I do not know nearly as much as a lieutenant should. I hope I will be able to close that gap before I disgrace myself or run into a court martial!" This was a steady, ominous theme at the training center: "There is a continual fund of anecdotes from instructors here on the subject of improvident officers losing their commands, commissions, or liberty—such as 'Well, that got back to the Admiral—and there were a few draughts on that ship.' or 'He can consider himself lucky that he got off with a court-martial!' All good morale-building doctrine, and it's really amusing to see what the next version will be."

The course lasted eight weeks and only got tougher as it went along. In early April my father let out a cry of near despair—"This week has been another bitch. The way they load the examinations on here is a joke. This morning the seamanship dept, just before the ASW exam, the climax of the whole course here, decided it would be fun to throw in a little 50-question exam on the rules of the road—so they did—And the gunnery department thinks nothing of scheduling its only examination in the whole term the afternoon before. They've got us on the ropes."

But he made it through. One evening toward the end of the ordeal he and several other larval officers were standing on a pier when a vessel none of them had ever before seen materialized out of the twilight, nosing in toward them past the little YPs. "To us," he told me years later, "she looked like a battleship." It was the USS *Brennan*, DE-13, a destroyer escort.

The fact that the new ship struck him as enormous was a good indication of how urgently it was needed.

"It was a staggering, towering thing compared with what we were studying," he told me, "the little sporty ships that we were supposed to be practicing on. We didn't know. Nobody had told us in the courses, which were all taught from mimeograph things by guys who had been in the navy six months longer than we had, they didn't know what was going on. And then all of a sudden the whole scale of our operation changed."

The Smallest Major
War Vessel

Inventing the destroyer escort, 1942

First there was the snake—or eel—in Alfred Thayer Mahan's orderly garden of battleships. For a long time it stood to reason that the only thing likely to hurt a battleship at sea was another battleship. The torpedo buzzed in and spoiled that.

It was largely the invention of a British engineer named Alfred Whitehead. He built his first torpedo in 1866. It had an explosive at one end and a propeller at the other, but nobody knows exactly what it looked like because he was so anxiously protective of it that no plans survive. His anxiety was perfectly justified, for his plans *were* eventually stolen, by a German who was visiting his factory, but not before he had sold his device to the Royal Navy.

As soon as it became clear that this troublesome prodigy actually worked, nations began building ships to carry it within striking range of an enemy. These were, naturally, called torpedo boats, and beginning in 1890 the U.S. navy commissioned thirty-five of them within a decade.

Torpedo boats were lightly armed, but fast. Some of the first

generation of American ones could boil along at nearly thirty
knots. That meant that any vessel hoping to discourage them
would have to be equally fast and carry more and bigger guns.
The first American torpedo-boat destroyer—these new vessels
were named for their job—was the USS *Bainbridge,* launched in
1901: four hundred tons, a flank speed of twenty-eight knots,
two three-inch guns, five six-pounders, and for good measure
two torpedo tubes.

Fifteen years later the Great War was on, the torpedo boat
had learned how to sail underwater, and American destroyers
were averaging 1,150 tons and mounting twelve torpedo tubes
and four-inch guns. These ships had evolved beyond their original mission of chasing down torpedo boats, and that part fell
away from their name. They were just *destroyers* now.

The World War I four-stackers hunted submarines, but they
also scouted and screened the fleet, including battleships. With
the Davids now guarding the Goliaths, they inevitably grew bigger. No destroyers were laid down during the 1920s, but by 1935
forty-five new ones were on order, the largest of them eighteen-
hundred tonners with five-inch guns. These evolved into the
two-thousand-ton Fletcher class, which became the standard—
and a high one—for the navy during the latter part of the war.
They were fast and heavily armed, and expensive.

As the destroyers' capabilities expanded, so did the calls made
on them. There was no mystery about their scarcity along our
coasts in 1942. As Churchill had badgered Roosevelt, so did the
president badger King, who was doubtless irritated—or, being
King, infuriated—to receive in July a memo that said, "I still do
not understand the long delay in making all ships sail under
escort. I realize the problem of making up escorts for convoys
but . . . frankly, I think it has taken an unconscionable time to
get things going, and further I do not think that we are utilizing
a large number of escort vessels which could be used, especially

in the Summer time. We must speed things up and we must use the available tools even though they are not just what we would like to have."

"I am in entire accord with your view as to the advantages of escorted convoys," King's impressively temperate reply began. He reviewed the difficulties involved and said, "I have used vessels of every type and size that can keep up with the ships they guard. I have accepted the smallest vessels that give promise of a reasonable degree of protection." He ended by telling the president, "My goal—and I believe yours also—is to get every ship under escort. For this purpose we (the United States and Great Britain) need a very large number—roughly 1000—of seagoing escort vessels of DE or corvette type. I am doing my best to get them quickly."

What he was asking for was, put bluntly, a ship that was cheaper and weaker than a destroyer. But for the job it was to do, weakness wouldn't be such a disadvantage. The destroyer escort would not have armor thick as a destroyer's, it would have fewer guns, and it would be at least ten knots slower. But it would not have to slug it out with real destroyers; the German destroyers were gone. The destroyer escort was designed specifically to fight U-boats, and to cope with them it carried equipment the equal of that on any of its burly Fletcher-class big brothers.

Or, more accurately, *would* carry, because there weren't any DEs yet.

The destroyer escort program, said Secretary of the Navy Frank Knox, had been "all bitched up from the start." The start had been in the spring of 1940, when FDR told Knox that he wanted four experimental destroyer escorts of 750 to 900 tons. The Bureau of Ships, responsible for all building, buying, and fixing the navy's vessels, had plans drafted in three months, which was quick work, but work largely wasted because it turned out that a 775-ton DE would cost $4.7 million and carry only two five-inch guns. The Bureau of Ships came up with a better design, but it cost more: $6.8 million to a sixteen-hundred-ton destroyer's $8.1 million. FDR lost interest, and the navy stayed with the conventional destroyers.

Admiral Harold Stark, however, did not lose interest. He convened an informal board to consider how to make something between YPs and fleet destroyers. It recommended "fifty escort vessels for the sole purpose of protecting convoys against submarines and for use in the western part of the North Atlantic." The new plans still made for a feebler ship that cost almost as much as a real destroyer, but the yet-unborn DE kept a hold on life because the British got word of it and pushed for it to be built under Lend-Lease. They wanted one hundred of them.

Captain Edward L. Cochrane, in charge of the Preliminary Plans division of the Bureau of Ships, believed in the DE and brought to his belief the practical skills of a first-rate naval architect. He designed a 1,085-ton destroyer escort that would cost a little more than half as much as a destroyer. The five-inch guns became three-inch, the theoretical ship shed some of its more expensive features, and in the summer of 1941 FDR approved the building of fifty DEs, and the contracts were let that December.

Then came Pearl Harbor, and the pressure for Liberty ships, and landing craft, and the DE kept being jostled farther back down the line. It took the enterprise of Doenitz's captains to get them back on order, but by then pressure was on to build everything, and although there would, in time, be a great many DEs, all of them would be built in haste and on the cheap.

The DE shaped up as what my father liked to say, with a mixture of pride and irony, the navy classified as its "smallest major war vessel." At fourteen hundred tons, the largest of them was six hundred tons lighter than a Fletcher-class destroyer. They carried a crew of about two hundred—at least one hundred fewer than a destroyer—and, at twenty knots or so, they could move

maybe two-thirds its speed. But they were fast enough to over-
take U-boats on the surface, and agile enough to stay on top of
one when it was underwater. A destroyer had a turning circle
nearly nine hundred yards wide; a DE's was four hundred.

Once we decided we wanted them, we wanted a lot. What
with priorities, this meant the DE would be built out of spare
parts, by amateurs.

Take the matter of engines. American maritime tradition
held that steam alone was a ship's proper motive power. "Some
of the DEs were steam and had regular boilers and water tenders
and had to get steam up," my father remembered, "They were, of
course, the classy ones. You know, the Europeans—the Scandina-
vians, or the Germans in particular—thought a helluva a lot of
diesel, so it's always been chickenshit in our navy. Steam is what
we drive our ships with. So we had steam turbines with reduction
gear, steam turbines that drove generators, and the shafts were
turned by motors. And in diesel, there was diesel with reduction
gear, which we were. And there was also diesel electric. So there's
four basic power systems. They all got the same speed, they all
did the same chores, it was the darndest thing. Steam is more
difficult in a way, but it's classier. And the diesels—they were
not marine diesels. When you're saying *diesel* in a DE, you're not
talking about those big, deep, long diesels that drove the Scandinavian ships and the German ships all over the world, these
were railroad diesels." The six different classes would be differ-
entiated by the kind of power plant they contained. The Edsall
class—my father's—was driven by six-thousand-horsepower Fair-
banks Morse diesels.

The DE would closely follow Admiral King's injunction to
make do with whatever was at hand. The big stuff, the cruisers,
the battleships, were built like cathedrals, piece by piece, in such
long-established shipyards as the one at Mare Island, California. Mare Island was fully booked when the DE contracts came

through, but its directors remembered a hungry decade well enough not to be likely to turn away any business. Sure, they said, we'll build your destroyer escorts.

They decided to do it in a town eight hundred miles from the sea. Most of the residents of Denver, Colorado, had never seen an ocean, let alone an oceangoing ship. But, like Mare Island, they wanted the work. The shipyard sent men with blueprints, and a battle fleet began to take shape up there in the mountains.

They built the ships in segments, forty-ton LEGO blocks that would be snapped together hundreds of miles away. This method was picked up across the country as the program gathered momentum. Like Henry Kaiser's Liberties, they were welded. Women did a lot of this work, which came to be disparaged as "lipstick welding" by those who distrusted it; but it passed every test nature and the Germans could devise.

DEs were not unconventional ships, but they got built in unconventional ways. Someone in the Devoe yards in Bay City, Michigan (who may have remembered what everybody who has hung a ceiling light knows: working with your arms above your head is a pain), got the idea of making DEs upside down. Bill Devoe, whose father founded the yard and ran it during the war, said, "Since it was easier and faster to weld downwards, we saved very many hours at work, and our workmanship improved greatly. The process virtually eliminated ninety percent of all overhead welding." The ship lay on a cradle deckside down while the workers moved downward from the keel, fastening every piece of machinery that needed to hang overhead. That done, two semicircular steel arcs, looking like the trusses on a bridge that carried a nonsensical roller-coaster dip of roadway, clamped on to the hull and flipped it right side up so that engines and deckhouses and guns could be applied in the conventional manner.

The hulls made their way to the sea, occasionally across the breadth of the whole country. Some DEs built on the Great

Lakes went through a labyrinth of locks and rivers and canals to the Mississippi, where, their masts and propellers strapped to their decks for later installation and riding on pontoons that reduced their draft from thirteen to eight feet, they were floated down to the Gulf of Mexico.

In time, seventeen shipyards were building destroyer escorts, and doing it quickly. Bethlehem Steel's Hingham, Massachusetts, yard delivered ten DEs in a month and got one completed in four and a half days—more impressive, even, than Henry Kaiser's four-day Liberty-ship coup because these vessels were built to naval standards, which were stricter than those for freighters.

Some of the yards, such as Mare Island, were navy-owned, some were private, and a few were brand-new, built by the government to meet the current crisis. One of these was the Consolidated Steel Corporation building yard in Orange, Texas. That's where Lieutenant Snow was sent after he finished sub-chasing school, and it was not much like Miami.

LIEUTENANT EDWARD P. STAFFORD arrived in Orange to commission a destroyer escort a little less than a year after my father did. Consolidated was sending off a new DE every eight days when he got there, and five ships were under construction by the long wooden dock on the Sabine River. Cocooned in electrical cables and acetylene hoses, comic with banana-yellow priming paint, simmering in the smell of creosote rising from the dock and the coal smoke exhaled by the self-important little yard locomotives fretting their way along the tracks just ten feet inshore, the ships nonetheless looked great.

"It was obvious that when the tangle and mess of the yard were cleared away," wrote Stafford, "the DE would be beautiful in a clean-cut, deadly, efficient way. . . . The short, raked single stack just abaft the mast added a touch of dash. . . . The clean, straight sweep of the deck from the anchors at her high, sharp bow to the depth-charge racks low on her fantail and the ordered symmetry of her armament made her as graceful as a yacht. Her appearance inspired a feeling of pride and promise, an itch to stand on her bridge and feel her take to the sea."

Eager though he was to get seaborne, when his ship, the *Abercrombie*, was commissioned, Lieutenant Stafford was sorry to leave, and so were most of the men aboard. "The people of Orange had been good to them, in marked contrast to the treatment they had received in Norfolk where the crew was formed. While public buses ran from the gate of the Consolidated yard into town, it was unusual for a sailor to have to take one because normally a passing motorist would provide a ride before the bus arrived. Nor was it unusual for the motorist to invite the sailor to his home to meet his family and share a meal."

This was not the town my father experienced. Forty years later, no trickle of sentimentality had softened his memories of it. "It was just an absolutely crappy, miserable, tenth-rate Texas town which raised chickens primarily. But they stopped raising chickens because the chicken houses were needed for the personnel that were building the ships. It was the damnedest thing."

To be fair, he was angry that he had been sent there rather than to sea. His profession was to blame. The fast-building navy needed men with an architect's understanding of structure more than it did hastily trained amateur watch-standing officers.

Now came a restless, cranky eternity that is perhaps the most universal of all military experiences. He wasn't just waiting: he was doing real work. But he chafed at designing shore installations, and more at helping fit out DEs only to send them off without him. "I can see," he wrote my mother, "no indications that I will not end this war a complete misanthrope."

First, there was Orange itself: "the only place I've ever been in my life that I would not have the slightest desire to revisit. I used to think that Lowell, Haverhill, and Ayer, Massachusetts were the most boring and unattractive cities in the country. Now they seem fraught with picturesque interest and solid New England virtues." Part of this disaffection came from seeing firsthand one of the great internal contradictions of America's war. "A staunch southern defender of our way of life and world democracy (I assume him to be such, as he is giving all his time for considerable money to the shipyard driving a truck, and the shipyard is providing our government with the implements necessary for setting the world to rights) told me today that they were going very soon to have to kill all the 'black bastards' around here to teach them their place—getting ideas in their heads, etc. It seems one has recently raped a nearby queen of Southern chastity, and there have been other incidents indicating that Negroes have been giving themselves all the airs of the local white criminals. There must be other things besides absenteeism (administratese for loafing) which cause the Axis to smile."

It got worse. Race riots broke out in the nearby town of Beaumont and grew "so serious that it is completely out of bounds; a nice little situation in the arsenal of democracy." This continued to trouble and anger him, producing for a while a far more intemperate man than I ever knew. "On account of the race question they've stopped all liquor sales here, but I imagine that won't be for long. Next to lynching a Negro, I gather Texans love drinking whiskey best. So after they have had their fill of one they will be ready to return to the other."

Nevertheless, the work went on, and much of it was satisfying. "I missed a day in letter writing because I had to work all night Friday and all through Saturday. A steering engine went out on one of the new ships which was about to leave. The men in the yard were wonderful about it. Never a murmur about there being anything even unusual about working like beavers all night and the next day too, just part of the job. It was extremely interesting to watch the operation, which was entirely successful. The ship got away on time."

Still, he was fretting about everything: from money ("we are going to need it after the war, and we should try to put it by if possible during. If we win the war it will be handy—and if we lose it won't matter anyway—so it's a better bet to try to lay by what we can. If anything happens to me, in the popular phrase, a little ready stuff would be a convenience to you") to the new uniforms that had become a curious idée fixe of Admiral King's. These were a source of annoyance to every U.S. navy man everywhere. They were a slate gray confection of King's own design—"We'll be as smartly turned out as bus drivers," my father groused—and they were one of the few fights the admiral ever lost. My father's mood, as he made his way across the griddle of Orange in July, surely reflects itself in his thoughts about an ailing relative: "It's too bad about Aunt Florence, in that a stroke is always too bad— but she has talked so goddam much for the last 20 years that it is only fair for her to have to listen a while, if she can stand it, which I doubt." Then, a few days later: "Have you seen Aunt Florence? I don't give a damn what happens to that evil old woman, but thought it was polite to ask." (Who was Aunt Florence? I'd never heard her name before I read his letters, and now there's nobody left to tell me.)

Even the reliable distraction of books tended to fade under the Texas sun, and he had the slightly paranoid thought that my mother was teasing when she sent him some: "Was your tongue in your cheek when I suggested a little diverting reading, possibly some biography, and you snap back with three volumes of Plutarch?" Movies, however, almost as important to morale as mail for every American sailor throughout the war, were more cheering. He found *Random Harvest* "the most enchanting picture I've ever seen. One of the most exciting and moving—I remember it seemed like a lot of baloney to you but I adored every bit of it." He was less enchanted by an Andy Hardy sequel: "Mickey Rooney has outgrown any lingering childlike charm, and is incredibly repulsive. The little squirt, I noticed in a BOQ [bachelor officers' quarters] copy of a movie magazine, has had the effrontery to get married to an attractive whore, and divorced." Although my father was irritated by the prospect of seeing *Sherlock Holmes in Washington* ("I imagine contemporary Washington is indicated, though how they have continued to keep the sage of Baker Street alive and active as long as this I don't know"), he came back buoyed by a joke in it: "Dr. Watson, played by the inimitable Nigel Bruce, on his first visit to America is seen closely examining the American comic sections. Holmes asks him what he is doing. 'Reading about Flash Gordon,' says Watson seriously. 'Seems like a very capable fellow.'"

Orange, for all its dolors, was producing capable fellows. My father was learning his business. After spending a day on a DE in the Gulf, he wrote, "The captain I was out with is developing a very fine ship. He has been hard working and able in his preparation and it shows. There is quite a difference in the attitudes and application of commanding officers, and it does show up in their ships. The way he brought his alongside the dock under difficult circumstances was reassuring and instructive to watch. It's very ticklish handling ships as large as these. The slightest wind or current alters the problems of coming alongside. Everything happens very slowly but inevitably. You have no brakes to step on and stop dead, and if things are not planned right there is the possibility of doing severe damage which you have to stand and see happen with no way in the world of controlling it, and see it happen slowly, over a period of what seems like many minutes. With so much weight behind them the ships can be apparently dead in the water, and yet put enough strain on a steel hawser to snap it with no perceptible motion. There is so much to be learned about handling them."

As the summer burned on, my father began to be happier with his work planning the stowage of hose and line and ammunition in the virgin hulls of the new ships. "As things get squared away here I can see that the detail is an absolute necessity in getting the ships to sea from the yard here and as I learn more about my job I feel more useful. The ships are coming along much more smoothly than when I got here, as the yard and everyone in it buckles down to the concentrated job of producing DEs. I feel there is no comparison between what I was doing in New York and what I am doing here, both in the work itself, and as a preparation for my job at sea when I get to it."

What he really meant was *if* he got to it. After a brief but intense spell of worry that he was going to be sent to design buildings in Bay City, Michigan, Lieutenant Richard B. Snow received orders to proceed to Norfolk, Virginia, and join DE-150, the USS *Neunzer,* for Atlantic duty.

"Set the Watch"

The birth of a warship, 1943

Most destroyer escorts were named for men who had already died in the war the ships were going to help fight.

Machinist Weimar Edmund Neunzer was killed in July 1942 while dive-bombing a Japanese submarine. The ship that would carry his name was built by Consolidated—my father saw it taking shape while he was trying to get to sea—and on April 27, 1943, Ruby Iris Neunzer, the flier's widow, broke a champagne bottle against the newborn's bow. The *Neunzer* slid backward into the Sabine River and bobbed and steadied, riding very high in the water because she was still just a hull, not yet both a working town and an engine of destruction. Accomplishing that meant not only adding the guns, but typewriters, filing cabinets, staplers and mimeograph machines, radios and anchor chains and blowers, soup pots and soup bowls, fire hoses and life jackets, signal flags and elegant, hand-wound chronometers that kept time at sea just as their forebears had when our new heavy frigates were alarming England in the War of 1812.

The start of this familiar process on DE 150 would have had no special significance for my father, but then his superior, who liked him, hinted he might be assigned to the *Neunzer*. The moment it happened, he was sent up to firefighting school in Norfolk, Virginia. This was a serious and spectacular course: "Today we put out great big oil and gasoline fires and got hot wet and dirty during it. The instructors are fine, all experienced firemen from various big metropolitan fire departments, and they are eager to help and advise."

Then he brought his singed eyebrows to New York for three weeks' leave with my mother—*Oklahoma!* was a particularly bright moment of it—before heading back to Orange, where he found the *Neunzer* the brief center of attention in that whole great forcing-bed of warships. She was still enmeshed, as she had been for months, in hoses and cables, but the tempo of the work had increased and engineers and officers with clipboards and flashlights moved among the welders and painters.

On September 26, my father wrote, "Our crew arrived today and we were busy all day loading the ship. I have a very young skipper, Lt. Greenbacker, U.S.N., and I am very nervous about satisfying him." And everything else, too: "I am nervous as a cat about the way things are going to go. There is so much that only experience afloat can teach me, and I am shy on that."

So were most of his shipmates. Of the 209 officers and men who had just arrived aboard, perhaps 30 had seen sea duty. John Greenbacker most definitely had. The son of a Connecticut dairy farmer, he had been so eager to join the navy that as early as junior high school his friends were calling him Annapolis. He got to the academy in 1936 and, as soon as he graduated, was posted to the carrier *Yorktown*. The ship ran convoys in the Atlantic before Pearl Harbor, then went to the Pacific and the Battle of the Coral Sea, where a near miss ruptured a fuel tank, and to Midway, where Japanese torpedo planes sank her.

Greenbacker, one of the last men off, was ordered to the new sub-chasing school in Miami and eventually transferred to the *Stewart*, becoming executive officer of the first destroyer escort built by Brown Brothers of Houston. Brown Brothers was a good example of the pressure of war measures at the time: before the company bid its way into the DE program, the closest it had come to building a ship was winning the contract to put the concrete capping on the locks of the Panama Canal. The neophyte builders took a while to get the hang of it. "I went to Houston," said Greenbacker, "and got there in February of 1943 and the ship didn't go into commission until something like the first of June." After a shakedown cruise, he was ordered back to Texas, this time to Orange, to take over another brand-new DE. Consolidated made a faster job of finishing its ship than its Houston rivals had theirs: "I was only there for four weeks before we went in commission."

By the early afternoon of Monday, September 27, 1943, the last of the hoses and welders and men with clipboards had left the ship. A theaterful of folding chairs had sprouted on the dock by her stern. They were occupied largely by friends and family of the crew, and by a band. Behind the chairs stood the workers who had put the ship together. The crew was gathered on her fantail, and her officers stood at attention by a podium set up there. The band played in the cool September sunshine, and my father was surprised to realize that he would miss Orange—or, he hastily modified this extravagant reaction, the friends he had made working on the shore detail there. A little after two o'clock the band subsided. A Consolidated official approached the podium and turned over the ship to the U.S. navy in the form of Captain J. M. Schelling, USN, representing the commandant, Eighth Naval District. Captain Schelling read aloud the orders authorizing him to accept it, did so, and said, "Hoist the colors."

At the bow the Union Jack blossomed—white stars, navy blue field—while aft a sailor ran the American flag up the staff. Amidships, the commissioning pennant, a long ribbon with one red stripe, one white one, and a narrow blue field with seven bars, broke from the mast. In that moment the *Neunzer* became the USS *Neunzer*. Captain Schelling turned her over to Captain Greenbacker, who gave his first order as commanding officer: "Set the watch."

"Set all regular port watches," begins the DE 150's log, which would be kept hour by hour, day by day, all the years she was in commission. But even before that the first entry reads, "The following men were received on board for duty (see attached list)." The roster of those who were to give a soul to the machinery begins, "ADAMOVICH, John 646 40 49 [the serial number of the "name, rank, and serial number" that is all the information you're supposed to give your captors], USNR; ADAMS, Trenouth A., 875 49 20, FC3c, USNR"; and right on through two hundred names until "WHITMAN, Arthur R., 245 03 59 S2c, USNR; WINIEWSKI, Louis F., 224 10 80, SF2c, USN [a valuable man: that USN as opposed to USNR means he is regular navy, not just called up as part of the naval reserve; so is his successor]; ZON-FRELLO, Peter, 376 58 15, S2c, USN."

The log makes the next day sound awfully quiet, although it had to be one of constant tumult as people were set to new jobs and put into new accommodations. But the whole entry, under the frowning "CONFIDENTIAL" that will head every page for the rest of the war, begins, "0000–0400. Moored stbd side to dock at City Docks, Orange." At four-hour intervals this is followed by the stolid phrase "Moored as before." It concludes with the final watch report of the twenty-four-hour day: "2000–2400. Moored as before." This is signed by my father, and it is a thrilling surprise for me to see his handwriting, which would change not a bit for the rest of his life, fresh, black, immediate, put down there on his spanking new ship, with the familiar glare and clamor of all-night Orange already part of another existence. He had a sense of the occasion. In the months ahead he would sign all the hundreds of log entries he made "R.B. Snow Lt USNR." But for this, the last watch of the ship's first full day in commission, he is "Richard Boring Snow Lieutenant USNR."

Everyone from Adamovich to Zonfrello was busy the next day as the ship absorbed all the proteins of war. The log's sparse report says, "0822 commenced loading ammunition; 0947 commenced fueling ship."

With the ammunition they would likely have started with the 20mm rounds, which came in olive-colored magazines. Once they were stowed, sailors carried aboard shells for the three-inch guns, each man cradling a single tall, brass-jacketed cartridge while constantly being instructed to "keep those noses up now, goddamn it." When the ready ammunition had been housed near the guns, the rest came aboard in wooden crates, the 20mm magazines in square boxes, the three-inch rounds in long, coffinlike ones.

The job took a little less than three hours. Meanwhile a thick black hose came aboard and the DE sucked in diesel oil, eighty-two thousand gallons of it in four hours.

Then came the first of what would be many hundreds of general-quarters drills: the alarm agitating in shrill bursts, sailors punching their arms into life jackets, running past each other to their battle stations, putting on helmets, while, on the bridge, the telephone talker relayed reports from the stations—"Condition Able set forward. Depth charge manned and ready. Engine room manned and ready"—until the ship abruptly fell silent, and the perpetual noise of the Consolidated yard insinuated itself again, and the talker said, "All stations manned and ready."

The ship secured from the drill forty-five minutes later and hurried on toward another milestone. "Made all preparations for getting underway," the log records.

"Now go to your stations, all the special sea details." This was a bosun's mate, over the ship's loudspeakers. Once again men swarmed the decks; once again, the bridge talker passed along reports. "Fo'c'sle manned and ready, sir. Fantail manned and ready. Engineering spaces manned and ready." When everything was manned and ready, Captain Greenbacker gave the order: "Single up your lines."

Twelve paired lines held the ship to six bollards along the dock. Consolidated-yard men threw off one from each mooring post. "All lines singled up, sir," said the bridge talker. Greenbacker spoke again, the remaining lines fell from the dock into the Sabine to be quickly pulled aboard, and the log reported, with "Captain conning and Navigator on the bridge," as the *Neunzer* moved out from the dock.

It wasn't much of a voyage, just a few hundred yards to tie up alongside another DE, the *Peterson,* still at the capacious City Docks, but the ship had been under her own power and worked by her own crew.

Nobody spent any time celebrating the maneuver. My father went back to his endless tasks. On the twenty-ninth he spoke of the routine in the first letter my mother received whose envelope carried the return address "USS Neunzer (DE 150) Fleet Postmaster NY." It was also the first to bear the rubber-stamped PASSED BY NAVAL CENSOR circling the initials of the censoring officer.*

His inaugural shipboard letter was brief and far from happy. "Another very busy day! Not as much accomplished on the ship

---

*Every piece of mail that went off the ship had to be read by an officer and certified innocent of any information that might possibly be useful to the enemy. My father found this duty both oppressive and touching. "We do our level best to work the boys to death and still they find time to write prolifically. It's admirable, even though it's a lot of work for the officers." He added to his wife, "It is very moving to read the men's expressions of affection for their wives and families, as they exactly counterfeit (in the Shakespearean sense) our own."

as I should have liked but will have a crack at it tomorrow. . . . My gear is all crammed into various drawers in an ungodly fashion. When the ship gets straightened out I hope to do likewise but I'm afraid it will be not until! . . .

"What a stupid letter. I guess I AM tired."

A few days later he was just as busy, but more cheerful about it: "There must be something very dire impending—because it isn't normal for me to have twenty minutes to myself—Ever since I talked with you on the phone from Orange we have been on the run—myself perhaps more than some of the others, for there have been so many small hull items to design, rip out, or finish up which involved telling somebody how long or how wide at all hours of the day and night. I have a splendid chief boatswain mate who runs things admirably from the seamanship point of view and of course I'd be making a monkey out of myself without someone like that to help out. Among other pedestrian jobs which have fallen to my lot is that of sorting and distributing about 500 keys, something that would try the patience of the most hardened shipping clerk. Other items which weigh very heavily on me are a leaky toilet, a leaky steam valve, more shelving, less heat etc. etc. So you can see the life of a First Lieutenant is in some respects not very different from that of an architect. However—a watch on the flying bridge is another story. Our executive officer is an ideal person to have charge of the shaping up of such a motley crew of officers and men as are in his charge—patient, experienced and tactful. I feel he fully appreciates whatever capabilities his officers already have and is very willing to work to develop those which come only with experience."

This exemplary officer was Virgil Gex, and my father's regard for him did not wane during the war, or for the rest of his life. The son of a Missouri farmer, Gex was appointed to the Naval Academy, but a failed eye exam put him into the Naval Reserve. He took a job at Procter and Gamble, but by December 1940 the increasingly hard-pressed navy decided his eyesight wasn't so bad after all, and he was sent as an ensign to the four-stacker *Chew*. December 7, 1941, found the *Chew* in Pearl Harbor moored four hundred yards away from the *Arizona*. Gex saw the bomb that exploded the battleship's magazine pierce her deck. The Japanese aim was all too good, and they weren't interested in World War I destroyers, so the *Chew* survived to operate out of Pearl for the rest of the war. Virgil Gex, risen to a gunnery and senior watch officer, was detached in May 1943 to help put the *Neunzer* in commission.

"Our Captain and Executive Officer being both absolutely of the first rank in experience and ability (although both are only slightly too old to be my nephews!) the ship's organization should develop very satisfactorily."

Quickly, too, because when my father wasn't occupied with the familiar tasks of formulating measurements and attending to plumbing, he found himself put into the swim of naval life with unusual speed. Reminiscing years later, Captain Greenbacker said he and Lieutenant Gex "and, I think, the chief engineer, were the only [officers] that had ever been to sea at all. I knew that in some of these cases the captain and the exec would stand off-and-on watches"—that is, one relieving the other in four-hour rotation. "I didn't do that. I said, 'You get on out there, you be officer of the deck. Call me if there are any questions. Call me if you sight anything.'"

It was a new world, and not a simple one to my father. "The ship organization is hardly less complicated than the social structure of India, and castes among the petty officers must be as strictly observed. Any deviation from the proper chain of authority causes ripples which eventually rock the whole ship—and it is of great importance to learn the proper channels of activity as soon as possible."

A couple of weeks later, in a letter he hoped was "not too

expository," he gave his wife an admirably clear account of shipboard routine. "We have had a good deal of steaming since I last wrote you, and all of us have had to stand deck watches night and day, as our turn comes up. The officers are divided up into groups of two, an Officer of the Deck and a Junior Officer of the Deck, and watches are usually four hours, during which the normal operation of the ship is in charge of the O.O.D. The Captain and the Executive Officer come to the bridge from time to time and are always there in any unusual situation, but in normal steaming the OOD has charge of the handling of the ship and her routine. Of course this is intensely interesting—always a grave responsibility and a job in which experience counts for almost everything, and with the constantly recurring watches, experience is the one thing of which there is plenty to be had. Off watch all the officers are busy with organizational and administrative affairs. My departments are Construction & Repair (C&R) and damage control, and I am Division Officer of the First Division—in general the Deck ratings forward. What a lot of detail there is to be straightened out in all that! I am fortunate in having a seasoned and very able Chief Boatswain's Mate, who has the happy faculty of instructing me under the guise of conferring with me. He has never even so much as hinted that he has forgotten more seamanship than I've ever known, which I think indicates great good feeling, and is probably more than I could manage under reversed circumstances. He is well satisfied with the assortment of green but willing seamen under his charge—and the boys are all coming along extremely well in their line handling, and chores about the ship."

He concluded, "Good night, my dearest—I love you and think of you 'at all times'—which is the Navy way of saying 'Always.'"

Despite this authoritative summary, he wrote a few days later, "Time certainly rolls along—but I don't feel my age as I should. Just when I might begin to feel a certain degree of achievement and settledness (no such word I presume) I wander into an entirely new trade, start in at the bottom of the ladder in competence, if not in rank, and spend my waking hours (and they are many) with youths in their early twenties. However, any doubts I may have held as to whether I am growing old were dispelled by a glimpse of the commissioning picture of the *USS Neunzer*, in which I look like a not too able character actor of 50, surrounded by ruddy and unlined adolescents not yet approaching the prime of life."

Still, there were compensations: "I have a very snug little cabin forward of the wardroom. My cabinmate is a very long and attractive young man, who has to fold up like a jackknife to get in the upper bunk, but as he is junior to me, that's where he goes (the advantage of my great age)."

My father had finally got his belongings—shirts, shoes—"put away in a magnificently orderly fashion." He was in good company: "Mr. Gex is extremely attractive and so are the other officers. I don't know whether it is just because they are my shipmates or whether they actually are as a group superior to some of the others I've seen. In any case, they all seem O.K. to me." And "our food continues to be excellent and plentiful."

The food *was* good. The first supplies to come aboard the freshly commissioned *Neunzer*—before ammunition, before fuel—were, the log records, 210 pounds of bread "received from the Fehr Baking Co . . . inspected as to quantity by R.M. Turner, Jr., Lieut, and as to quality by Y.R. Tate, PhM 1/c [pharmacist's mate first class]." Three hours later Turner and Tate were called upon to inspect "8 gal ice cream from Stewart Dairy Co." The navy had long had the reputation of being the best-fed service, and meals improved throughout the war.

The 1940 edition of *The Cook Book of the United States Navy* is a skinny 164 pages. Although it reflects a diet far better than many Americans were enjoying in the final years of the Great Depression, the recipes—"ALL FOR 100 MEN"—are workmanlike to the point of drabness: "Cut 60 pounds of mutton into 5-pound pieces and wipe with a clean damp cloth. Place in boiling water and boil for five minutes. Then reduce to a simmering temperature and let cook until tender. When about half done season with salt." In fairness to the Supply Corps officers who assembled the book, the result should be "serve[d] with caper sauce," but this is also pretty rudimentary: "2 pounds flour. 3 pounds chopped pickles or capers. 2 pounds butter or shortening. Salt and pepper to taste." Many of the recipes are even less inspiring—"Lima Bean Loaf"—and some are actually dire: "Canned Creamed Codfish" (which employs the only fish mentioned by name other than "Canned Salmon"; the rest of the piscine world is covered by the twin entries "Baked Fish" and "Fried Fish"). One of the seven sandwiches recommended is this imaginative confection: "Put between these slices [of bread] three slices of crisp lettuce leaves."

The *Cook Book* of 1944 has grown to 430 pages, nine of them devoted to dozens of sandwiches. The lettuce filling has been augmented with tomatoes and bacon; the mutton recipe has disappeared. There are fifty pages of desserts. Fish are cited by species: "Fillet of Flounder," "Baked Halibut and Tomatoes." The creamed codfish remains among the manifold hardships of war, but a typical "winter menu" runs:

> Navy Bean Soup
> Fried Pork Chop Gravy
> Hominy Spoonbread
> Buttered Green Peas
> Apple Cole Slaw Salad
> Lemon Cream Layer Cake
> Bread Butter Coffee

Among the *Neunzer*'s crew were hill-country boys who had got the worst of the Depression since they had been three or four years old. My father remembered them ballooning under the impact of their new diet, giving the ship a population of fat men for a few weeks until their young metabolisms caught up.

A month after Consolidated turned the *Neunzer* over to the navy, Lieutenant Snow described a scene in which food and shipmates and growing competence had combined to produce, for the moment at least, an obviously contented man: "Last night I had the mid watch with Lt. Gex—midnight to 4AM—or 0000–0400 in navy figures. It was a long watch, but uneventful, and we stood all the way topside on the ship under the stars. It was most impressive to look back occasionally and see the tall mast swaying back and forth against the dark star-lighted sky. When I came down off watch I found the steward had left steak and potatoes in the pantry oven, so I had a very early breakfast before I went to bed for two or three hours sleep."

The Heartbeat of the Pings
The importance of sonar, 1941–45

The *Neunzer*'s sea career had begun on October 1, when she left the Orange City Docks, bound for Galveston: down the Sabine River, past Port Arthur, shimmering in the perpetual stink of its oil refineries, and out into the Gulf of Mexico, where for the first time the ocean swell lifted the new ship. The sea was not running high that day, but those who were going to get seasick began to. My father could report with satisfaction to my mother, "It appears that whatever other limitations I may have to contend with (and they are legion) sea sickness will probably not be one of them."

The men went to general quarters, and for two hours the ship steamed through a racket of its own making as all the guns were tested and the torpedo tubes swiveled this way and that. By late afternoon the DE was moored at Galveston, and the next day she ventured into the maw of the Todd construction company's Floating Drydock 3, a topless, steel shoebox hundreds of feet long and half full of water. The *Neunzer* inched in amid an ecstasy of shouted instructions and orders between dock and ship. Tall steel gates closed behind her stern, and pumps began to empty the dock, gentling the ship down to rest on keel blocks and cradles. In less than half an hour the *Neunzer* was standing like a model on a mantelpiece.

For two days it was like Orange again, with workers everywhere and the ship drawing its power and water from shore while final adjustments were made and weaknesses disclosed by the brief voyage set aright. Then the DE was refloated and put to sea, bound for Bermuda and her shakedown cruise.

At 2202 on October 15, with supper already hours in the past and taps just sounded, the sonarman made a sound contact.

The navy had been trying to listen for submarines underwater since World War I, when operators strained to make sense of the noises picked up by an "S.C. [sub-chaser] tube," which was more advanced than a tin-can-and-string telephone, but not by much. Between the wars the British and American navies developed what they called asdic and we called sonar (for "sound navigation and ranging"). This could passively listen for engine noises, but it also had the capacity to hunt a submarine by emitting a sharp ping from a retractable dome in the ship's hull. If this pulse of noise hit an object, it would bounce back an echo, which the gear amplified and transmitted to the sound shack up near the bridge. The man listening to the echo could tell from its pitch where and how far away the object was. That is, he could tell if he had an exceptional ear and a lot of training.

By the late 1930s our old four-stackers were being fitted with sonar, and two schools had been established to train operators. The first students helped develop the technique even as they learned it: "Everybody in antisubmarine warfare at that time was an inventor," one of them remembered happily. This was surely what my father was referring to when, during his training days in Florida, he had written my mother cryptically, "In one of the courses my accurate sense of relative pitch (not to be confused with my intonation when performing on the violin) is going to be a great help. Isn't that a surprise!"

The electronic chirp became as much a shipboard constant as the engines or the sea itself. Wirt Williams, who served in the North Atlantic aboard a four-stacker and wrote a novel about it called *The Enemy*, remembered, "Each ping was like the sound a rock makes dropped into a lake, silvery, searching, and finally vanishing but never dying. The pings were seconds apart, like a dead-slow heartbeat. . . . They were our eyes, and ears, and nose, under the sea." To Williams, the sonar was the most important piece of equipment on his destroyer: "The heartbeat of the pings was her reason for existence. When they stopped, she was nothing."

Now the pings had told the *Neunzer*, on her nineteenth day in commission, that a submarine might be out ahead of her under the night waters. The alarm began its clamor and sailors rushed to their stations.

When he was still outfitting destroyer escorts my father had written his wife that "the DE which just left had on board two of the tiniest most appealing little kittens you ever saw. They were not fluffy ones, but thin wistful little things with large ears and beautiful ascetic faces—they are very tiny, and very calm, don't scamper about, but walk around deliberately or lie in what shade they can find. There was something delicious in seeing one of them carefully select the shade of a 300 lb. cylinder of TNT to lie down for a little rest. Somehow the kitten looked normal and made all the rest of the show look a little absurd—but don't say I said it."

I'll bet the cylinder of TNT didn't look absurd to him that night. The kitten had been taking its ease beneath the DE's main antisubmarine weapon, the depth charge. A sailor would have referred to it as an ash can, and compared with other fixtures on the ship—the sonar, for instance—it was as primitive as the nickname makes it sound. For the first years of the war our ships had been outfitted with the Mark 6, which, unlike the sound gear, had changed scarcely at all since Armistice Day 1918. Rolled off racks at the stern of the ship, or shot out from its sides with K-guns, it would tumble down to a preset depth, where water pressure ignited it.

If simple, the weapon was far from feeble. E. J. Jernigan had received a vivid demonstration of its potency while he was still aboard his new battleship *Washington* in the North Atlantic. His ship was sailing through heavy fog in company with four British destroyers some two hundred yards astern of the battleship *King George V*. One of the destroyers blundered across the bows of the *George V* and, said Jernigan, "the huge battleship cut her completely in two." As the *Washington* steamed between the two halves, the destroyer's depth charges began to explode. Their effect on the accidental and unsubmerged target—one of the largest and heaviest warships afloat—was that "all 1900 tons of the number 2 turret jumped the track. The range finder went out and two-thirds of all the light bulbs were broken. The after-steering engine room crew was so badly shaken . . . that they got out in a hurry thinking we had been torpedoed. . . . The screws came out of the water while exploding depth charges drove us high in the air. We finally began to settle by the stern and felt like we were falling. The screws ran away until they bit into the water again."

By the time the *Neunzer* put to sea the Mark 6 depth charge had been replaced by the Mark 9, which was streamlined (it looked like the atomic bomb envisioned by newspaper cartoonists in the 1950s), sank faster than its predecessor, and ignited with a far greater concussion. The Mark 9 was said to be lethal to a submarine if it exploded within thirty feet, but nobody knew this for sure, and there were other problems. Throughout the war, sonar could tell where a submarine bore on the pursuing ship, but not how deep it lay, so setting the proper depth on a charge was largely a matter of instinct; sonar lost contact when it got within 150 feet of its target; and when the charge burst, it deafened the equipment for long enough to allow a good U-boat commander—and they were all good—to pivot and sneak off in another direction while the shattered water gave the listeners only scuffling, sterile noise.

So the *Neunzer* went into its first attack with hedgehogs. As the homey descriptive name might suggest, the British had developed this weapon, an odd, busy-looking machine. Twenty-four steel "spigots" reached up from the cradle in which it was mounted, each one topped with a projectile that carried thirty pounds of explosive. That was a tenth as much as a depth charge packed, but still enough to crack open a submarine with a direct hit. Contact-fused, unlike the depth charge, it would explode only if there *was* a direct hit. Because of this, and because the bombs fired forward, throwing their projectiles in a semicircle 250 yards ahead of the ship, sonarmen could keep contact with the target while it was under attack.

The *Neunzer* had all her battle stations manned and ready eight minutes after the alarm and began her first run. The hedge-hog projectiles went off in pairs, quickly, throwing a lariat of twenty-four splashes. That was all they accomplished. The contact remained strong. Another twenty-four rounds went out into the dark. They, too, failed to disturb whatever they were fired at, and the *Neunzer* made one more unrewarded hedgehog run four minutes later.

Captain Greenbacker decided to shift to the depth charges and dropped eight of them. The sea bulged and then broke into hundred-foot-tall spars of foam behind the ship. The contact disappeared but, the log says, "with no evidence of damage to target."

Sonar was a highly exacting discipline. The *Neunzer* could have been attacking a shoal of fish, or a stream of colder water flowing beneath the surface, or any number of the other bounte-ous distractions the ocean had to offer (among them "snapping shrimp," whose conversations produced a noise that could confound the inexperienced operator). "There was a lot of activity with whales," Greenbacker said of those early days aboard. "The whales took a lot of beating, I'm sure."

The *Neunzer* secured from general quarters half an hour after midnight and steamed on, if unvictorious also unharmed, to learn its business in Bermuda waters.

"How Many Germans Will It Kill?"

Learning to use radar, 1940–43

Whatever Captain Greenbacker had expended his seventy-two hedgehog projectiles and eight depth charges on, it almost certainly wasn't a German submarine. Just a month earlier Admiral Doenitz had ordered his captains to launch a new offensive against convoys in the North Atlantic. The days of easy gleanings in the western part of the ocean were long past, he believed. And what he believed, he could act on, for Doenitz had recently become the most powerful man in the German navy.

On the last day of 1942, far north in the arctic storms, a German force of six destroyers, the heavy cruiser *Hipper,* and the pocket battleship *Lutzow** had attacked an eastbound Murmansk convoy defended by a few British destroyers. Two British cruisers steaming with a westbound convoy heard the firing and rushed

---

*This was the same vessel that had hijacked the *City of Flint,* no longer called the *Deutschland* because the Kriegsmarine did not want to risk the humiliation of losing a capital ship named for the German nation.

up, but they had only six-inch guns to oppose the *Hipper*'s eight-inch, let alone the eleven-inch giants *Lutzow* mounted. By naval logic this encounter should have meant the end of the convoy, of the destroyers, and of the two cruisers. Instead, for the loss of one aged destroyer and a minesweeper, the British sank a German destroyer, roughed up the *Hipper* so badly that she never fought again, and scared away the *Lutzow*.

A U-boat commander who had been on the scene somehow managed to pass along to Berlin that Germany had just gained a decisive naval victory. Hitler was preparing to incorporate the triumph into a New Year's Eve speech when he heard a London radio broadcast report what had actually happened, right down to the fact that the convoy had lost not a single merchant ship.

It is difficult to imagine news that would be more disagreeable to Hitler (but not impossible: the Stalingrad surrender would come a month later). He "flew into an uncontrollable rage," wrote Erich Raeder, that correct, aloof champion of a powerful surface fleet at whom the rage was directed. "He announced his intentions of immediately having all the heavy ships laid up, and recorded in the War Diary his view that the heavy ships were utterly useless. . . . He would not listen to any explanations . . . but ordered me by telephone to report to him immediately."

Raeder gave his report on January 6, 1943, at Wolfsschanze, the gloomy concrete headquarters in East Prussia where Hitler was directing his war against the Soviet Union. There, under the pious gaze of Field Marshal Wilhelm Keitel, one of the Führer's most pliant yes-men, Raeder received a lecture on the history of German sea power. Hitler, he wrote, attacked "the Navy in a vicious and impertinent way. He disparaged its founding, belittled its every role since 1864 and stated that except for the submarines the entire history of the German Navy had been one of futility."

Hitler went on for an hour, Raeder remembered (one of the

two stenographers on hand said it was actually an hour and a half), and "it was glaringly obvious to me that this whole diatribe against the Navy which I commanded was intended but for one thing—to insult me personally."

Raeder took it all in silence, and when Hitler finally ran down, asked if he could speak with him alone. Keitel and the stenographers left the room, and Raeder, "very quietly" by his account, requested to be relieved of his command.

"Hitler—as he always did when faced with firmness—began to calm down and try to smooth over his remarks." Raeder was adamant. He had been on active duty for half a century, but now the time had come "for a parting of the ways."

Compared to the frequent and abrupt firings of the generals on the Eastern Front, it all went decorously. Raeder gave three radio broadcasts summarizing his role in the growth of the Kriegsmarine, saying poor health had forced him to seek a different assignment, praising Hitler, and concluding with a valediction: "I know that the navy will carry on this battle under its new commander in chief with the same obdurate determination, with the same unshakable will to conquer, and with the same loyalty as heretofore."

That new commander in chief was Karl Doenitz. Though the two men had often quarreled, and there was little warmth between them, Raeder had faith in his fractious subordinate and gave him a warm recommendation. As soon as Raeder was through speaking, his successor came on the radio. "To the U-boat arm," Doenitz said, "which I have been hitherto privileged to command, I extend my thanks for its courageous readiness to fight to the death and for its loyalty. I shall continue personally to command the U-boat war.

"I intend to command the navy in the same firm martial spirit. . . . Gathered about our Führer, we will not lay down our arms until victory and peace shall have been won. Hail our Führer!"

Doenitz took up his new duties on January 30, 1943.

Hitler liked Doenitz, liked his utter devotion to his boats and his confidence, which was not a matter of martial propriety, but perfectly genuine. Also, Hitler really had nowhere else to turn. Whole armies had disappeared into the terrible white vastnesses of the Eastern Front. The Americans had taken him completely by surprise with a successful landing in North Africa, and his big surface ships were sunk or, it seemed to him, useless. The Luftwaffe, sucked like the armies into the annihilating void of the Russian front, was no longer the offensive weapon it had been. Formidable though it remained, nobody thought anymore that it could win the war. The U-boats might.

Things were getting tougher for their crews, though. The "air gap"—that stretch of ocean that lay beyond the reach of Allied bombers—was growing narrower and the planes that chewed away at its edges more effective. German sailors had begun calling the passage across the Bay of Biscay, so recently a welcome time-saving convenience, the Valley of Death.

Peter Cremer, on the bridge while *U-333* was starting out for Florida the year before, had gotten a premonitory glimpse of what lay ahead. "My eyes were in top form, the lookouts on the bridge were wide-awake, there was good visibility with gathering cumulus clouds, and even so we were surprised, our third day at sea, when from those very clouds an aircraft descended with total suddenness and came directly at us."

Captain and watch rushed below into the already diving boat. They were one hundred feet down when two bombs exploded. "All the electric lights went out, bulbs and fuses jumped from their sockets. The repeater compass on the control-room bulkhead smashed into fragments, flap valves and hull valves sprung a leak, and a stream of oil three fingers broad poured from a crack." The rudders were knocked out, all the radio tubes broken, and the conning-tower hatch took such a pounding that for the rest of the voyage "a crash dive brought a stream of water into the boat as from a shower." Such were the rigors of his service that Captain Cremer ended his account, "All in all the air attack had not caused any considerable damage."

Still, the incident continued to worry him. "Six pairs of eyes on the bridge—the lookouts, the officer of the watch, and myself—but none had seen the aircraft in time. On the other hand it must have spotted us long before—but with what?" He talked it over with his officers. They'd heard rumors that enemy airplanes were mounting radar, but they'd dismissed them, thinking the equipment far too heavy to take aloft. Now "we did suspect though that, somehow, the epoch of the bare eye, however good, was coming to an end and that the new era of technology . . . was upon us."

Cremer and his officers had every reason to be skeptical about the existence of radar-equipped airplanes. Radar was real and radar worked: Cremer's airborne colleagues had been dealt a war-changing reverse by it. In the last years and finally in the last hours of peace, Britain had built a chain of radar stations along its east coast. These emitted radio waves and, when the waves hit a distant airplane, could pick up the faint signal that echoed back. When the German bombers came in the summer of 1940, the stations were working. They looked across the Channel and the North Sea and saw where the bomber groups were headed in time to alert the British fighter squadrons, whose masters could thus hoard their planes and send up just enough to blunt the successive attacks. In the early fall, without acknowledging defeat in any way—and in later years even saying there had been no such thing as the Battle of Britain—the Germans gave up. That is, they gave up the effort that had been a prelude to an invasion of Britain. They didn't stop sending their bombers.

The radar that had made possible a victory in one of the decisive battles of the west was not portable. The transmitting

masts stood 250 feet tall; the receivers that harvested the frag-
mented echoes of the ever-widening radio signal were a hundred
feet higher. Transmitting equipment weighed several tons. To be
carried in an airplane, a radar set could not weigh more than two
hundred pounds.

Also, those stations transmitted waves meters long; their
broad curves bounced sloppily off everything. They yielded
information good enough to save a nation, but nowhere near
sufficiently precise to closely track a single plane.

The British badly needed to be able to because the Germans
had shifted to night operations. The radar stations could see in
the dark, but the pilots sent up to intercept the bombers could
not. The scientists had anticipated this. As early as 1937 they
had an airborne radar with a wavelength of just over a meter,
which gave the promise of homing on an attacker with unprecedented precision. But they needed a device that emitted far
greater power from a much smaller source. Four months before
Germany knocked France out of the war, they had invented it.
The resonant cavity magnetron is something of a miracle, by
far the single most important advance in the history of radar.
It was smaller, lighter, and allowed more accurate readings than
any previous system, firing out much shorter waves. Although
these were actually 9.7 centimeters, the development was called
"ten-centimeter radar" or, more economically, just "centimetric
radar." In late August 1940, after having produced just twelve
magnetrons, Britain sent one to America.

On a September night, a group of British and American scientists and military men gathered at a Washington hotel discovered that both countries had walked similar paths developing
radar. The Americans were appreciably ahead in receiver technology; and they had a ten-centimeter system, but it was woefully
underpowered.

The British said they'd been working on that as well. They

produced a wooden box, twisted loose the thumbscrews that held it shut, and took out the magnetron. Like so many of the century's momentous inventions, it did not appear impressive in its natal form. The historian Robert Buderi, who half a century later spoke with many of the people who'd brought it into the world, wrote, "Small enough to fit in the palm of a hand, the magnetron looked like a clay pigeon used in skeet shooting, with a few couplings thrown in." But once those couplings were hooked up, it could put out ten kilowatts of power at ten centimeters. This was well over a thousand times more than its American counterparts could generate.

The British scientific mission was working with American military and civilian organizations alike, and since the military already had meter-length radar, the magnetron went to a civilian agency, the National Defense Research Committee. The NDRC had been coaxed into being just a few months earlier by the head of the Carnegie Institution, Vannevar Bush. As a young engineer working on submarine detection during World War I, Bush had seen enmity between civilian scientists and the military blight one promising initiative after another. Hoping to prevent that from happening again, he devised an agency that could serve as a bridge between civil and military spheres, distilled his plan into four paragraphs on one sheet of typewriter paper, and handed that piece of paper to Franklin Roosevelt. The president liked the idea, and no man had more relish for working outside established channels. Within ten minutes Bush's synopsis had "OK, FDR" written on it.

This seminal document swiftly led to the establishment of a research and development organization with five sections, the one devoted to radar colonizing ten thousand square feet of laboratory space at the Massachusetts Institute of Technology. Initially called the Microwave Laboratory, the name was soon changed to the Radiation Laboratory, on the premise that this would persuade any spies that its job was doing nuclear research, of purely theoretical military utility and thus innocuous.

The Rad Lab—as it was immediately known—recruited young physicists and engineers from across the country, as well as Isidor Isaac Rabi, forty-two years old and dedicated to doing all a scientist could to stop Hitler. Confronted with a new piece of equipment or a new idea, his first question was almost always "How many Germans will it kill?"

All the recruits were amazed by the cavity magnetron. One of them, Luis Alvarez, said of it forty years afterward, "A sudden improvement by a factor of three thousand may not surprise physicists, but it is almost unheard of in engineering. If automobiles had been similarly improved, modern cars would cost about a dollar and go a thousand miles on a gallon of gas."

The Rad Lab men spent a lot of time speculating about how it actually worked. Clouds of electrons rotated inside it, accelerating through six or eight holes set like the chambers in a revolver—the cavities—until they generated the energy to shoot out a tremendously strong signal. Early in the program, a group of physicists stood around a disassembled magnetron, speculating on its occult power. "It's simple," Rabi said breezily. "It's just a kind of whistle." "Okay, Rabi," a colleague shot back, "how does a whistle work?"

What was clear was that it *did* work, but as Elting Morison pointed out, "Any strange device that alters the familiar procedures tends to disturb the military society." Radar most dramatically altered familiar procedures. George Marshall didn't particularly want to hear about it, and neither did Hap Arnold, head of the Army Air Forces. But Henry Stimson got word of what was going on in the Rad Lab, and he listened. In the spring of 1942, with the East Coast under attack, he went on an inspection tour of Panama and was impressed by the radar he saw in airplanes stationed there: it was crude, but it could spot approaching ships. Back home, he had a plane with better radar take him out to sea. The set picked up three ships fifty miles away. Stimson watched "until we were right over them and I could look out at the little window . . . and actually see the ships right under us." It was, said the secretary, "interesting and wonderful."

Stimson had no yearnings for modernity. Once he received a letter from a horse soldier decrying the "destruction of our fine old cavalry" and urging the secretary to restore the arm. Stimson wrote the man that some of his "oldest and choicest recollections are pervaded with the smell of horse sweat and saddlery . . . that goes with a good cavalry unit," but that "nearly all of us have to see some of the things we love remorselessly replaced in the modern mechanized world—a world that is just as repellent to me as I think it is to you." Repelled or not, Stimson had the breadth of mind to see that this war was germinating new weapons and systems of communication that held within them the means of winning it. He had been impressed enough by his flight to issue what a colleague called "the closest approach to an order" he ever gave Marshall and Arnold. Both generals found this note on their desks: "I've seen the new radar equipment. Why haven't you?" By the summer some hundred B-18s were being outfitted with centimeter sets and their crews taught how to use them.

Those were army planes. Admiral King proved a more resistant customer for radar. Shown a new set installed on one of his destroyers, he said, "We want something for this war, not the next one." Convoy was the way to fight submarines, King now firmly believed. It had proved its effectiveness, and developing radar-equipped airplanes as a primary weapon of attack in the middle of a war would be an enervating distraction. "Admiral King has a terrible blind spot for new things," Vannevar Bush wrote, "about as rugged a case of stubbornness as has been cultivated by a human being." Still, Bush was as determined a man as

King, and he approached the admiral directly, with a tactful but forthright letter sent on April 12, 1943:

"Antisubmarine warfare is notably a struggle between rapidly advancing techniques. It involves, to a greater extent than any other problem I could name, a combination of military aspects on one hand, and scientific and technical aspects on the other." Bush followed with some emollient thoughts on how no scientist can hope to understand naval tradition, but then he added that scientific training, too, takes a lifetime to master and must be respected. "Recent advances in airborne weapons greatly increase the potential probability of a kill of a submarine after aircraft sighting. These are of such striking nature as to warrant a review of our plans in regard to the balance between seaborne and airborne attack, and a re-orientation of our strategy."

King called Bush in for a meeting, and the men talked for two hours. Finally, King said something that sounded close to acquiescence: "Wouldn't our problem be met if one of your scientists sat with Admiral [Francis] Low and participated in planning with him . . . ?" Bush pressed his advantage: three scientists, who would have complete access to every aspect of the U-boat campaign, and the guarantee that their recommendations would go straight to King and Low. Agreed, said King.

OUT IN THE ATLANTIC, the new radar was already making its presence felt. The U-boats had been carrying what the sailors called the Biscay Cross, an assemblage of wood and wire that hung from the conning tower like some inscrutable piece of folk art. Primitive though it looked, it could pick up metric radar beams from an approaching airplane in time for the ship to save itself (the cross had to be pulled apart and bundled below once it had given its warning). The Biscay Cross was blind and deaf to centimetric radar.

The May 20, 1943, entry in the war diary kept by German

naval command chronicled a futile pursuit of an eastbound convoy: "It was not possible to maintain contact and proceed in the vicinity of the convoy owing to continuous surprise attacks from low-lying cloud. These attacks are explicable only in terms of very good location gear that enables a plane to detect the boat even from above the clouds." The report concluded, "The loss of *U-954* in the vicinity of the convoy is taken as certain as this boat reported making contact when up to the convoy, possibly lost in underwater attacks."

The tone is straightforward; nothing suggests that Doenitz's son Peter, just turned twenty-one, was the second watch officer aboard *U-954*.

Doenitz's response, if response it was, came in his message redirecting the submarines that had survived the costly attack—five boats lost, out of forty-one that would be destroyed that month—to engage another convoy. "If there is anyone who thinks fighting convoys is no longer possible, he is a weakling and no real U-boat commander. The Battle of the Atlantic gets harder, but it is the decisive campaign of the war. Be aware of your high responsibility, and be clear you will answer for your actions."

The Fleet without a Gun

Admiral King remakes his command, 1943

If it seems surprising that the obdurate King could be swayed with such relative ease by a civilian scientist, it may largely be because Bush approached him at a time when the admiral was considering a whole new way of running the Atlantic war. In March alone German submarines had sunk 627,000 tons of merchant shipping. King had been thinking this over.

When he told Bush to have his scientists sit with Admiral Low, he wasn't merely fobbing off a pest on a subordinate. Just a couple of weeks earlier he had made Rear Admiral Francis "Frog" (at least it's not "Froggie") Low his assistant chief of staff for antisubmarine warfare.

Low had served on submarines in World War I and later worked on torpedo research. He joined King's staff in 1940 and left two years later to command a cruiser in the Pacific. He was as tough as King, but calm and understated.* The Hungarian-born journalist Ladislas Farago, who worked with him in the war, wrote that Low was "a proper Bostonian (although he was born in Albany, New York). . . . A bookish-looking man with some bulk in his build and a ponderous big head, he resembles more the dean of men in an Ivy League school, or my image of Samuel Johnson, than the professional naval officer he was. He never sought the limelight and made every grade on the way up so quietly and effortlessly that his growth was hardly noticed."

King charged Low with studying the way the antisubmarine campaign was being conducted. He did and suggested that the various scattered commands, the sea frontiers and naval districts, all be placed under Admiral Ingersoll, Commander in Chief Atlantic Fleet. King agreed with the plan, except for putting Ingersoll in charge of it.

On May 1, 1943, King issued a statement to the Joint Chiefs of Staff: "It is† arranged to set up immediately in the Navy Department an antisubmarine command to be known as the Tenth Fleet.

"The headquarters of the Tenth Fleet will consist of all existing anti-submarine activities of U.S. Fleet headquarters, which will be transferred intact to the Commander Tenth Fleet. . . . In addition"—and here are the fruits of scientists getting together with Low—"a research-statistical analysis group will be set up composed of civilian scientists headed by Dr. Vannevar Bush."

The fleet's commander was "to exercise direct control over

---

*So understated that to this day even close students of the war don't know he came up with the idea for the Doolittle air raid against Japan that was the sole gleam in the half-year succession of American defeats that began with Pearl Harbor.

†"Note well the verb," observed Samuel Eliot Morison; clearly King didn't think he needed to get permission from anyone.

all Atlantic Sea Frontiers, using sea frontier commanders as task force commanders. He is to control allocation of antisubmarine forces to all commands in the Atlantic, and is to reallocate forces from time to time, as the situation requires." The enumeration of powers went on to give the Tenth Fleet absolute authority over every American plane and vessel involved in the Atlantic campaign.

King made Low chief of staff, but was slow to choose the commander who would wield such power. Days went by. Low chafed and fretted and finally cornered the admiral to tell him, "The Tenth Fleet commander should be a naval aviator."

King had clearly been fretting, too, and Low's statement brought him up short. After a few seconds he said, "He is."

"Who?"

"Me." And that was that. "There were not the proper people available," King said later, "so I wanted to keep it under myself."

A fleet, of course, means ships. The Tenth Fleet had no ships; indeed, the whole enterprise cost less to run than a single destroyer. It consisted in its entirety of about fifty people in a grubby Washington office building. "There never was anything like the Tenth Fleet in the U.S. Navy," wrote Farago, who was on its intelligence staff, "nor for that matter in any navy of the world."

Low gathered the brightest people he could find, and he pushed them hard. Like an actual guns-and-steel fleet, Tenth Fleet worked a twenty-four-hour day.* But if he had King's determination, he was not so grim. "Low mellowed an iron rule with the traits of his own personality," Farago remembered. "He was

---

*Once, Commander Kenneth Knowles, the head of Low's intelligence operations, stepped out into the corridor and came upon such a press of hurrying people that he thought there might be an air raid; it never occurred to him that it was simply five o'clock, quitting time.

always kind and considerate, urbane and cordial in his relations with his subordinates."

With its absolute authority to direct the Atlantic naval war, the operation he ran grabbed ships and planes as it needed them, telling them where to find U-boats, or diverting convoys far from their planned routes so the boats wouldn't find them.

Out in the Atlantic on his destroyer, Wirt Williams would look at little X's drawn on a chart, each one representing a U-boat, and wonder "for the hundredth time, by what sort of intelligence men sitting at desks before map-covered walls in London and Washington could say, 'there are so many submarines operating here,' and make a pinpoint in the ocean. But they did . . . they were not infallibly right. But they were good. They were very, very good."

In part, those men at their desks knew where the Germans were because the Germans told them. The close hold Doenitz kept over his submarines meant a constant crackle of radio traffic between boats and shore—"They were always too goddamned chatty for their own good," my father said—and their opponents had ways to listen in.

A line of high-frequency direction finders—HF/DF, or Huff Duff to every sailor who ever had occasion to talk about them—rose along Atlantic coasts in the Shetlands, Greenland, Newfoundland, Africa . . . twenty-six of them in all. If one picked up a transmission from a U-boat at sea, it learned in which direction the submarine lay; if two or more did, the bearings could be laid over a chart and show by their intersection the boat's exact location. Huff Duff eventually went to sea on escort vessels and got more and more precise in its findings all through the war.

The Germans knew the Allies were using HF/DF, and the Allies knew they knew. But behind Huff Duff, behind every other intelligence tool and technique, lay one of the most closely guarded secrets of the war. The British had broken the German naval code.

In the 1920s a German inventor named Arthur Scherbius

developed a coding machine. It was meant not for the military, but rather to protect confidential business messages from the nosy freemasonry of the telegraph office. It did its job far beyond what any commodities trader had the right to expect.

The machine, called Enigma, sent no messages itself. Rather, it enciphered them. At its front was a typewriter keyboard and, directly behind that, a battery of electric lights, each bearing a letter of the alphabet and laid out identically to the keyboard. When the user pressed a key, one of the letters would light up. Much had gone on before it did, though. The current passed through an electromechanical maze whose twists involved three interchangeable rotors ringed with the alphabet, with twenty-six pins on their faces, one for each letter, and veined with internal wiring to connect them randomly with contacts on the opposite side, a "plugboard" whose scramble of wires could be shifted like those in a telephone switchboard of the era, and a reflector, which, like the rotors, contained a pattern of wires that further diverted the current. The letter punched in would be converted five times— by the three rotors, by the reflector, by the plugboard—before its corollary letter blinked on.

To encode the message an operator set the rotors and plugs in position, typed it in, and copied down each letter that lit up. Then the resulting gibberish would be broadcast to a recipient who would key it into another Enigma machine and copy down the decrypted letters that showed up on his machine. But those letters would be decrypted only if the recipient had the same rotors and had set them and the plugs identically to those on the machine that had encoded the message.

Though the engine itself was basically a piece of late-Victorian ingenuity, the messages it produced inhabited the last way station short of infinity. When the German navy added a fourth wheel, the machine could dispense for each of our paltry twenty-six letters 150,000,000,000,000,000,000 substitutions.

Scherbius and his military clients, who adopted Enigma in the late 1920s, had every reason to believe its ciphers were impregnable.

They weren't. Poland, the object of a resurgent Germany's most strenuous enmity, put mathematicians to work on Enigma intercepts nearly as soon as the German army started using the machine. The Poles attacked the endless wilderness of possibilities with no tools save pencil and paper. In a feat of intellectual heroism unique in the war, and perhaps in the history of mathematics, they broke Enigma.

They built working models of the German Enigma machines, and in the summer of 1939, suspecting their nation was on the verge of a fight it would likely lose, they gave one to Britain. By that time the Poles had moved beyond pencil and paper to build machines to sort through the possible settings. They called them *bombas*—bombs—but nobody knows why; perhaps because they ticked during their cogitations.

After Poland went down, the British largely pursued the mechanical solutions. In their Code and Cipher School at a redbrick estate some fifty miles northwest of London called Bletchley Park, ten thousand staffers tended ranks of what were by then called bombes as the machines pulled coherent messages out of all the billions of permutations.

The bombes made the work possible. It was still excruciatingly repetitive, always intense and frustrating, often baffling. The codebreakers got considerable help in their work in the spring of 1941, when the *U-110* torpedoed two ships in a westbound convoy. A corvette immediately set upon the submarine and forced it to the surface with depth charges. The crew abandoned the boat as soon as it broke water and were picked up by the corvette. A Royal Navy destroyer arrived on the scene, saw the submarine still afloat, and sent over a boarding party. The British sailors found the U-boat deserted and made a hasty, skillful search. Before it sank, they took off a sheaf of papers and an oblong wooden box.

When the destroyer made port, this harvest was handed over to waiting Naval Intelligence officers. One of them exclaimed, "What! This . . . ? And this . . . ? We've waited a long time for one of these." It was an Enigma machine, all its settings just as they had been when the first depth charge exploded.

Everyone kept quiet about this capture for decades. The British official history, *The War at Sea,* published in 1954, came no closer to explaining its significance than that mention of "one of these," and quoting the first sea lord's congratulations, which ended, "The petals of your flower are of rare beauty."

The man who had inadvertently made those petals available to his enemies disappeared with the *U-110.* He was Captain Fritz-Julius Lemp, who had opened the long fight by sinking the *Athenia.*

The British named the information gained from their Enigma decryptions Ultra. Although they'd been openhanded with their magnetron, they didn't tell the Americans they'd cracked Enigma until after Pearl Harbor. Throughout the war they used the shrewdest gambler's instincts in playing the cards Ultra dealt them. Any move too obviously spurred by knowledge gleaned from orders enciphered by Enigma could have let the Germans know that someone had learned how to listen to them.

King was less cautious about the information flowing into the Tenth Fleet than his British colleagues thought he should be. He wanted to take after the *Milchkühe.* These were Type XIV U-boats, nicknamed "milk cows" because they dispensed liquid sustenance. They were big submarine tankers, carrying provisions and ammunition and, most important, diesel oil. A Type VII could take on enough fuel from one to double the length of its war patrols. By the time the Tenth Fleet began its operations, the Type XIVs had met and refueled some four hundred U-boats, and ten of them were at sea.

King intended to use what he'd learned from Ultra to destroy them. The keepers of the oracle said the operation would be too risky. King wrote the first sea lord, "While I am equally concerned with you as to security of [Enigma] information it is my belief that we are not deriving from it fullest value. The refueling submarine is the key to high speed, long range U-boat operations. To deprive the enemy of refuelers would at once decrease the effectiveness and radius of entire U-boat deployment. With careful preparations it seems not unlikely that their destruction might be accomplished without trace."

As usual, King got his way, saying that he'd disguise the true source of the whereabouts of the U-tankers by sending over planes. The Germans would think they'd been caught solely by air reconnaissance. By midsummer, only three of the tankers were left, and two of them were in home ports being overhauled. The U-boats got hungrier, their patrols shorter.

The air ruse worked; the Germans never did discover that Enigma had been penetrated. Doenitz thought something was wrong, though. His boats seemed increasingly to be chasing convoys that evaded them and attacked by enemies that couldn't have found them with radar alone.

His own country's intelligence service was superb, almost always able to supply the sailing date and destination of a convoy. Still, the convoys somehow disappeared between making sail and making port. German Naval Intelligence—which was more meticulous than that of the country's army or air force—insisted its system could not have been compromised. There had to be an agent, albeit a supernaturally good one, somewhere in the Kriegsmarine. Erhard Martens, who ran Naval Intelligence, conducted an investigation so thorough that only Doentiz himself and his chief of staff for submarines, Admiral Eberhardt Godt, were spared its scrutiny. When Martens reported that there was no possible leak, Doenitz made what seems to be the only joke ever attributed to him. Turning to his chief of staff, as loyal and dutiful a lieutenant as any commander could wish, Doenitz said gravely, "Now it can be only you or me."

The bombes ticked away in Bletchley, still, always, unheard in Berlin. In 1943 Ultra revealed that the Germans had developed a torpedo that could follow the sound of propellers. All the U-boat captain had to do was fire one in the direction of a ship, and the eel would take care of the rest. Tenth Fleet got the news and, among many other measures, sent the *Neunzer,* still on her shakedown cruise in Bermuda, to help.

Steaming as Before

The essence of Atlantic duty,
1943–45

An assignment to sail around off Bermuda sounds like soft duty, but it wasn't. From 0545, when the bosun's pipe, made even less dulcet by the ship's loudspeakers, and followed by the bosun's voice—"Now reveille! Now reveille! Up all hands! Mess cooks down to the galley!"—woke the crew, the days were at once densely eventful and monotonous, filled with repetitive rehearsals for any ill fortune that might befall the ship: man overboard, collision, fire, steering gone, fire again. . . . In between the drills, more drills: gunnery practice, and torpedo launches, the costly missiles shot from their tubes amidships and set so that at the end of their run they would bob to the surface to be collected. Every day brought the ancient order "Sweepers, man your brooms," and the eternal chipping away at the rust that would silently and ceaselessly attack the ship for the rest of her life. All this activity culminated with the captain in charge of the Bermuda training group coming aboard for a final inspection, with formalities such as side boys and saluting and a solemnly exacting tour of the ship while officers and seamen alike stood nervously waiting for the judgment. "The ship passed a big inspection Monday,"

my father wrote in relief, "for which we were really beautifully scrubbed up." The *Neunzer* was deemed ready to fight the war.

But first she went north, out of the coddling mildness of the Gulf Stream and into the stiff, black-green waves off Quonset Point, Rhode Island, in Narragansett Bay. Here, in late November, the log gets cryptic: "Underway pursuant to orders to run measured mile and assist Mr. Burgess in research project." That was the torpedoes.

The British had gotten it wrong when they thought Ultra had told them the Germans were building an acoustic homing torpedo. The Kriegsmarine was about to deploy a "curly" torpedo, which, toward the end of its run, would start speeding around in circles. It couldn't hear, but its final flurry greatly increased its chances of hitting a ship in the close ranks of a convoy. The error turned out be fortunate for the Allies, however, because when the Germans did begin building actual homing torpedoes, work on how to defeat them was well along.

In Narragansett Bay the *Neunzer* helped develop ways to outfox the torpedoes. Given the technological sophistication of the attack, the defense was almost absurdly simple. While he was on this duty, my father made a drawing showing a DE towing a calliope mounted on an ornate little swan boat. An officer is pounding away at a keyboard on the fantail while torpedoes gambol about the organ like happy dolphins as a convoy steams safely past. This whimsy (which was so well received by his shipmates and then his superiors that it eventually found its way to FDR's desk) was not all that wide of the mark. What the navy scientists came up with was nothing more than a length of line towing metal rods that clanged together just under the surface a few hundred feet astern of the ship. The British called it foxer, the Americans FXR, and the Germans the buzz saw, because, they claimed, it made ten to a hundred times the noise of a ship. However loud it was, it did the job.

The torpedoes successfully beguiled, the *Neunzer* set off on the work she'd been designed to do. On New Year's Day 1944, at Norfolk, she joined up with TF (Task Force) 62, headed with a large convoy for the Mediterranean.

Here was the essence of the Atlantic War: convoy work, dull, trying, and anxious. The routine is reflected in thousands of *Neunzer* log entries. On January 5, ending his watch at 1800, my father opened his report with the universal prefatory phrase "Steaming as before," followed by "1721 convoy changed course to 1160 T speed increased to 8 kts." What a world of potential disaster lies in that "changed course." Following a preset zigzag pattern, the vessels in a convoy would turn in one direction, steam in it for a while, then in unison turn again and continue on a new course. Dozens of ships, not one showing a light, swinging around together, trying to keep track of their neighbors on the firefly glow of the radar screen, each a potential danger to the next, a vast choreography of two-, six-, and ten-thousand-ton machines, all toyed with by the wind and the set of the sea and human inattention, struggling to maintain an intricate pattern in the winter dusk.

To the end of his days my father spoke with gratitude of the helmsman who one night murmured to him in a matter-of-fact way, "Still on course 120, sir." The mundane report may have saved a hundred lives, two ships. My father had made the zig but not the zag: he'd given the routine course change, then forgotten to correct it once the ship had reached the new bearing. For a little while he was sailing back into the columns of merchantmen and was at least as great a danger to the convoy as any tracking U-boat. Then, with the five words from the helmsman, he came up on the proper course and was just steaming as before.

Alarms were plentiful on the voyage, lots of standing to general quarters, but no real trouble, and the routine was made more pleasant because "in our last port we picked up a baker, and have been living on the most wonderful bread and rolls I have ever eaten. The bread is a little like Pepperidge Farm, *fresh every day* and a little more homemade even than that."

On January 21 my father was able to follow some mighty ghosts into port. "Cape Trafalgar light sighted bearing 010T," he entered in the log, and soon the *Neunzer* was moored beneath the great fortress-rock of Gibraltar. Ships present, my father recorded, included along with "various merchant ships and units of the British Fleet" the "USS *Pillsbury* (DE-133), USS *Pope* (DE-134), USS *Chatelain* (DE-49)."

We had a lot of DEs by then.

The *Neunzer* took on depth charges from the Royal Naval Ammunition depot, then patrolled the straits to keep submarines from entering the Mediterranean. "We have been operating in some perfectly magnificent waters," my father wrote my mother without being able to tell her where. "Some of the scenery is so superb as almost to form a distraction for the officer of the deck, but no disasters have actually occurred." Indeed, "I am very well and very much on the job. The Navy is beginning to get some return on its investment in trying to process me into a naval officer, the picture of my duties and what is expected of me becomes clearer every week."

His next duty, if not momentous, was unique in the war. "Italy had turned coat, come in on our side," he told me, "and there were these five Italian submarines. They'd seen pretty tough, demanding duty in the Mediterranean. Then all of a sudden they were our great friends." The *Neunzer* was detached from "our division and formed a task force of one—everything was a task force in those days—to escort these submarines to Bermuda."

He found the crossing with his former enemies a fascinating extended lesson in flexibility and improvisation.

"Greenbacker was a bold, creative thinker," he said, and paraphrased his captain's idea: "I've got these sub skippers, they know more about it than I do, let's do some training activities."

The Italian officers were all genial cooperation, but "they said we can't do it, we've just got fuel enough, if that, to get across the Atlantic. We can't fool around.

"They had, of course, never fueled at sea in the Mediterranean. Italian submarines didn't have to fuel at sea, they were always twenty minutes away from home base.

"But this was so ingenious—we had to get an elaborate lash-up where our engineers fueled them through fire hoses." With twelve thousand gallons of fresh fuel, they could "show Green-backer what a real submarine could do when it was under pressure."

Which was a good deal. The log includes the entry "At 1500 commenced one hour of ASW (antisubmarine warfare) runs with submarine VORTICE. . . . A new type of submarine evasive tactics was encountered during these runs. After the first simulated attack, sound contact was extremely difficult to establish and maintain. The target seemed to be completely surrounded by wake interference, and it was usually impossible to establish and maintain a definite contact outside of a range of 500 yards. Interrogation of the VORTICE after she surfaced disclosed that she had backed down most of the time, thereby completely surrounding her hull with screw currents, which so quenched the Sonar beam as to make any submarine echo almost unrecognizable. This tactic had never been encountered in any training runs with U.S. submarines, nor heard mentioned by U.S. submarine officers. It was extremely effective as employed by the VORTICE, and is considered worthy of mention as a possible maneuver to be encountered against enemy submarines, and as an evasive tactic to be considered by our own submarines."

My father went on, "They were fine mariners. They were instinctive mariners. I remember the sub skipper coming alongside on the surface with this great big evil-looking diving plane a foot, two feet away from our eighth-inch plating. He didn't do it [give his helm orders], 'Right standard rudder, left fifteen degrees.' He'd just go—" And smiling at the memory more than forty years later, my father raised an index finger and moved it left and right across a short arc like a piano teacher instructing an advanced student. "Honestly, we were all agog. We were scared stiff. And he didn't turn a hair. He might have been watching a traffic light on Fifth Avenue."

The Americans could answer this daunting professionalism with some clever extemporizing. The submarines had been at war since 1940, and they were wearing out. "We had a communication by blinker. Somebody in the submarine sent the blink in English—they were better linguists than we were. The *Marea*, which was maybe a mile away off our port beam, said she was experiencing difficulty with an injector fitting, and she couldn't make twelve, or even ten knots—the most you could get if you were probably down to one diesel, because they simply had no parts, no replacements.

"Now, ours was a new ship with a nice little machine shop and some good machinist mates aboard, so we said—blink, blink, blink, blink—'Send us your fitting and some brass stock and we'll try to duplicate it.'

"And the blink blink blink came back, the quartermaster writing it down—'From *Marea* to *Neunzer*. There is no brass stock aboard the *Marea* or in the entire Italian Royal Navy.'"

Send over the part anyway, said the *Neunzer*: "We had a couple of blowtorches aboard and any number of forty-millimeter shell casings. So what did our guys do? Really, we were awfully good in World War Two. They put a blowtorch on fifty shells, melted down their own stock, got a little chunk of brass, put it on the lathe, and sent back the *Marea* this fitting that it needed to make twelve knots."

The Italian skippers took their boats close in, and "the guys got out on their fo'c'sle—their fo'c'sle is about six inches above the Atlantic—and sang us some lovely songs." The *Neunzer* sent them over the even better than Pepperidge Farm bread. They came to Bermuda. "And I think that was a marvelous way to get involved in the Atlantic and the submarine warfare."

The *Neunzer* left the submarines and headed, my father was happy to learn, for New York. On the morning of February 15, the log records, "0610 turned on running lights, passed Ambrose Light Ship abeam to starboard, entered Ambrose Channel." As Hardegan and his *U-123* had before it, the *Neunzer* passed along the beach of Coney Island, emptied by winter. My father watched the still clockwork of the Wonder Wheel as it slid past, the shrouded rides.

"I'm a son of a bitch!" he exclaimed.

Why? the others on the bridge wanted to know.

He pointed to the long glass-and-iron shed of Steeplechase amusement park, looking as industrial as a munitions plant under the February sky. Its owners, the Tilyou family, had evidently bought his wheatstalks when the World's Fair closed, and there they were, a quartet of hundred-foot-tall steel shafts rising above the roof of the park, still gleaming in the winter light, sending their superseded advertisement for peaceful husbandry to the officers of the USS *Neunzer*.

After the men got shore leave and the ship got drydocked, the *Neunzer* rejoined Task Force 62. She took another convoy to the Mediterranean, stayed at Casablanca for a week, helped shepherd a westbound convoy to New York, returned to the Mediterranean with another convoy, bringing it through to Tunisia. My father went ashore at Bizerte and visited some of the places where the army had fought the year before.

"There were evidences of not too recent violent military activity in which the quarrels of civilized nations had accomplished the destruction of most of the structures they had produced, leaving the natives very much in status quo ante—all at great expense." He went for a long walk, "sight-seeing in a dead city, a little man-made Pompeii, quiet and deserted, the shop fronts still with their signs up—some with the shutters open for business, some closed, but no one there to buy or sell. All the stock gone—old ledgers lying around on the floors and all the innards gutted with high explosives. From the water this looked like a thriving capital city, but from the streets and walks it looks like last season's fair. We passed one building militarily occupied and a cool and refreshing Mozart piano concerto rolling out from a radio—the only thing we heard except the military vehicles which are no more than part of the landscape. The boys played a ball-game with another ship today, and although they got trimmed in a double header everyone had a good time."

Then it was back west with another convoy. My father left Tunisia not exactly weary of his job, but far beyond being able to find in it any pleasing residual novelty. "It's hot as Tophet in the wardroom today, but that's only one reason why I hope we shall soon be heading home. . . . There is much about this life that is tiresome to everybody, even though our ship is really very well organized now, and runs without too much trouble. The delightful variety of life as it is lived at home, and the opportunities to live just the kind of life you want to, with help from just the people you want to see. The books you want to dabble in— of course that is almost absolutely impossible here and now. In many ways I appreciated it before, but what a colossal difference there will be to appreciation if I am ever able to resume where we left off."

The ship ran into heavy weather. There were always storms, or the imminence of them, in the Atlantic, and bad weather was rough on DEs. The shaggy-crested waves with great webs of foam seething down their flanks could run sixty feet high, and a destroyer escort was lively even in relatively calm seas. After hitching a ride on one the war correspondent Ernie Pyle wrote,

"So now I'm a DE sailor. Full-fledged one. Drenched from head to foot with salt water. Sleep with a leg crooked around your sack so you won't fall out. Put wet bread under your dinner tray to keep it from sliding.

"And you don't know what a DE sailor is? A DE, my friends, is a destroyer escort. It's a ship, long and narrow and sleek, along the lines of a destroyer. But it's much smaller. It's a baby destroyer. . . .

"They are rough-and-tumble little ships. . . . Their forward guns sometimes can't be used because of waves breaking over them. They roll and they plunge. They buck and they twist. They shudder and fall through space. Their sailors say they should have flight pay and sub pay both because they're in the air half the time, under the water the other half.

"The boys talk mostly about the storms they've been through, for when you've been through a storm on a DE you've been somewhere. They toss off angles of rolling that are incredible. They tell of times when the ship rolled all the way from 65 to 75 degrees, which is almost lying flat on the side.

"There are little things all over the ship to indicate how rough she is. Fiber rugs are fastened to the steel decks of cabins with scotch tape so they won't slide. Ash trays are tied to stanchions with wire. There are hand railings the entire length of the narrow decks. (My ship never had a man washed overboard.)"

The *Neunzer* did, early in 1944. Officers and crewmen knew the drill; the ship came about, tossed over lifelines, lowered a boat. It did no good. The sailor disappeared. "We lost him," my father said. "We'd been trained, we went though the right motions, but we were still all too green. We didn't *know* enough yet."

The weather taught them.

"We took an awful cuffing around from a storm a while ago," my father wrote in one letter; in another: "We have had stormy weather, a real tossing around. . . . It is really very fatiguing to go through several days of rough weather, for you are using your muscles 24 hours a day, awake or asleep. It takes almost as much agility to stay in the bunk as to keep your feet on deck, so everyone gets tired and discouraged, and it's impossible to keep ship effectively."

A storm meant day after day when the galley fires couldn't be lit, so there was nothing to eat but cold corned beef and "horse cock," the amply supplied bologna sausage that found few admirers on the ship. It meant broken crockery and small accidents: "The wardroom china has suffered a severe beating this trip, and we are reduced to drinking our coffee and soup from eggcups— fortunately the standard Navy egg cup is capacious, and so we do very well. Our only casualty occurred in the wardroom when Quiner [a steward's mate] had a beaker of freshly boiling coffee slop into his face and chest during a severe roll. . . . He made very little fuss about it, save for a mighty burst of rage and surprise when it happened."

The ocean offered harsher caprices than Quiner's scalding. Louis Auchincloss, the novelist-to-be, wrote of bucking westward from Plymouth, England, to Norfolk, Virginia. "The winter Atlantic was frightful, and our crossing took more than thirty days, more than Columbus took on his fourth and final voyage. One morning in the chart room, as the ship rolled and pitched, the commander steadied himself by catching hold of the side of an open doorway. I saw that the heavy door was loose and swinging. I shouted at him, but he only looked at me, and as he did so, the door closed, shearing his thumb away as a razor might cut through a piece of rope."

The storms always passed, of course, the hectic, jagged landscapes replaced by the vast flat, dully-glinting disk whose center the ship perpetually inhabited. Steaming as before: the *Neunzer* was under way for all but sixteen hours during the entire month of October 1944. "It is so terrible tiresome to be out of sight of land for weeks at a time," my father wrote on the thirtieth: "Salt water without a little entourage is the most dismal spectacle in the world. Even the most magnificent sunrises or sunsets—cloud effect and all that hoopla—are desolate for want of a stretch of beach or mountain in the distance, or even the hope of it in a few days' time. Like Dr. Johnson's dictum to the general effect that the finest landscape in the world could not but be improved by the inclusion of a comfortable inn in the foreground. This morning I did see a spectacular arrangement of sun's rays, however, which was quite impressive. The rays were really arrayed as symmetrically as a sunburst in ormolu around a mirror or clock—appearing out of dark clouds beyond which the sun had risen. I wish I could trade all the sunrises over the ocean I have been compelled to witness on the morning watch for a half dozen over some nice mountain or meadow scenery. The only thing they reveal on the ocean is a few whitecaps, a bit of kelp, or a porpoise or two."

Not always, though. The Atlantic had been a battleground for five years, and every now and then even the all-concealing ocean would yield up a remnant of old violence.

One midwinter day lookouts aboard the destroyer escort *Sims* spotted a dozen life rafts with four or five men on each, some waving to the ship. The captain, Lewis M. Andrews Jr., wrote, "I instinctively gave the order to bear down on them and, at the same time, heard the commodore telling us not to waste too much time." Andrews was surprised by this callous order, but the commodore had been at sea longer than he had, and "when we came alongside, I could see the gray of death in the faces of men frozen from life, still lashed together in sitting positions, some of the lifeless frozen arms still waving. It was the same with the rest of the rafts. The animation was caused by the rolling rafts in the sea. Our commodore knew this from prior experience but let us learn for ourselves lest we fret that we had abandoned castaways." The *Sims* left them to their long voyage.

★ ★ ★

THE ATLANTIC WAS A battleground still, but the war was changing. Doenitz's boats were there, although the wolf-pack attacks were all but over. They had become too costly for the Kriegsmarine.

Faced with the increasing effectiveness of airborne radar in the Bay of Biscay, Doenitz had responded with a tactic that was anything but timid. He had his boats outfitted with heavier batteries of antiaircraft guns. No more skulking across underwater now, he ordered: bring on the planes to fight. He had the boats cross in company, on the surface, in daylight. They would blast their way through.

It didn't work. A plane sighting a group of boats could stay out of range while it called in support, then launch an attack that overwhelmed even the massed antiaircraft fire. Doenitz was offering his enemy battle on his enemy's terms.

Soon, even this suicidal measure would be impossible. The Allied forces had come ashore on the Normandy beaches, and before long the Biscay ports, with their immortal bunkers, would change ownership.

Doenitz did not lose faith in his weapon. He did change tactics. Now, he said, rather than conducting the war against tonnage, his boats' role was "tying down" the enemy. "The U-boat," he said, "was the sole instrument that, with a few men on board, could make a wholly disproportionate contribution to success in war by sinking, for instance, just *one* ship laden with munitions, tanks, or other war material, even if it was itself lost in the process. How many soldiers would have to be sacrificed, how great an endeavor made, to destroy on land so great a mass of enemy war material." He would fight a holding action, at least until he could send new boats and improved equipment. This was in the works. His enemies knew how to use technology, but so did he.

When the world learned of the Normandy landings, my mother wrote her husband, "I worried so much when I saw a report from Germany that a convoy had been sunk in the Mediterranean on May 13. I thought it might involve you. I still think so—at last D-Day has arrived and again I worry that you are taking part in it."

In fact, my father had just left Gibraltar, headed for Virginia, and an entirely different kind of work. On the morning of July 15, 1944, the *Neunzer* sailed from Norfolk in the company of her fellow DEs *Pope, Pillsbury,* and *Frederick C. Davis,* and a newcomer, the USS *Guadalcanal.* Unlike her coterie, the *Guadalcanal* was not a pretty ship. She was a boxy, ungainly dwarf aircraft carrier, an escort carrier, a "jeep." Her presence changed the kind of war the DE-150 was fighting. Heretofore the *Neunzer*'s job had been to guard. Now it was to hunt.

Combustible, Vulnerable, and Expendable

The escort carrier joins the fight, 1944

Our Atlantic war was being won by a succession of discoveries and rediscoveries. Convoys protected the supply lines, industry supplied the ships to make up the convoys, radar could see above the water and sonar hear beneath it, Ultra could tell where the U-boats were bound before they left port.

Yet victory's complex recipe demanded one final ingredient, and the *Neunzer* had just joined up with it.

David Bradley Duncan, who graduated from the Naval Academy in 1917 and spent much of his early career in carriers, was an executive officer at the Naval Air Station in Pensacola in the spring of 1941 when he was ordered to Newport News to become captain of the USS *Long Island*. The ship did not yet exist. On the way, Duncan stopped in Washington and looked up a high-ranking friend in the Bureau of Aeronautics. "What is this thing I'm going to command?"

It turned out that Admiral William Pratt, a former chief of naval operations, had got word about the backs-to-the-wall British expedient of equipping their escorts with a single airplane, which would take off at a crucial moment. The moment had better be crucial because the plane could make just that one flight. It had no place to land. The pilot was to bail out after his single sortie. Admiral Pratt thought the U.S. navy should be doing something like this, and he said so in a *Newsweek* article. This caught the president's ever-restless eye, and FDR summoned a somewhat nonplussed Pratt to say he'd thought it over, and rather than just using the plane once and throwing it away, why not get a merchant-ship hull and convert it into a cheap little carrier? And—presidential speculation swiftly changed to presidential order—get it done in ninety days.

Duncan found his new command already well along. He looked over the plans with misgiving yielding to relief. "I felt the ship would be operable and useful," he said decades later. "She had the three elements needed to make an aircraft carrier: she had the hangar space, which could hold about a dozen airplanes; she had an elevator to get them up and down; she had a catapult to get them in the air and an arresting gear to get them back on deck. Those were the basic things, and that was it."

Basic was the word. Many of these carriers were built by Henry Kaiser, which meant they became available quickly, but were constructed below navy specifications. Most had inexpensive, cranky Skinner Uniflow steam turbines that navy mechanics knew nothing about, and far fewer watertight compartments than any navy-built fighting ship.

Halfway through watching his prototype take shape, Duncan got a telephone call from Harry Hopkins: the president wanted to see him. Duncan found FDR in bed, drinking coffee and reading newspapers. "He welcomed me very cordially and asked me to sit down and tell him about my ship. So I did, very frankly and completely, including my difficulties in getting a few things done."

The president heard him out and said, "Well, that's fine. Is it going to be done on time?"

Duncan said it was.

"Now this is the important thing. This is why I wanted to see you. Is it going to be operable and is it going to be useful? Can it get the airplanes on and off, and can they carry depth bombs, and will it be able to look for submarines?"

Duncan again said yes.

The president was pleased. "That's what I really wanted to find out." With Duncan sitting there FDR picked up the phone and called Admiral Howard Vickery, head of the Maritime Commission. "Vickery, about those eight ships—the C-3s [freighters] that are building, that you told me about. I want them converted into aircraft carriers right away. That can go forward right now and we'll take care of all the paperwork and so forth."

The ships got built—seventy-eight of them eventually—and officially designated "escort carrier (CVE)," but nobody called them that; they were "Woolworth flattops," "one-torpedo ships," "Kaiser coffins"; and as for the CVE, that stood for "combustible, vulnerable, and expendable."

With a flight deck of less than five hundred feet, they were half the length of a fleet carrier and, at eight thousand tons, weighed slightly more than a quarter as much. They carried twenty-four to thirty planes.

A newspaperman who sailed in one wrote, "A jeep carrier bears the same relation to a normal naval vessel that is borne to a district of fine homes by a respectable, but struggling working-class suburb. There is a desperate effort to keep up appearances with somewhat inadequate material and not wholly satisfactory results."

"They were just barely good enough," said Captain Daniel V. Gallery, "but they *were* good enough."

Just as the DE was a budget destroyer, so was the CVE a budget carrier, and the ships were built the same way—"by farmers, shoe clerks, and high school gals," wrote Gallery; "all over our country, factories accustomed to building bridges, oil tanks, and farm machinery, built miscellaneous sections of ships. These sections poured into Vancouver by rail and were put on an assembly line as if they were automobile parts." Gallery went on, "A bunch of amateurs, setting up assembly-line production for any kind of a ship, are taking a long chance. To do it for a specialized type like an aircraft carrier seems like a miscalculated risk. But the fifty-five jerry-built ships that crowded down those building ways in Vancouver performed at sea like professional men-of-war."

Vancouver was where Gallery picked up his CVE, the *Guadalcanal*. He had been transferred from Iceland and was "bitterly disappointed" when he got orders to take his new ship to the Atlantic: "After my year and a half up in Reykjavik I figured I had served my time in that ocean and should be eligible for parole to the Pacific, where the fighting was much more exciting than the monotonous grind of anti-submarine warfare." Later he changed his mind, realizing that in the Pacific "the jeeps usually were very small fish in a big pond. In the Atlantic they were the big fish in the pond. There was plenty of sea room, and the CVEs still had a big job to do in clinching the victory over the U-boats." And Gallery managed to bring a good deal of excitement to the Atlantic with him.

The CVEs changed the way things could be done. The rule of convoy had held for two wars that it was a waste of effort to chase after a submarine. The odds of turning one up were infinitesimal. But now the odds were shifting. During its first month of life the Anti-Submarine Warfare Operations Research, a branch of Vannevar Bush's National Defense Research Committee established in 1942, calculated the effectiveness of search patterns. A destroyer equipped with radar could check seventy-five square miles of ocean in an hour; in the same amount of time a plane with meter radar could cover one thousand square miles, and a plane with microwave radar, three thousand.

As more and more escort vessels became available, some of

them were sent not to protect convoys but rather, gathered around the nucleus of a jeep carrier, to go looking for U-boats. These groups had a name with a snarl to match *wolf pack: hunter-killer.*

The CVEs initially proved yet another irritant to Admiral King, but that didn't last. An early example, the *Bogue*, CVE-9, arrived in the Atlantic just before the Tenth Fleet opened for business on May 20, 1943. Two days later, following Tenth Fleet instructions, planes from the *Bogue* sank the *U-564*. It was both the *Bogue*'s first victory and the Tenth Fleet's.

After the war Captain Gallery wrote a series of highly popular books about his career. My father never much cared for them, and this puzzled me when I was younger, for I knew the *Neunzer* had spent a good deal of time in company with the *Guadalcanal*. Reading the books helps explain his coolness. The historian Clay Blair, probably the greatest authority on America's war against the U-boats, calls them "self-serving." I'd say self-satisfied might be more like it, but without question Gallery was the real thing.

Not long after the *Guadalcanal* was commissioned, Captain Gallery was talking with the chief boatswain's mate. What, Gallery asked, did the chief think of the draft of new men who had arrived yesterday from boot camp? "Cap'n, I'd swap 'em all for a bucket of oily rags." In three cruises, Gallery built from this unpromising material a crew capable of pulling off something the U.S. navy hadn't accomplished since 1815.

In early June 1944, the *Guadalcanal,* almost out of fuel, was heading back to port when the destroyer escort *Chatelain* reported a contact on its sonar, and then, "Contact evaluated as sub. Am starting attack."

THE *U-505* WAS NOT a lucky ship. Continually beset by mechanical problems, the submarine had barely been able to start its current war cruise, the crew still unsettled from a weird event unique in U-boat annals. A few months earlier, running three hundred feet below the surface under the buffeting of a depth-charge attack, the crew heard what they thought was some electrical equipment giving way in the conning tower. It wasn't. The captain had shot himself.*

Now the first hint the crew had that they were in trouble was the hammer of the *Chatelain*'s depth charges dousing the lights and knocking their Sunday dinner into the scuppers. Desperate voices reported that the torpedo room was flooding. The captain decided to abandon ship.

The *U-505* blew her tanks and shot up to the surface. Captain Gallery told his DEs to fire no heavy stuff at the submarine: "I want to capture this bastard."

Then came—probably for the only time ever over a loud-speaker—the order "Away all boarding parties." The *Pillsbury* churned up, launched a boat, and with the Germans all in the water, Lieutenant Albert David jumped onto the sub's deck. Followed by torpedoman's mate A. L. Kripsel and S. E. Widomaik, radar man second class, he scrambled down into the lightless, alien intricacies of the submarine's interior, where, everyone knew, explosive charges had surely been set, and the sea cocks opened to flood the boat just in case it didn't blow up.

Half of this was true: a solid rod of water six inches across was cannoning into the vessel, which had only minutes more to live. The boarding party managed to stanch it. The *Guadalcanal* ordered the *U-505*, the first enemy vessel captured by Americans on the high seas since the War of 1812, taken in tow.

The *Pillsbury* moved in so close that her quarry dealt her the injury the men on the *Neunzer* had feared from the Italian submarine. One of the diving planes pierced the DE's hull, but she stayed afloat.

_____

*The boat's first watch officer took charge and got the badly shaken crew safely home to Lorient.

All the *U-505*'s codebooks and papers were seized intact. David received the Medal of Honor, one of just two given for the Battle of the Atlantic. Admiral King was angry, of course, this time because he was certain that the news would leak out and Doenitz would change his codes. But miraculously, every single one of the hundreds of sailors involved in this spectacular coup kept his mouth shut about it until after the war was over.

In fact, King himself almost let out the secret. Gallery found on the submarine a book called *Roosevelt's Kampf,* which detailed the president's plans for world domination, and sent it to King. The Fleet Admiral, much amused, passed it up the line to FDR, who replied with a thank-you note. Somehow that note reached Francis Low, who immediately became furious at Gallery for cavalierly endangering the secret. Gallery naturally was quick to explain to Low that King had sent the book, and, Gallery remembered happily, "They dropped the idea of teaching anybody anything about security."

ONCE THE *NEUNZER* JOINED up with the *Guadalcanal,* she became part of a hunter-killer group. Wirt Williams was irritated when his four-stacker was assigned to an escort carrier. "That's her, that's our baby," he has one of his officers say when the CVE first comes into sight. "The white hope of the Yer-ninted Stytes Nyvy. Look at her, boy, look at her. Get used to her. We're going to be her foot-servant and vassal from here on."

Nobody aboard the *Neunzer* minded this servitude. Attending flight operations was far more interesting duty than riding herd on thirty-year-old freighters. Their counterparts aboard the *Abercrombie* felt the same way when that DE left Orange for the Pacific in the company of CVEs. "There was inherent drama," wrote Edward Stafford, "in the burst of bright bunting at the signal halyards; in the sharp, fast turnaway from the crawling convoy and the welcome breeze over the bridge and deck as speed built up; and in the roar of aircraft engines on the carriers' stubby decks that rose to sustained successive snarls as the blue-winged planes made their short runs and took to the air, the agile Wildcats leaping skyward, the heavier Avengers lumbering level with the deck or sinking slightly as they picked up speed."

Those navy planes rasping off a runway the size of an ice cream truck's roof accounted for the only excitement the *Neunzer* had that summer and fall, save for the storms. In a half year of hunting, there was no killing at all. Yet the empty months were themselves a kind of victory, emblematic of the way things were going in the Atlantic, just as the *Guadalcanal*'s exploit had been.

Two days after Gallery captured his U-boat the Allies went ashore in France on D-day ("Boy, oh, boy!" yelled one happy sailor on the *Guadalcanal* when the news came through. "Look what Eisenhower had to do to top us!"). Two years earlier the Germans had been able to keep a hundred boats at sea at one time; now it was half that number. American yards were turning out a million tons of new shipping each *month*.

ON DECEMBER 25, 1944, my father began a letter by pasting a picture of a sprig of mistletoe over the emblem at the top of the stationery, appending the rueful caption "Nothing under here but the Navy seal."

He thought, naturally, of past Christmases: "I remember a wonderful magic show performed one Xmas afternoon in Sacramento by a mysterious magician in a kimono. Also a new and beautiful little steamboat baked to death in an oven after its maiden voyage in the tub. There is also the smell of the little alcohol lamps burning under new steam engines."

He imagined the scene back home: "I know you will be surrounded with loving members of the family—and probably about now things will be rather quiet (4:00 pm)—one or two people perhaps feeling a little sleepy, or at any rate comfortably full. Well, it's exactly the same on board—the post-prandial lull has set in—two hardy players are keeping a card game going and all is quiet. Everybody is thinking of home and family—in other words they would rather be dozing off with them than with their fellow officers. But it does seem like Christmas, even though we spend it floating around in this fighting machine in a thick fog.

"Today there was a magnificent meal served for the boys—and at a leisurely pace so there was time for them to enjoy it. It's holiday routine, and a movie, which was passed over to us on a line early in the day. We also had a lovely Christmas dinner just as filling and almost as good as the home-cooked variety, and managed with some Christmas wrapping paper and other odds and ends to achieve very gay decorations in the wardroom.

"We had a carol sing last night on the fantail. It was darken ship [all exterior lights doused] but the moon was out, the fog not too thick, and everybody turned out and really had a good time. I played the violin for the singing and it seemed to be much appreciated. I enjoyed it and so did all the men. It was really rather touching to me how willingly and spontaneously they all congregated topside at the mere announcement that there would be a little carol singing for anyone who cared to participate."

I suspect he was right about the men having enjoyed it. Some fifty years later I was surprised and pleased to get a letter from one of his shipmates talking about how well he remembered that evening—the violin and the singing on the fantail in the moonlight, that last Christmas of the war.

Captain Just's Last Fight

The final days of the Kriegsmarine, 1945

A month earlier *U-1230* had ghosted along the coast of Maine and into Frenchman's Bay, where the boat put ashore two spies: Erich Gimpel, who had been an effective Nazi agent for a decade, and Willie Caldwell, a Connecticut boy with such passionate pro-Axis sympathies that the German secret service had smuggled him to Berlin by way of Lisbon. Although the landfall had been perfect, the mission was planned with ludicrous crudity. Soon the two men found themselves trudging through a blizzard along Route 37 in their summer shoes, carrying $80,000 in cash—American cash, but bound in wrappers that read "Deutsche Reichsbank"—and a suitcase with a German radio transmitter in it. The FBI trailed them as far as New York, arrested them, and found Gimpel much more talkative than might be expected for one of his calling.

More agents were on the way, he said, to be followed by U-boats that were even then "being fitted out with a rocket-firing device for guided missiles, which would enable them to bomb the coast from positions well under the horizon." Vice Admiral Jonas Ingram, the new commander in chief of the Atlantic fleet, thought enough of this to call a press conference. "Gentlemen," he told the reporters, "I have reason to assume that the Nazis are getting ready to launch a strategic attack on New York and Washington by rocket bombs."

The Tenth Fleet was skeptical (they'd heard such rumors long before, but believed reconnaissance photos of what looked like rocket launchers being fitted to submarines in fact showed something more prosaic: wooden planks laid to help load torpedoes), but the presence of the spies proved that U-boats were back in our coastal waters.

In fact, Doenitz was gathering his boats for Seewolf, as he named this final cast of the dice against the American enemy.

The technology he'd been counting on had come through, but slowly. The Type XXI, powerful and heavy, could carry twenty-three torpedoes and swim underwater on its batteries for three days straight. It also was capable of a submerged speed of seventeen knots. But only two of them would ever become operational.

What the admiral did have on hand was the snorkel. This allowed the boat to breathe as it ran on its diesels with only a tiny piece of apparatus showing, one so small it could escape radar detection. Like the escort carrier, it was just good enough. Crews detested it. The device had a ball float that automatically closed when the snorkel dipped beneath the water. This was supposed to last for only a few seconds at a time, but one German sailor remembered what happened when the ball got stuck and the voracious engines vacuumed up the oxygen in the boat: "The men gasped for air, their eyes bulging. The Chief lowered the boat, bringing the *Schnörkel* head below the surface in an effort to loosen the float. To no avail. Breathing became ever more difficult; suffocation seemed imminent. The Chief gesticulated wildly, trying to tell his men to lay down the air mast, which might result in unlocking the float. With agonizing effort, the mechanics turned handles, lowered the mast by cable, then erected it again with the primitive winch. Painful minutes passed, but then the mast drained and the seawater gurgled down into the bilges. The float cleared with a snap and air was sucked into the boat with a long sigh. The sudden change in pressure burst many an eardrum. Some of the men covered their faces in pain and sagged to the deck plates."

Despite playing such tricks, the snorkel offered the only real chance a U-boat now had to get to sea undetected. In March 1945, seven submarines, all outfitted with it, assembled along the Norwegian coast; they would sail in two groups of three with one going alone. When they arrived off the United States, in April, their commanders were to open sealed orders and go into action.

PAUL JUST, CAPTAIN OF the *U-546,* had begun his military career as a flier. Many German submarine officers had started out that way, despite the near-total difference of conditions in the two services, the endless blue acreage of the sky, and a world where sweating rivets were never more than a couple of feet from your face.

Just had commissioned *U-546,* a Type IX, in June 1943 and taken the boat on two war patrols. He'd sunk no ships, but his voyages had not lacked for incident. On the first, he left Kiel in late January 1944. Two weeks later he was attacked by a British Sunderland flying boat. It killed a man in his gun crew and damaged the boat's engines, but Just continued his patrol. Coming home across the Bay of Biscay in April, he was attacked from the air three nights running. The boat suffered no harm, shot down a B-24 Liberator bomber, and got back to base late in May.

Two months later, with a snorkel fitted, it set out again and again got in a fight with an airplane. Neither plane nor boat was harmed, but the *U-546* used up its entire store of antiaircraft ammunition in the encounter. Captain Just had to return to France to replenish the supply and fix the misbehaving snorkel. The boat went back out, attacked a carrier, and in turn got depth-charged for three hours. It was a long cruise—150 days—and it ended in Germany because the French ports had been taken. At Kiel, the now constant air raids delayed the overhaul for weeks, but the boat was ready when Doenitz's orders for Seewolf came through.

Every one of the men in *U-546* knew what the odds were. Doenitz was taking casualties of more than 70 percent. In January 1945 he had sunk seven ships and lost six boats, an insupportable rate of exchange. "Our situation is desperate," Just wrote later. "The commander can no longer guide us as he did during the successful group tactics of the battles of the Atlantic. The aircraft carriers and destroyer formations have been brought into combat. A single carrier group can police thousands of sea miles."

But if Just didn't have much hope, he did have fourteen torpedoes, and *U-546* put to sea on March 21.

SEVEN BOATS: PERHAPS NOT much of an armada, but look what only five had accomplished in the weeks after Pearl Harbor.

Everything had changed since then, however. Once we could be taken completely by surprise when German submarines appeared off our coast; once we had the *Atik* and the *YP-438* and the *Kitsis* to throw into the breach. Now the Tenth Fleet knew what Doenitz planned, and Admiral Ingram knew what to do about it. For Operation Teardrop, the last and largest antisubmarine effort of the war, he had four escort carriers and forty-two DEs at his disposal and would, he said, "bar off the entire Eastern Seaboard of Canada and the United States to a phalanx of snorkel boats." His cordon would consist of two "barriers." The carriers *Mission Bay* and *Croatan* and their attendant DEs would make up the first one, the northern barrier; *Core* and *Bogue* the southern barrier.

The *Neunzer* would be part of the latter. She was in Miami on April 9 when she got orders to dash north to Argentia, New-foundland, in company with her fellow DEs *Chatelain, Pillsbury, Pope, Flaherty,* and *Frederick C. Davis.*

The day before, my father had written my mother a relaxed, high-spirited letter that ended with "P.S. the baker gave us all a slice of delicious hot apple pie tonight which he had just taken out of the oven. The rigors of war!" Now, apparently feeling some sort of sad prescience, he dashed her off a note that concluded, "There undoubtedly will be some break in my letters after this one, dear. . . . Darling, I do love you so much and always will. It would make me so happy just to have your companionship once more. This is number 1 of all the important things I must forgo in these times. War is such a wretched thing—extravagant, destructive, nerve wracking—and monotonous. The wrong appli-cation of so many distinguished abilities, and so much material."

The *Neunzer* had a new skipper now. Captain Greenbacker had been assigned to a Pacific command, and his exec, Virgil Gex, relieved him. He took the *Neunzer* out of sunny Miami back into winter. "It has been a normal week aside from rough cold weather," my father wrote, "to which we are by now accustomed, but which certainly cracked down on us with very little prepara-tion. Now we look on cold whitecap churned water, and right now on bleak craggy mountains." The ship left the bleak crags of Argentia to take up the barrier patrol with its fellow DEs and the carrier *Bogue.* These sentries had a bitter time of it. This was the April Atlantic at its worst: steady winds of forty to fifty knots, green water solid over the decks, spray and drizzle melding into a stinging gray haze that never lifted. While they were at sea, the navy lost a staunch friend. On April 12 Franklin Roosevelt died. "We had our memorial services for the President today," my father wrote on the fifteenth. "I was on watch and couldn't attend, but understand it was fine."

On that same day, destroyer escorts of the *Croatan* group in the northern barrier sank the first of the Seewolf submarines; the next day, two more. Then it was the southern barrier's turn.

April 23, 1945, found fourteen DEs combing a hundred miles of ocean between Newfoundland and the Azores. Early in the afternoon a plane from the *Bogue* spotted a submarine running on the surface about seventy miles from the *Pillsbury*, where Commander F. S. Hall was in charge of the DE Task Unit 22.7.1: DEs *Pillsbury*, *Otterstetter*, *Flaherty*, *Pope*, *Keith*, *Chatelain*, *Frederick C. Davis*, *Neunzer*, *Hubbard*, *Varian*, *Otter*, *Hayter*, *Janssen*, and *Cockrill*. Commander Hall formed a scouting line, the ships three thousand yards apart, and headed toward the place where the submarine had, predictably, submerged. As a darkening in the wind-driven murk indicated nightfall, the ships steamed along, their sonar flinging out its unceasing query. Just before midnight, my father recorded in the log, "All hands manned battle stations, proceeded to assist USS DAVIS on possible sonar contact . . . negative results."

But they'd very likely made contact with the *U-546*.

"Although we try our best to conserve electricity and every man moves as little as possible," wrote Captain Just, "after twenty-four hours of silent running we must surface, raise the mast of the snorkel, and face whatever immediate danger awaits us. For four weeks we had to alternate between creeping and snorkeling in order to avoid a carrier group in this part of the sea. Now the hydrophones register screw sounds. They swell up and down until at last they fade away."

Hours later, on the morning of April 24, the screw sounds returned.

"Go to periscope depth," ordered Just, and he took in a "quick panorama view. The wind has abated, the stormy sea has changed into a high, long swell. The view is good, there is no enemy in sight. At the horizon however stands a large dark square. I recognize the silhouette from another trip: an aircraft carrier. Its protectors, the destroyers, are nowhere to be seen, no airplanes in the sky. . . . It would make no sense to become targets without first having an opportunity to launch an attack ourselves. So we dive down to ninety meters. And listen."

The propeller noises returned. Captain Just ran up his periscope again. "It's the protectors," the DEs.

"Now we can be the ones to launch a surprise attack. Another quick look over the entire horizon to determine whether any danger looms from behind. All is clear. The carrier is nowhere to be seen. The destroyers are running at full speed. They are lean and beautiful, cutting through the swells like knives. It is a magnificent, a dangerous sight.

"Every man is stationed, all torpedoes poised to fire. Suspense. Concentration. The motor of the periscope purrs softly. . . . Enemy speed twenty-eight knots—distance nine hundred meters—bearing forty."

Just's first watch officer put the captain's estimates into the range calculator. "Time seems to creep, sweat beads my forehead. 'Distance six hundred—bearing seventy.' Waiting just a few more seconds, the breath falters, the mouth is dry. . . .

"Now he shows almost his entire broadside.

"'Tube two—GO!'

"Slight recoil on the calmly floating boat. 'Torpedo launched!' It's time to get out."

THE *FREDERICK C. DAVIS* was a veteran; she had beaten off air attacks in the Mediterranean, taken part in the invasion of southern France, won the Navy Unit Citation for her work during the Anzio invasion. Her men called her the *Fightin' Freddie,* and this was not just bumptious alliterative provincialism: sailors aboard other ships also used the nickname. (The men of the *Neunzer* liked to call DE-150 the *Mighty Buck-and-a-Half,* but it is unlikely this usage ever spread beyond the ship's own crew.)

Dawn came up on the twenty-fourth to show everything as it should be, the *Hayter* three thousand yards to starboard, the *Neunzer* three thousand yards to port. The *Davis*'s men were at breakfast.

At 0829 the soundman got a contact, "very sharp and clear," he reported. The ship rode over it as Lieutenant Robert Minerd, the JOOD, called the captain, J. R. Crosby, in the wardroom where he was still with his eggs and coffee, to tell him, while the OOD ordered "right standard rudder." "Am investigating possible contact," the *Davis* reported. Five minutes later she picked up the contact again. At 0840 the submarine—if that's what it was—lay only 650 yards away.

The *Davis* knew her job as well as any ship in the navy. Perhaps the crew's seasoned expertise had made them all a little casual. Afterward, my father heard that the *Davis* hadn't really buttoned itself up for action, hadn't gone to general quarters.

The torpedo killed everyone in the wardroom in one red second. Bulkheads and decks tore apart. The engine room was a roiling molten pool—two men made it out, neither lived long—and the mainmast fell. Some men escaped from their quarters up a ladder whose rungs were so hot they glowed. Lieutenant Minerd made his way out of the smoke-filled pilothouse, past a lookout hanging dead from a belaying pin on the signal bridge. The executive officer, wearing no life jacket, jumped off the bridge and disappeared forever. Seawater shorted out the service generators, which killed the pressure on the bilge pumps and the fire hoses. That didn't make any difference, though. The *Davis*'s back was broken, and she split in half. Some of the crew tried to man their battle stations, but it was too late.

Seven minutes after she'd regained that promising sonar contact, the *Davis* was gone. A few minutes later, her depth charges exploded; some had been set on safety, but some couldn't be reached. The explosions were violent enough to knock out the

Flaherty's sound gear as she steered into the spreading oil slick to pick up survivors. She couldn't launch a boat—the seas were too high—but her men threw lines over the sides, and *Davis* crewmen on a raft had just reached one when the *Flaherty*'s sonarman, who had his equipment running again, said he'd picked up a submarine. That's the sinking *Davis* you're getting, an officer told him. No, said the sonarman, he had the *Davis* and the submarine both, "positive submarine, very deep." The captain knew the priorities of the situation. He ordered the rescue lines cut and went after the submarine. The *Hayter* was sent to help the survivors. "The HAYTER commenced a circular sweep," her action report reads, "around the outside of the area where the survivors were located. Individual survivors were first brought to the side of HAYTER by members of the HAYTER crew who thoughtless of their own life or injury jumped from the side of the ship into rough and shark infested waters." The *Hayer* got a boat launched, and it returned to the ship nearly foundering, with only six inches of freeboard showing. It took an hour and a half to gather in sixty-six survivors and eleven corpses. "Shock, chills and acute anxiety greatly predominated and obscured practically all other symptoms until they diminished. About one third were in good shape and needed no treatment other than dry clothes. About one third were shaking so badly that they couldn't undress. About one third were unconscious or semiconscious." Most of them "snapped back to normal with amazing rapidity under warm blankets with a dose of brandy" administered by the crewmen who "rendered emergency aid with alacrity and wisdom and nursed the patients with tenderness and a rough good will that played a large role in restoring the boys' morale as well as their bodies to normal."

THE *DAVIS*'S DEATH WAS identical to many so prodigally dispensed by the Kriegsmarine since the distant summer of 1939. What happened afterward was not. The U.S. navy had been fighting

U-boats for a long time now, and the action that followed has come to be seen as a sort of final exam that ratified the service's long and costly education.

Captain Just knew what was coming: "Hell awaits us." He ordered every man not on watch to his bunk, to conserve air, and moved away at one knot. "The instinct to flee makes us wish we could take off at full speed . . . but a slowly turning screw is almost inaudible." He had gone half a mile when the radioman reported, "Five strong points of sound can be heard. What is happening above us is unmistakable. The five destroyers are separating and positioning themselves in formation. Their screws are switching on and the hunt for us begins."

The destroyer escorts followed him, lost him, picked him up again. They attacked with depth charges and hedgehogs.

Just took his boat as deep as it could go, to nearly six hundred feet. "Here and there the wood of the inner lining crackles. It sounds creepy in the breathless silence. Nineteen atmospheres of water press together the iron pipes in which we live.

"Crashes envelop us. Six heavy bombs very near. The entire boat is shaken, glass clinks, objects fly through the rooms, the lights go out."

As planes from the *Bogue* circled in the gray sky, the DEs went in on creeping attacks, a tactic developed by the British in which one ship keeps sonar contact, guiding the other when the crash of exploding depth charges briefly deafens the ship that dropped them. Here is a fragment of the group's battle report:

1254: VARIAN *reported a large air bubble.*

1255: DE NEUNZER *was ordered to the scene of contact.*

1259: HUBBARD *reported indications that U-boat was at depth of 600 feet.*

1314: *Another creeping attack delivered.*

1320: JANSSEN *relieved by* FLAHERTY *at scene of contact.*

1341:   *Creeping attack delivered.*

1346:   DE CHATELAIN *ordered to scene of attack.*

1418:   *ComtCortDiv 62,* in OTTER, *and* DE HAYTER *left scene of* DAVIS *torpedoing to deliver survivors to escort carriers* CORE *and* BOGUE. DE OTTERSTETTER *remained on scene of torpedoing to continue search for any remaining survivors.*

1515:   VARIAN *reported depth indication that U-boat was at depth of 580 feet.*

1516:   *Another depth-charge attack delivered.*

1545:   DE COCKRILL *ordered to scene of contact.*

1549:   *Creeping attack delivered by* NEUNZER, VARIAN, *and* HUBBARD, *with* CHATELAIN *as directing ship.*

And so the long day wore on.

Despite all the spaciousness of sky above them, the men aboard the destroyer escorts felt something of the cramped anxiety the German crew below experienced in having to do everything for hour after hour, always slowly. The DEs were tied to the speed of the submarine as they took turns dropping depth charges and everyone stood at his battle station, cold and tense and remembering what had happened to the *Davis.*

It was worse for the men they were hunting.

"The deathblow threatens us once more," wrote Just. "The screw sounds become clearer. One wants to close one's ears, to scream, to wish oneself away. . . . Like a terrible storm it thunders down upon us. Five bombs arrive hard and so damn close that the boat rolls and shakes. . . . Water leaks are reported everywhere. The rudder is stuck hard a-port. But no matter; we are more or less trapped in place anyway. The inside of the boat is devastated."

The *546*'s crew worked in the faint, dying shine of the emergency lights. "The eyes of the men hang on me. Another attack.

Again the thundering and cracking breaks down upon us. 'Large water leak in the engine room!' Now it is serious. . . . No longer does a jet of water stream in; it is an unbelievable amount, an avalanche of white water. . . . In no time the weight presses into the boat by the ton. The bilge, the room under the floorboards fills up in minutes. *U-546* is sinking."

1700:   As VARIAN *fires Hedgehog on his target,* HUBBARD *starts in for Hedgehog run,* NEUNZER *holding contact also.*

1718:   VARIAN *commences dropping,* NEUNZER *still holding contact.*

"The destruction and devastation on the boat are indescribable," wrote Just. "Inch-thick screw joints have been severed from the steel walls. Big electronic devices have been torn free and hang from the ceiling by their cables. All of the lockers have burst; clothes, shoes, and kitchenware are heaped together in chaotic disarray."

His chief engineer, who had been on thirteen war patrols, told the captain, "I've been through a lot, but I've never been banged up as badly as this." Seawater was mixing with the hydrochloric acid in the broken batteries, and a lethal tang of chlorine gas added itself to all the other reeks in the thick, spent air.

The crew had been at action stations for thirty hours, had eaten nothing for twenty-four.

"The end is here. We must go up."

The men gave the boat a tense, weary cheer, then "the valves are ripped open. Hissing, the air presses the water out of the diving tanks. Thank God, we still have compressed air left over, the pipes are in order. We rise. Now—the boat is out. It rocks amid the swells."

1838:   *U-boat surfaced.*

There it was, a few hundred square feet of dour metal, dingy under its brief sea-glaze, a strangely humble sight to have drawn so many people so very far, to have taught them so many new trades, before they could be privileged to see it.

Every ship in range opened fire, and the *Flaherty* got off two torpedoes. The submarine had been badly wounded; the first torpedo missed but the second passed right over the now-sinking stern.

Captain Just and his crew crawled out into this. He had thought of trying to man the deck guns, but gave that up before the crescent of vengeful DEs. "We would be unable to reach our guns even if it had made sense to do so."

He gave his last order—"Abandon ship"—and "I slide down the oily wet deck, want to hold tight, tumble into the water." The *U-546,* still driven by its electric motors, moved away from him.

He tried to count his sailors in the water, lost track of them, then saw his boat: "*U-546* will no longer swim. There—now: slowly the bow tips, cuts downward, the stern continues to fall, until the bow stands almost vertically for a few seconds and then silently, faster and faster, glides into the deep. I stare at the spot. *U-546* is no more."

As the sea blossomed with little one-man life rafts, Captain Gex on the bridge of the *Neunzer* gave the order to cease firing. "So we did," my father told me.

"The hell we did," Bill Epstein told me. He'd manned one of the twenties on the *Neunzer* and, thinking of my father one day half a century later, had looked his name up in the phone book and got me. A lot of destroyer-escort men—like sailors on any class of vessel—would get into boasting rivalries and then fistfights about the comparative virtues of their ships, but, Mr. Epstein told me (and I'd had no idea of this), the *Davis* and the *Neunzer* saw themselves as brothers. They even had a saloon where the crews mingled on leave, a bar on West Forty-fourth

Street named the Palace; pictures of the *Davis* and the *Neunzer* hung on the wall together there. "So when the cease-fire order came, we took our time."

Nonetheless, the *U-546* fared better per capita than the *Davis*. The DE lost over half her crew, and Lieutenant Minerd was one of only three officers who survived. Most of the *U-546*'s fifty-nine men were pulled, cold, shaken, dripping, aboard the destroyer escorts.

"The destroyers have ceased firing," Just wrote. "I lie on my back on the rubber dinghy—a small living creature raised and lowered by the mighty waves beneath the wide sky. For a brief moment I feel myself set free in nature, gripped by its beauty. Life itself has me again, but soon I become conscious of reality. I am soaked to the bone, shaking with cold and exhaustion. Will we be saved?"

Yes, but not without yet one more scary moment for Captain Just.

"An American ship moves forward. Over her side hangs a cargo net. Faces stare down upon us, the detested enemies." Just was too weak to get up the net. Tied to his raft with a "safety leash," he found himself being raised by the roll of the ship, then dragged back down under the surface. "A tree-tall Negro, a knife between his teeth, climbs down to me over the rail. Muscles seemingly made of steel play under his white shirt. Leisurely he takes the knife out of his mouth—and cuts the leash."

"Free—upwards . . . ," and Captain Just lived to never fight another day.

THE *NEUNZER* GOT ONLY one of the prisoners. His raft had been clustered with those of other survivors, at the mercy of the wind, which blew him away from the group. The rafts drifted away from him; a ship stood in toward them. He tried to catch up, failed, then, realizing that being among strangers on the closer

Neunzer was a far better prospect than rowing to the Azores, paddled frantically to it.

He was Machinist Mate Second Class Waldmar Gaseyk, an amiable man, and everyone on the *Neunzer* took a shine to him. Captain Gex put him in a cabin with the baker, who, along with his mastery of bread and pie, spoke fluent German. Gex had hoped that the intimacy thus established would coax some military secrets out of Gaseyk.

No such luck, and the captain was a little sulky about it when, just before being put ashore at Argentia, Gaseyk delivered a speech of thanks for the good treatment he had received from his captors.

He gave away nothing about his service, but he did give my father a pair of German-navy cuff links. They're not showy. They look to be made out of a modest composition material. But the anchor on their faces is still strong and crisp these sixty-five years later, and somehow they suggest both the tenacious courage and the desperation of the Kriegsmarine in its last days.

Along with the prisoners, many of the *Davis* survivors were transferred back to the States from Argentia.

More than sixty went there aboard the *Hayter,* and before going ashore they prepared a statement for the officers and men of the destroyer escort: "The survivors of the U.S.S. F.C. DAVIS, (DE-136) wish to thank all of you for the many things, big and small, which you did during the disaster which befell our ship; for your gallant conduct, your selflessness, your excellent and tender care, your spirit of sympathy, warmth and understanding. . . .

"We feel that you know what it was like; you saw the ship go down; you were in the water with us; you administered first aid to the injured and those suffering from shock; you were beside our bunks cheering us up and giving freely of everything you had; you made every possible effort to save the dying; you buried with reverence our dead. . . .

"We cannot think of the sinking of the U.S.S. F.C. DAVIS except as the bitter loss of our ship and our shipmates. In the tragedy, however, there is one thing which we can count as a gain; and that is the experience of knowing in time of greatest need how kind fellow Americans can be."

Do Hostilities Ever Cease?

After the convoys, 1945

Early in the morning of April 29, Hitler, having just married his mistress Eva Braun in his besieged bunker, withdrew from his entourage to dictate his last testament. In it he said for one final time that the war was solely the fault of the Jews and those in their thrall, and ended with "In order to give the German people a government of honorable men to fulfill the duty of continuing the war by all means, I, as Führer of the nation, name the following members of the new cabinet: Reichpresident, Doenitz . . ."

The next day Hitler killed himself, and Doenitz was in charge of the shards of the riven, surrounded real estate that was all that remained of the Third Reich.

He was amazed. He publicly called for the fight to continue, but he meant only the fight in the east while as many Germans as could manage it surrendered to the English and Americans. What boats he still had, he used in the Baltic to take German soldiers and civilians away from the advancing Russians, in whom his countrymen had sown implacable ferocity. He did as well as he could until the end, then he surrendered and was arrested.

★ ★ ★

TWO SUBMARINES MADE IT through Admiral Ingram's cordon. *U-805*, commanded by Richard Bernardelli, sailed at snorkel depth to Cape Race, Newfoundland, ready to go to work. The orders from Doenitz, when they came, were not at all what Captain Bernardelli had expected. Hostilities had ceased at midnight on May 8; all U-boats were to surface, signal their positions, and wait for an Allied ship to come collect them. Bernardelli went up on deck. He had left the ugly weather behind in the Azores; here everything was smiling spring. The captain looked around at the sunny blue immensity that was the grave of 768 U-boats less fortunate than *U-805*. After a while he spoke. *"Verdammter Atlantik!"*

IN LATE MAY, MY father sailed with the final eastbound convoy of the war. Germany had surrendered, but the navy calculated that it would be more costly and disruptive to cancel the convoy than simply to send it off according to schedule.

Every sailor found it a strange crossing because now there was no reason to have the ships blacked out. A hundred times Lieutenant Snow, keeping the watch at night, would glance up from some chore and be shocked afresh to find lights enough to equip a small city shining all around him, bright enough to dim the Atlantic stars.

The freighters that contributed to the glow, steaming now in perfect safety, were carrying to Britain the last of the Lend-Lease cargoes, which at the final accounting had come to cost $50 billion.

THE TENTH FLEET CLOSED up shop with the same efficiency it had brought to all its tasks. By June the ramshackle offices stood empty.

ON SATURDAY, JUNE 16, 1945, the *Neunzer* was at Pier 35 in Booklyn, New York. The log reports it "moored in a nest of ships—in order from dock: USS FLAHERTY (DE135), USS CHATELAIN (DE149) and USS NEUNZER (DE150)." During the 1200–1600 watch, at 1417 exactly, "Richard B. SNOW, USNR, in accordance with BuPers orders 13-6412 left ship, detached from duty."

He thought he'd surely see the ship again—it had been his home for nearly two years, after all—but he never did.

THE *NEUNZER* IS AT Pier 35, riding little eruptions in the greasy water as her various systems twitch and snort into life. "Now go to your stations, all special sea details." The navigator is on the bridge, the captain has the conn. The lines are singled up. The lines are cast loose, whipped smartly on board. She backs away from the pier. She is out in the stream. She is gone.

RICHARD B. SNOW, USNR, is in Miami, teaching damage control. It is August. The city looks down-at-the-heels to him, worn dingy by all the eager martial life that has poured through its schools for so many seasons now.

He wants to get back to his architecture job. And, somewhat to his surprise, he wants to see his ship. "One bright spot in the picture is that the *Neunzer* appears to be due in here as a training ship one of these days. It amuses me to think how greatly I look forward to that—and the friends it will bring me, the same ones over whom I have fretted so often cooped up in the wardroom with them."

The *Neunzer* doesn't come. Instead she goes north and then, to his amused indignation, is chosen to loaf along the East Coast accompanying the *U-505* on a war-bond-selling drive: "What do you think of that soft duty the Neunzer walked into! I couldn't be more surprised than I was to hear of that. There'll be some long tiresome deck watches in port for the boys, and I can hear the wardroom saying alternately 'If this is all they have for us to do, why don't they let us go home!' and 'Well, it's better than the

Pacific!' It makes me feel a little less useless in my present job to learn what the Mighty Buck-and-a-half is up to. I'll bet the captain doesn't like it a bit. Being heart whole and fancy free, and with a certain amount of military ambition, he has been talking hungrily of Pacific duty for many months."

When my father thinks about the ship now, it's never about six straight days of horse cock and corned beef choked down on vertical decks; it's about coming home from England with the merchantmen's running lights bright around him for miles, in that final convoy of the war. "We have just completed a very calm and pleasant crossing," he had written my mother in his last letter mailed from sea, "which I really believe everyone enjoyed. . . . I was relieved of my duties as watch officer and 1st Lieutenant for this crossing, and acted as navigating officer—You know how much I enjoyed that. If you remember my sitting up until all hours three years ago to finish my navigation lessons you can imagine how I welcomed this opportunity to make an application of my lessons to a transatlantic crossing. We made a very good landfall, with no unpleasant surprises, and the weather all the way across was a dream. This is the only time I ever left New York without a feeling of despair and unbearable loneliness. The short duration of the trip, and the vast change in the feeling of things due to the conclusion of the European war made a great difference in our feelings on putting to sea. . . . The work I have done on board I have enjoyed more than any I have done on this ship ever before."

When I was just old enough to understand it, my father read me *The Caine Mutiny*. Herman Wouk's service was very different from his: the *Caine* is a 1918 four-stacker converted to a minesweeper and operating in the Pacific. No matter: he felt that no other novel to come out of the war chimed so closely with his own experience. He called my attention especially to this passage, about Wouk's hero, Willie Keith, cocktail-piano-playing college twerp turned warship commander, on his final voyage home, leaving scorched coral atolls for Manhasset, Long Island: "He spent long hours on the bridge when there was no need of it. The stars and the sea and the ship were slipping from his life. In a couple of years he would no longer be able to tell time to the quarter hour by the angle of the Big Dipper in the heavens. He would forget the exact number of degrees of offset that held the *Caine* on course in a cross sea. All the patterns fixed in his muscles, like the ability to find the speed indicator buttons in utter blackness, would fade. This very wheelhouse itself, familiar to him as his own body, would soon cease to exist. It was a little death toward which he was steaming."

The classes go well enough: "The Damage Control training is really excellent, far superior to anything you can develop on board your own ship where you can't punch holes in bulkheads and pipes at critical places."

It's hot; the streets are hot, the vegetation exhales its remote spiciness; at night the palm leaves clack like dominoes. He finds two coconuts fallen on the lawn of a vacant house. With considerable effort he cracks one open and is amazed how sweet the meat is. He sends the other to Caroline McCagg, the small daughter of Martha, the woman whose husband arranged for him to get to sea.

One evening he looks up from paperwork into an earlier war: "I thought tonight for the first time in months of the beautiful old Civil War song 'Tenting Tonight'—because of the refrain 'Many are the hearts that are waiting tonight to see the dawn of Peace.' That's what we all are doing now. Time has softened the outlines of the Civil War and its horrors and miseries for the men and women who lived through it—so the tender old song has a feeling of peace in it, which even with the cessation of 'hostilities' (do they ever cease when one nation wins and another loses?) we will probably be long in achieving. It is only an illusion seen through a haze of sentiment, of course. Times were just as rough and bitter then as the reconstruction period surely shows. But if you have your nose right to the grindstone in any job, it's hard to see the more picturesque aspects of it as posterity may see them. I have heard what I'm sure would be regrettably little discussion of the spiritual values of this war by the men engaged in fighting it. I believe that to appreciate the ethical grandness of a modern war you must keep a safe distance away from the actual theaters of operation."

He teaches more classes and begins to think about applying for Pacific duty. "It's funny how tired I used to get of all the disadvantages of life at sea, and at the same time, how much finer and more rewarding the feeling of serving afloat can be than any duty ashore."

And then it is August 16: "My darling. What a wonderful thing it was to be listening to the radio for once! This evening at just seven o'clock PM I heard the statement from the White House announcing Japan's complete military surrender—promises to sign the terms—turn over their war machines and put themselves in our hands. I felt my face contorted by a broad grin, which I made no effort to control, but I'm sure I looked like anything but a conqueror. Everyone crowded around the radio was smiling with delight, the reputedly impassive Orientals, our Chinese officers, obviously as enraptured as anyone else. One young Chinese ensign stood with his arm around the shoulders of one of our boys, listening to the declaration in a very alien tongue, whose words I know were a little strange to him, but whose purport he could not miss. After a very vivid account of the surrender, an orchestra played the National Anthem. I never heard it sound more majestic and authoritative, and then I think I was closer to tears than laughter.

"One Labor Day weekend I heard Prime Minister Chamberlain tell the world in a voice heavy with tragedy that all his efforts had failed, and that Great Britain was at war with Germany. There we were together listening to our symphony program when the broadcast was interrupted to announce the bombing of Pearl Harbor, and I remember that we neither of us took it in at all and had no real idea of what had happened until we came out of the ballet that evening. And now the cycle of fighting and bombing is completed, and the process of setting things to rights again must be undertaken. I learned the military business well enough to serve effectively in it, and now I daresay I must learn the reconstruction business."

But he doesn't seem quite in the mood to take on the reconstruction business: "I suppose downtown now the sailors are busy tearing the town apart, and I must say, I hope they do a competent job. It seems the Chamber of Commerce or some such civic body treated with the Navy here to have all the sailors restricted to the base as a precautionary measure. I am happy to say the Navy turned them down flat. It occurs to me to wonder what Miami might look like these days if it hadn't been for the Army and Navy. I think they will make a very good trade of a few windows and restaurant chairs, as against an occupation or bombing. But with the job done, the populace is beginning to get very impatient with the brutal, blundering, avaricious military services and wish them to the devil. I see numerous little remarks, statements, and speeches in the paper to that effect, of which the concern of the Miamians for their plate glass is typical."

This does not sound like an architect talking.

On September 5, 1945, my mother got this telegram: due friday 9:15 am. dont both[er] meeting will rush right home—through with navy orders and sailing dates. dearest love.

When Daylight Comes

From then to now

Karl Doenitz went on trial for war crimes at Nuremberg in November. Douglas Kelley, an American psychiatrist who examined him before the trial, wrote that "he was bitter in pointing out that his seven days of Führership netted him nothing except an opportunity to hang with the other German criminals." He had brought about peace as quickly as possible, he said, but now he was threatened with the gallows: "This seems to be an example of American humor." Was that extraordinary remark an example of Doenitz's own bleak humor?

The admiral said he said he had fought a clean war and that like so many others in the German High Command he was as ignorant of the atrocities against the Jews as he was appalled by them. The navy, he said, had always been the least politicized of German arms.

There is some truth in this, although it is also true that Doenitz had no quarrels with Hitler that didn't revolve around the apportionment of steel. He had spoken of "the spreading poison of Jewry" and declared that he dreaded the idea of his grandson being brought up in "the Jewish spirit of filth."

Other German naval officers repudiated the policies of their state. Peter Cremer told an interviewer that if he'd known about the camps, he would have resigned his command. But, then, a highly successful skipper, Joachim Schepke, wrote a book called *Submariners of Today* that explains the U-boat custom of calling the youngest crew member "Moses" in this jolly passage: "Now, quite contrary to what you, a conscientious Aryan might think, Moses doesn't mean that we have a Jew on board. No, my dear friend. In the first place you don't find any Jews at sea at all; and secondly, the seamen would hardly share their space with such an aberration of nature."

Doenitz was given ten years, among the mildest of the Nuremberg sentences. He served his time and during it became deeply interested in developing a kindergarten system that would help disadvantaged children by pairing them with a pet. He lived long enough to be told about the breaking of Enigma when it became public knowledge in the 1970s. He had all but believed it in 1943, but he refused to in 1973. When he died in 1980, his government would not let uniforms be worn to his funeral.

During his trial he found an unlikely defender in Admiral Dan Gallery. Doenitz, Gallery insisted, had been following exactly the same rules of engagement in his Atlantic campaign that American submarines had in the Pacific, and it was hypocrisy for us to prosecute him.

This wasn't Gallery's last gesture toward the Kriegsmarine. After its bond-selling tour down the East Coast in company with the *Neunzer*, the *U-505* was laid up in Portsmouth, New Hampshire. One by one its fellow U-boats were destroyed, most as target ships. But Gallery got it into his head that this one—the one *he'd* captured—should be saved, and he backed the plan with all his energy and promotional zeal. His hometown was Chicago, and he wanted his prize to go there. After a great deal of arguing about who would pay for it and an absurd squabble with Milwaukee, which suddenly decided the boat belonged there (this debate descended to the two cities' deriding one another's football team), the *U-505* made its last voyage, to the Chicago lakefront. In a bravura piece of tricky engineering, the submarine was winched out of the water, hauled across Lake Shore Drive, and deposited at the Museum of Science and Industry, where it reposes today in somewhat surreal splendor, magnificently restored, and the only U-boat in the United States.

THE DEs, MOST OF them, suffered the same fate as the vessels they had defeated. With the war over barely a year, an ad appeared in a rather squalid precinct of the *New York Herald Tribune*'s real estate section:

VESSELS for SALE

FOUR DESTROYER ESCORTS (DE)
Total Estimated Weight: 2,800 Gross Tons
LOCATION: Anchorage 29, Antioch, Calif.

Bids Accepted Until 15 November 1946
For Complete Details Ask For
Catalog B-60–47AVH

NavyMaterialRedistribution and
DesposalAdministration

Other DEs were torpedoed or sunk by gunfire; the *Camp*, DE-251, made it to Vietnam and was left there; the *Bright*, DE-747, was given to the French navy; and so it went. The *Neunzer* was decommissioned in January 1947 and succumbed to the wrecker's torch in 1973. But one, the *Slater*, DE-766—transferred to the Greek navy by the Truman doctrine and rechristened the *Aetos-01* (under which name she played a role in the movie *The Guns of Navarone*)—steamed on and on. In 1997 Greece gave her to a veterans' group called the Destroyer Escort Sailors Association, which raised $275,000 to hire a Russian tug to tow her back across the Atlantic. Today, stripped of postwar additions and carefully maintained, she rides out the years in the Hudson River at Albany, the last of her prodigious breed still afloat.

THE WAR NEVER LAID a glove on my father. The peace nearly killed him.

When it had become clear the Atlantic battle was winding down, government pamphlets warning of the impending difficulties of readjusting to civilian life began circulating on the *Neunzer*. My father read them with a sort of Olympian pity for the boys who had no jobs to return to. He was delighted to get back to his architectural office. He sat down at his drafting table, picked up a pencil—and froze. Days went by, weeks. When somebody said, "Draw a doorway here," he'd do a sure and lovely job. But he couldn't think on his own. Give it time, said his partner, who had carried the shop during the war. But the more time my father gave it, the more he despaired. As with tens of thousands of others who had stepped aside from their lives for the past few years, the momentous diversion had worked more deeply on his spirit than he knew. Everything he'd wanted to get back to seemed opaque, cold, changed. My mother told me that one afternoon he telephoned her. A surging clatter in the background let her know he was on a subway platform. "I called to say good-bye," he said.

She said no, come home, they would talk about it, he should have some supper. She did her best to summon up all the comforting fixtures of the workaday world, then sat in misery for hours until she heard him at the door.

Months went by. He got too embarrassed to stay at the firm he'd founded. He left it and reluctantly joined the staff of another.

Once at sea he had written my mother, "I like the morning watch best, in spite of having to get up at 3:15 AM to start it, for there is something very pleasant about starting the watch in total darkness—often with no visibility whatever, and gradually, imperceptibly have a little light steal over the ship, coming from no apparent source. Later it is intensified on the Eastern horizon— and finally if it is not too cloudy you see the sun rise." And that is just how his healing went: not by eastern windows only.

Slowly things began to lighten for him, and the hardest of all his watches drew to a close. He did fine at his new firm (even with the interruption of the war he ended up practicing architecture for nearly sixty years), eventually specializing in university and public buildings: the Barnard College library, the Firestone Library in Princeton, the Robert Frost Library at Amherst College, West Point.

A current convention holds that the veterans of World War II tend to be closemouthed, almost secretive, about what happened to them in it. In my experience, this is not so much the result of brooding over old horrors as it is the basic politeness of not wanting to bore someone. Whatever it may have done to his career, my father was glad he'd gone to sea and always seemed to enjoy talking about it, and visiting with his shipmates.

My mother died in 1976. Some time after, he remarried, to Martha, his architecture school friend of fifty years earlier, whose husband had swung sea duty for him. Her daughter Caroline, the little girl to whom he had sent the coconut, grew up to be one of America's foremost practitioners of rehabilitative medicine. When the sturdy constitution that had brought the old man of the *Neunzer* through the worst the Atlantic could dish out finally faltered in the last years of his life, Carrie and her husband, Michael, brought him into their home, where he received better care than any fleet admiral ever got. He died, at ninety-five, in the year 2000.

A decade before that, when the VCR had spilled its cornucopia of forgotten movies into the national lap, I brought home *The Enemy Below*. In it, beneath a turquoise South Atlantic sky, a Buckley-class destroyer escort under the command of Robert Mitchum fights a single-ship duel with a U-boat. Although the German skipper, Curt Jurgens, says the Hitler-is-a-madman-who-has-disgraced-our-profession-of-arms stuff that was evidently mandatory for World War II movies in the mid-1950s (when Germany was, as its former boss had once hoped, becoming our ally against the threat of communism), he is nonetheless a canny seaman who is determined to get out of the engagement alive, and the moves and countermoves become increasingly complex and perilous. As the film unspooled itself, my father said, "How the hell did I miss this when it came out?" He watched hypnotized as Mitchum dropped his depth charges and fired his K-guns. Every so often he murmured, "That's just the way it was."

When the movie ended, he sat in silence for a while. Then he exclaimed, with proprietary satisfaction, "Wasn't that DE a beautiful ship!"

Bibliographical Note
and Acknowledgments

Anyone who comes fresh, as I did, to the subject of the Battle of the Atlantic will be at once daunted and encouraged by the work of those who have been there before. There is a great deal of it, and the quality is high.

A glance at the bibliography I've drawn on will immediately reveal that much of it flowed from the Naval Institute Press, an operation remarkable not only for the scope of its publications—the titles cited here are the merest sliver of its long list—but for their clarity and verve. The most specialized material is vigorously presented, untarnished by jargon. You may never have occasion to seek out a book on, say, the World War I destroyer, but if you do, you will find yourself most enjoyably engaged by John D. Alden's *Flush Decks & Four Pipes*. You'll find the same quality right across the list, from the oral histories gathered by Jack T. Mason Jr. for *The Atlantic War Remembered* to the disastrous epic of the "mystery ships," told by Kenneth M. Beyer, who served aboard one.

Throughout writing this book, I've been fortunate in the reading that has, as it were, been forced on me. For instance, when I was editing *American Heritage* magazine, I had the good luck to become acquainted with the historian Elting Morison, and to publish some of his articles. I admired them—and him—greatly, but without this project I would probably have gone to my grave without reading *Turmoil and Tradition,* his biography of Henry Stimson, which is wise, rueful, subtle, beautifully written, and extremely funny into the bargain.

Other books that proved as diverting as they were useful included Thomas Buell's biography of Admiral King; *The Borrowed Years,* Richard Ketchum's engrossing panorama of America between the invasion of Poland and the destruction of our Pacific fleet; Philip Goodhart's survey of the destroyer deal; Michael Gannon's account of the 1942 U-boat offensive off our shores (a favorite of Elting Morison's, by the way: "a splendid book, moving in description, instructive in well supported analysis"); Peter Padfield's sympathetic but thoroughly unsentimental biography of Admiral Doenitz; Peter Elphick's history of the Liberty ships; *Count Not the Dead,* another winner from the Naval Institute, in which Michael L. Hadley examines how the image of the U-boat has chimed over the years with the spirit of the nation that developed it; *Little Ship, Big War,* Edward P. Stafford's memoir of life aboard a destroyer escort; Gerald Reminick's scrupulous reconstruction of the fight between the *Stephen Hopkins* and the *Stier; Unsung Sailors,* Justin F. Gleichauf's tribute to the Naval Armed Guard . . . I could cite just as many more with equal enthusiasm.

The Kriegsmarine has engaged the energies of deeply dedicated scholars. I am convinced that Jak Mallmann Showell knows enough about U-boats to command one in action; so too with Gordon Williamson and Lawrence Paterson. And Clay Blair, whose two-volume *Hitler's U-boat War* runs to over seventeen hundred pages. The German sea war is also the subject of two fine websites: uboatarchive.net and uboat.net.

I am in debt to all the above, but have some more direct debts to acknowledge.

My friend John Lukacs, who has an unparalleled grasp (at once poetic and rigorously factual) of what befell Europe during the twentieth century, has been wonderfully generous with his time discussing with me the annus mirabilis of 1940, Churchill, Roosevelt, and especially Hitler's decision to declare war on America.

I knew the National Archives likely held the logs of the USS *Neunzer*, but had no idea how to get at them. Martin Baldessari, a first-rate researcher living in Washington, D.C., did, though, and he retrieved them all from the Textual Branch and had them copied for me, as well as finding photographs of the ship in the Still Pictures Branch. Once the pictures for the book had been located, there remained the problem of acquiring in reproducible form the ones in the National Archives. For this I turned to the National Air Survey Center, Corp. t/a Visual Image Presentations. Michelle Pointin and her colleagues there have close ties with the people who work in the archives, and they achieved in days what would likely have taken me the rest of my life. In the mid-1990s my father's skipper Captain John E. Greenbacker was interviewed for the oral history program of the Special History Collections of the J. Y. Joyner Library at East Carolina University in Greenville, North Carolina; the Joyner produced a transcript with impressive speed.

I was amazed to discover that Paul Just, the captain of the *U-546*, had written a memoir. It existed only in German, but this obstacle was overcome for me by Saskia Miller, who translated the sections dealing with his last fight.

Two equally venerable but very different institutions have sustained me in this project. One is Volare, on West Fourth Street in Greenwich Village, which has been a restaurant for at least a century, and under its present ownership since the 1970s. Most of what became this book first emerged on yellow legal pads while I comfortably occupied the last booth on the right.

The other is Forbes Inc. The company owned *American Heritage* magazine; all four Forbes brothers are deeply interested in history (as soon as they bought *Heritage*, in the 1980s, I discovered to my mixed pleasure and alarm that my immediate boss, Tim, knew a lot more about it than I did), and this book began when, after a long, gallant struggle to keep the magazine afloat, Forbes finally had to sell it. I had worked for *American Heritage* for forty years and now, suddenly having no more articles to edit, was relieved to get something to do via a book contract. The Forbeses generously gave me a place to do it in. Admirable though Volare is, it is not an office, and I am deeply grateful to have been supplied one while this took shape.

I must also thank my agent, Emma Sweeney, first for approaching me to write a book, then for showing my proposal to Colin Harrison at Scribner. I could not have a sharper or more helpful editor, and I appreciate his gently getting me to impose more chronological coherence on the narrative. (I trust him on this: anyone who has read his riveting novels will agree that *nobody* tells a story better.) I am in Scribner's debt as well for recruiting a superb copy editor, Steve Boldt, whose keen eye and mind saved me from many small—and not so small—embarrassments.

Finally, my thanks to my friend of thirty years Scott Masterson, Senior Vice President and General Manager of Forbes. Through some mysterious bonhomie worked on the golf course, he made contact with Rear Admiral Richard J. O'Hanlon, Commander, Naval Air Force Atlantic, who arranged for Scott and me to spend two days at sea on the *Nimitz*-class carrier *Theodore Roosevelt*. I realize this is not an overwhelming qualification for one to write a book on a maritime theme—*Two Days before the Mast*—but it was a fascinating and valuable experience for me. During my brief time aboard, I learned that although the destroyer escorts and CVEs of World War II have gone to join the U.S. navy's frigates and ironclads in Valhalla, the spirit that animated them, the energy and intelligence and enterprise that allowed them to prevail in their long struggle, are still very much in our country's service.

Bibliography

Abbazia, Patrick. *Mr. Roosevelt's Navy: The Private War of the Atlantic Fleet, 1939–1942.* Naval Institute Press, 1975.

Adams, Stephen B. *Mr. Kaiser Goes to Washington: The Rise of a Government Entrepreneur.* University of North Carolina Press, 1997.

Alden, John D. *Flush Decks & Four Pipes.* Naval Institute Press, 1989.

Andrews, Lewis M., Jr. *Tempest, Fire & Foe: Destroyer Escorts in World War II and the Men Who Manned Them.* Narwhal Press, 1999.

Auchincloss, Louis. *A Writer's Capital.* University of Minnesota Press, 1974.

Bath, Alan Harris. *Tracking the Axis Enemy: The Triumph of Anglo-American Naval Intelligence.* University Press of Kansas, 1998.

Beyer, Kenneth M. *Q-ships versus U-boats: America's Secret Project.* Naval Institute Press, 1999.

Blair, Clay. *Hitler's U-boat War: The Hunters, 1939–1942.* Random House, 1996.

———. *Hitler's U-boat War: The Hunted, 1942–1945.* Random House, 1998.

The Bluejackets' Manual: United States Navy. Naval Institute Press, 1940.

Bravier, Robert N. Jr. "Introduction to a 'DE.'" *Yachting,* July 1943.

Buderi, Robert. *The Invention That Changed the World: How a Small Group of Radar Pioneers Won the Second World War and Launched a Technological Revolution.* Simon & Schuster, 1996.

Budiansky, Stephen. *Battle of Wits: The Complete Story of Codebreaking in World War II.* Free Press, 2000.

Buell, Thomas B. *Master of Sea Power: A Biography of Fleet Admiral Ernest J. King.* Little, Brown, 1980.

Bunker, John. *Heroes in Dungarees: The Story of the American Merchant Marine in World War II.* Naval Institute Press, 2006.

Campbell, John. *Naval Weapons of World War II.* Naval Institute Press, 1985.

Carse, Robert. *A Cold Corner of Hell: The Story of the Murmansk Convoys, 1941–1945.* Doubleday, 1969.

Caulfield, Max. *Tomorrow Never Came: The Story of the S.S. Athenia.* Norton, 1958.

Churchill, Winston S. *The Second World War.* 6 vols. Cassell, 1948–53.

Coale, Griffith Baily. *North Atlantic Patrol: The Life of a Seagoing Artist.* Farrar & Rinehart, 1943.

Cohen, Eliot A., and John Gooch. *Military Misfortunes: The Anatomy of Failure in War.* Free Press, 1990.

The Cook Book of the United States Navy. Government Printing Office, 1944.

The Cook Book of the United States Navy 1940. Government Printing Office, 1940.

Cooper, Joseph H. "The Hooligan Navy." *Nautical Quarterly,* Spring 1981.

Cremer, Peter. *U-boat Commander: A Periscope View of the Battle of the Atlantic.* Naval Institute Press, 1984.

Destroyers, Pacific Fleet: Armament Safety Precautions for Destroyers and Destroyer Escorts, May 1, 1945. No publisher.

Doenitz, Karl. *Memoirs: Ten Years and Twenty Days.* World Publishing Company, 1959.

Duffy, James P. *Target America: Hitler's Plan to Attack the United States.* Lyons, 2004.

Elliott, Peter. *Allied Escort Ships of World War II: A Complete Survey.* Naval Institute Press, 1977.

Elphick, Peter. *Liberty: The Ships that Won the War.* Naval Institute Press, 2001.

Farago, Ladislas. *The Tenth Fleet.* Ivan Obolensky, 1962.

Franklin, Bruce Hampton. *The Buckley-Class Destroyer Escorts.* Naval Institute Press, 1999.

Friedman, Norman. *U.S. Destroyers: An Illustrated Design History.* Naval Institute Press, 1989.

Gainard, Joseph A. *Yankee Skipper: The Life Story of Joseph A. Gainard, Captain of the City of Flint.* Frederick A. Stokes, 1940.

Gallery, Daniel V. *Clear the Decks!* Morrow, 1951.

———. *Twenty Million Tons under the Sea: The Daring Capture of the U-505.* Naval Institute Press, 2001.

Gannon, Michael. *Operation Drumbeat: The Dramatic True Story of Germany's First U-boat Attacks along the American Coast in World War II.* Harper & Row, 1990.

Gannon, Robert. *Hellions of the Deep: The Development of American Torpedoes in World War II.* Pennsylvania State University Press, 1996.

Gardner, W. J. R. *Decoding History: The Battle of the Atlantic and Ultra.* Naval Institute Press, 1999.

Gasaway, E. B. *Grey Wolf, Grey Sea.* Ballantine, 1970.

Gilbert, Martin. *Churchill and America.* Free Press, 2005.

Gleichauf, Justin F. *Unsung Sailors: The Naval Armed Guard in World War II.* Naval Institute Press, 1990.

Goebeler, Hans. *Steel Boats, Iron Hearts: A U-boat Crewman's Life aboard U-505.* Chatham, 2005.

Goodhart, Philip. *Fifty Ships That Saved the World: The Foundation of the Anglo-American Alliance.* Doubleday, 1965.

Gray, Edwin. *The Devil's Device: Robert Whitehead and the History of the Torpedo.* Naval Institute Press, 1991.

Hadley, Michael L. *Count Not the Dead: The Popular Image of the German Submarine.* Naval Institute Press, 1995.

Hickham, Homer H. Jr. *Torpedo Junction: U-boat War off America's East Coast, 1942.* Naval Institute Press, 1989.

Hornfischer, James D. *The Last Stand of the Tin Can Sailors: The Extraordinary World War II Story of the U.S. Navy's Finest Hour.* Bantam, 2004.

Hoyt, Edwin. P. *U-boats Offshore: When Hitler Struck America.* Stein & Day, 1978.

Isaacson, Walter, and Evan Thomas. *The Wise Men: Six Friends and the World They Made—Acheson, Bohlen, Harriman, Kennan, Lovett, McCloy.* Simon & Schuster, 1986.

Janeway, Eliot. *The Struggle for Survival: A Chronicle of Economic Mobilization in World War II.* Yale, 1951.

Jernigan, E. J. *Tin Can Man.* Vandamere Press, 1993.

Johnson, Rody. *Different Battles: The Search of a World War II Hero.* Sunflower University Press, 1999.

Just, Paul. *Vom Seeflieger zum Uboot-Fahrer: Feindfluge und Feindfahrten, 1939–1945.* Motorbuch Verlag, 1979.

Keegan, John. *Intelligence in War: Knowledge of the Enemy from Napoléon to Al-Qaeda.* Knopf, 2003.

Kershaw, Ian. *Fateful Choices: Ten Decisions That Changed the World.* Penguin, 2007.

Ketchum, Richard M. *The Borrowed Years, 1939–1941: America on the Way to War.* Random House, 1989.

Kimball, Warren F. *Forged in War: Roosevelt, Churchill, and the Second World War.* Morrow, 1997.

——. *The Most Unsordid Act: Lend-Lease, 1939–1941.* Johns Hopkins, 1969.

Knight, Austin M. *Modern Seamanship.* Van Nostrand, 1943.

Larrabee, Eric. *Commander in Chief: Franklin Delano Roosevelt, His Lieutenants, and Their War.* Harper & Row, 1987.

Lash, Joseph P. *Roosevelt and Churchill, 1939–1941: The Partnership That Saved the West.* Norton, 1976.

Lukacs, John. "The Dangerous Summer of 1940." *American Heritage,* October/November 1986.

——. "The Transatlantic Duel: Hitler vs. Roosevelt." *American Heritage,* December 1991.

Marolda, Edward J., ed. *FDR and the U.S. Navy*. St. Martin's Press, 1998.

Martienssen, Anthony. *Hitler and His Admirals*. Dutton, 1949.

Mason, John T., Jr., ed. *The Atlantic War Remembered: An Oral History Collection*. Naval Institute Press, 1990.

Massie, Robert K. *Castles of Steel: Britain, Germany, and the Winning of the Great War at Sea*. Random House, 2003.

Meacham, Jon. *Franklin and Winston: An Intimate Portrait of an Epic Friendship*. Random House, 2004.

Miller, Nathan. *The U.S. Navy: An Illustrated History*. American Heritage/ Naval Institute Press, 1977.

Monsarrat, Nicholas. *The Cruel Sea*. Cassell, 1951.

Morison, Elting. *Admiral Sims and the Modern American Navy*. Houghton Mifflin, 1942.

——. *Turmoil and Tradition: A Study of the Life and Times of Henry L. Stimson*. Houghton Mifflin, 1960.

Morison, Samuel Eliot. *History of United States Naval Operations in World War II: The Battle of the Atlantic, September 1939–May 1943*. Little, Brown, 1947.

——. *History of United States Naval Operations in World War II: The Atlantic Battle Won, May 1943–May 1945*. Little, Brown, 1956.

Mort, Terry. *The Hemingway Patrols: Ernest Hemingway and His Hunt for U-boats*. Scribner, 2009.

Mulligan, Timothy P. *Lone Wolf: The Life and Death of U-boat Ace Werner Henke*. Praeger, 1993.

——. *Neither Sharks nor Wolves: The Men of Nazi Germany's U-boat Arm, 1939–1945*. Naval Institute Press, 1999.

O'Reilly, Tim. *Purser's Progress: The Adventures of a Seagoing Office Boy*. Doubleday, 1944.

Outhwaite, Leonard. *The Atlantic: A History of an Ocean*. Coward-McCann, 1957.

Padfield, Peter. *Dönitz: The Last Führer*. Harper & Row, 1984.

——. *War Beneath the Sea: Submarine Conflict during World War II.* Wiley, 1995.

Parrish, Thomas. *The Submarine: A History.* Viking, 2004.

Paterson, Lawrence. *U-boat Combat Missions: The Pursuers & the Pursued: First-Hand Accounts of U-boat Life and Operations.* Chatham, 2007.

——. *U-boat War Patrol: The Hidden Photographic Diary of U564.* Greenhill, 2004.

Raeder, Erich. *Grand Admiral.* Da Capo Press, 2001.

Reisenberg, Felix Jr. *Sea War: The Story of the U.S. Merchant Marine in World War II.* Rinehart, 1956.

Reminick, Gerald. *Action in the South Atlantic: The Sinking of the German Raider* Stier *by the Liberty Ship* Stephen Hopkins. Glencannon Press, 2006.

Roland, Alex, W. Jeffrey Bolster, and Alexander Keyssar. *The Way of the Ship: America's Maritime History Reenvisioned, 1600–2000.* Wiley, 2008.

Roscoe, Theodore. *United States Destroyer Operations in World War II.* Naval Institute Press, 1953.

Ross, Al. *Anatomy of the Ship: The Destroyer Escort England.* Naval Institute Press, 1985.

Ruark, Robert C. "They Called 'Em Fish Food." *Saturday Evening Post,* May 6, 1944.

Runyan, Timothy J., and Jan M. Copes, eds. *To Die Gallantly: The Battle of the Atlantic.* Westview Press, 1994.

Sard, Ellis. "The Last Cruise of the *YP-438.*" *American Heritage,* June/July 1985.

Savas, Theodore P., ed. *Hunt and Kill:* U-505 *and the U-boat War in the Atlantic.* Savas Beatie, 2004.

Schofield, William G. *Eastward the Convoys.* Rand McNally, 1965.

Sherwood, Robert E. *Roosevelt and Hopkins: An Intimate History.* Harper, 1948.

Showell, Jak P. Mallmann. *Enigma U-boats: Breaking the Code.* Naval Institute Press, 2000.

——. *Hitler's U-boat Bases.* Naval Institute Press, 2002.

——. *The U-boat Century: German Submarine Warfare, 1906–2006.* Chatham, 2006.

——. *U-boats under the Swastika: An Introduction to German Submarines, 1935–1945.* Arco, 1977.

Simpson, B. Mitchel, III. *Admiral Harold R. Stark: Architect of Victory, 1939–1945.* University of South Carolina Press, 1989.

Sims, William Sowden. *The Victory at Sea.* Naval Institute Press, 1984.

Stafford, Edward P. *Little Ship, Big War: The Saga of DE343.* William Morrow, 1984.

Standard Oil Company (New Jersey). *Ships of the Esso Fleet in World War II.* 1946.

Stern, Robert C. *Type VII U-boats.* Brockhampton, 1998.

Stimson, Henry L., and McGeorge Bundy. *On Active Service in Peace and War.* Harper, 1948.

Suhren, Teddy, and Fritz Brustat-Naval. *Teddy Suhren, Ace of Aces: Memoirs of a U-boat Rebel.* Chatham, 2006.

Tarrant, V. E. *The Last Year of the Kriegsmarine, May 1944–May 1945.* Arms and Armor Press, 1996.

——. *The U-boat Offensive, 1914–1945.* Casell, 1989.

Taylor, Theodore. *Fire on the Beaches.* Norton, 1958.

Terraine, John. *The U-boat Wars, 1916–1945.* Henry Holt, 1989.

van der Vat, Dan. *The Atlantic Campaign: World War II's Great Struggle at Sea.* Harper & Row, 1988.

Vargas, Robert L. "The Gallantry of an 'Ugly Duckling,'" *American Heritage,* December, 1969.

Vause, Jordan. *U-boat Ace: The Story of Wolfgang Luth.* Naval Institute Press, 1990.

Veigele, William J. *PC Patrol Craft of World War II: A History of the Ships and Their Crews.* Astral, 1998.

Walling, Michael G. *Bloodstained Sea: The U.S. Coast Guard in the Battle of the Atlantic, 1941–1944.* McGraw-Hill, 2004.

Ward, John R. "The Little Ships That Could." *American Heritage of Invention & Technology*, Fall 1999.

Weinberg, Gerhard L. *Visions of Victory: The Hopes of Eight World War II Leaders*. Cambridge University Press, 2005.

——. *A World at Arms: A Global History of World War II*. Cambridge University Press, 1994.

Werner, Herbert A. *Iron Coffins: A Personal Account of the German U-boat Battles in World War II*. Holt, Rinehart and Winston, 1969.

Wiggins, Melanie. *Torpedoes in the Gulf: Galveston and the U-boats, 1942–1943*. Texas A&M University Press, 1995.

Williams, Wirt. *The Enemy*. Houghton Mifflin, 1951.

Williamson, Gordon. *U-boat Bases and Bunkers, 1941–45*. Osprey, 2003.

——. Wolf Pack: *The Story of the U-boat in World War II*. Osprey, 2006.

Wilson, Theodore A. *The First Summit: Roosevelt and Churchill at Placentia Bay, 1942*. Houghton Mifflin, 1969.

Winton, John. *Ultra at Sea: How Breaking the Nazi Code Affected Allied Naval Strategy during World War II*. Morrow, 1988.

Wouk, Herman. *The Caine Mutiny*. Doubleday, 1951.

Wragg, David. *The Escort Carrier in the Second World War: Combustible, Vulnerable, Expendable*. Pen & Sword, 2005.

Wylie, Philip, and Laurence Schwab. "The Battle of Florida." *Saturday Evening Post*, March 11, 1944.

Y'Blood, William T. *Hunter-Killer: U.S. Escort Carriers in the Battle of the Atlantic*. Naval Institute Press, 1983.

Index

About the Author

Richard Snow was born in New York City in 1947, and he graduated with a BA from Columbia College in 1970. He worked at *American Heritage* magazine for nearly four decades and was its editor in chief for seventeen years. He is the author of several books, among them two novels and a volume of poetry. Snow has served as a consultant for historical motion pictures—among them *Glory*—and has written for documentaries, including the Burns brothers' *Civil War,* and Ric Burns's PBS film *Coney Island,* whose screenplay he wrote. Most recently, he served as a consultant on Ken Burns's World War II series, *The War.*

(Author's collection.)